D1562615

Interfaith Just Peacemaking

Interfaith Just Peacemaking

Jewish, Christian, and Muslim Perspectives on the New Paradigm of Peace and War

Edited by Susan Brooks Thistlethwaite

palgrave
macmillan

INTERFAITH JUST PEACEMAKING
Copyright © Susan Brooks Thistlethwaite, 2012.

First published in 2012 by PALGRAVE MACMILLAN®
in the United States—a division of St. Martin's Press LLC,
175 Fifth Avenue, New York, NY 10010.

Where this book is distributed in the UK, Europe, and the rest of the world,
this is by Palgrave Macmillan, a division of Macmillan Publishers Limited,
registered in England, company number 785998, of Houndmills, Basingstoke,
Hampshire RG21 6XS.

Palgrave Macmillan is the global academic imprint of the above companies and
has companies and representatives throughout the world.

Palgrave® and Macmillan® are registered trademarks in the United States, the
United Kingdom, Europe and other countries.

ISBN: 978-0-230-33989-7

Library of Congress Cataloging-in-Publication Data

   Interfaith Just Peacemaking : Jewish, Christian, and Muslim perspectives on
the new paradigm of peace and war / edited by Susan Brooks Thistlethwaite.
      p. cm.
   ISBN 978-0-230-33989-7
   1. Peace—Religious aspects. 2. Judaism. 3. Christianity. 4. Islam. I.
Thistlethwaite, Susan Brooks, 1948–

BL65.P4I57 2011
201'.7273—dc23   2011024626

A catalogue record of the book is available from the British Library.

Design by Scribe Inc.

First edition: January 2012

10 9 8 7 6 5 4 3 2 1

Printed in the United States of America.

Contents

Christian Preface

I have been invited by friends and scholars whose work I respect to contribute a brief preface to this important book; I am happy to do so. I do so as someone who did not participate in the writing of the book or the broader process from which it emerged, but as someone whose work has been absorbed by the normative and strategic issues of war and peace for 40 years.

Writing from that perspective, this book is important for three reasons. First, along with its predecessors, it will find a place in the growing literature on the role of religion in international relations and world politics. For over three centuries the analysis and practice of world politics has treated religion as virtually a black box. During this time it surely has been recognized that religious convictions and participation in religious communities have been important motivations (for good and bad) in the lives of individuals, nations, and cultures. But that recognition has been joined with the apprehension that explicit inclusion of religious ideas and communities in the worlds of diplomacy, politics, and strategy would not only complicate all these fields, but likely would intensify conflict rather than ameliorate it. In the Western world, where the formal study of international relations and the diplomatic history of modern world politics are rooted, the specter of the religious wars in Europe of the sixteenth and seventeenth centuries has been the abiding memory. The lesson learned was that religion was best treated as a private reality but not a component element in the understanding or the practice of empires, states, or nations. In important and incremental ways that assumption has been challenged over the last 40 years. The driving force has not been an organized body of advocates "for religion." It has rather been the need to understand major substantive changes in world politics, which were largely unintelligible without some analytical role for religious ideas, communities, and leaders. From Saudi Arabia to San Salvador, from Israel to Iran, from Poland to the Philippines, and from South Africa to Sudan, the "religious factor" must be accounted for in explaining the problems faced, the outcomes in specific situations, and the persistence of religious themes in world affairs. This book will fit into wide-ranging discussions now under way not only among theologians, moralists, and students of religion but among foreign policy analysts, strategists, think tanks, and international organizations. Precisely because of the specific "practices" endorsed here and the complexity of the situations they are designed to address, the reception of this work will be mixed. It draws upon materials in the three great religious traditions that are virtually unknown to social scientists, strategists, and others; it makes claims of an empirical order that supporters and critics will want to test; it enters moral arguments about war and peace that have divided faith and politics for centuries. In this kind of terrain, a mixed reception is a compliment: it means the work is being seriously weighed and analyzed.

Second, as just noted, this work seeks to contribute to a long argument. The religious traditions have been significant sources of ideas about the moral judgments of war and peace. The classic arguments have focused on whether war could ever be a morally justified activity, and, if so, how could that judgment be made? In a world where war remains a constant factor in world politics, I believe the classic arguments remain important and needed. This book, however, is distinguished by a different perspective, a different objective, and a different style of analysis. It is based on the conviction that the religious traditions engaged here have more to contribute to the world than specific judgments on decisions to go to war or the way wars are fought. As the book's title indicates, the basic shift is from "Just War" ideas to "Just Peacemaking." The meaning of Just Peacemaking has been worked out in previous contributions of the project begun among Christians and extended to the Jewish and Islamic traditions. As someone who has spent years on the Just War perspective, I can first affirm that the authors are right that too little time has been given to the positive possibilities of religious discourse for building the fabric of peace. The theme has never been absent (peace as the product of justice is an ancient formula), but its development has always been overshadowed by the efforts to contain or limit the resort to force. In a world as complex as the global and globalized international system of today, both the old and the new arguments about war and peace are needed. That fact should not diminish the importance of the effort undertaken in this book. The "Just Peacemaking" project should be recognized as an effort of "development of doctrine" carried out on an interfaith basis. The traditional moral arguments are being stretched to new dimensions in the "Practice Norms" advocated here.

Third, two other characteristics of this work combine to make it important and distinctive. On the one hand the interreligious nature of its production is immensely important in a world where religious traditions often insulated from each other are constantly brought into contact with possibilities for either conflict or collaboration. This research obviously seeks to enhance the latter possibility, and it brings us back to the growing significance of religion in world politics. On the other hand, the specific recommendations explained and analyzed here in the Practice Norms will engage other disciplines and other analytical perspectives more concretely than the deep theoretical foundations of ancient religious traditions. This work, in its specificity, brings religious conviction to bear upon questions of life and death and the possibilities for peace.

For these three reasons and for many others this work should be widely studied, tested, and engaged by individuals, states, and organizations seeking to build a peace that will last.

—J. Bryan Hehir
Harvard Kennedy School of Government

Jewish Preface

This book is a testament to the benefits of interreligious communication among the so-called Abrahamic faiths—Judaism, Christianity, and Islam. By claiming membership in the Abrahamic faiths, we affirm that we share the belief in the God of Abraham and the mission of Abraham to make God known to all humanity. Abraham was the only biblical personage destined to become "father of many nations" (Gen. 17:4), and in fact only Abraham has achieved spiritual patrimony over about half of humanity. There is no figure in history to whom more people trace their lineage in one way or another than Abraham. Only God is called father by more.

Accordingly, the twelfth-century Arab Jewish philosopher Moses Maimonides deemed the biblical prophecy about Abraham that "all the families of the earth will be blessed through you" (Gen. 12:3) fulfilled by the fact that "his activity has resulted, as we see today, in the consensus of the greater part of the population of the earth in glorifying him and considering themselves as blessed through his memory, so that even those who do not belong to his progeny claim to descend from him."[1] For him, "Anybody who converts throughout the generations, and anyone who affirms the unity of God, as described in the Torah, becomes a disciple of Abraham our father, and all are members of his household."[2] There are thus two Abrahamic categories: the people of Abraham and the household of Abraham.[3] The former encompasses his progeny and those who have joined them; the latter encompasses all affirmers of God's unity.

For a faith to qualify as Abrahamic, however, it must advance not only monotheism, but ethical monotheism, which entails promoting the value of human life and working for the perfection of the world. Those monotheists who devalue, yea destroy, human life in the name of God *de facto* exclude themselves. In contrast, in the High Holiday liturgy, we are called upon to affirm that God is "King who desires life." In fact, the Talmud says, "Anyone who has mercy on people, is presumed to be of our father Abraham's seed; and anyone who does not have mercy on people, is presumed not to be of our father Abraham's seed." Maimonides codified this, saying, "If someone is cruel and does not show mercy, there are sufficient grounds to suspect his lineage."[4] Obviously, Abrahamic lineage also has an ethical DNA marker.

The project of this book shows the inadequacy of affirming God's unity without promoting the value of human life and working for the perfection of the world. The great divide among the Abrahamic faiths is not among Jews, Christians, and Muslims, but among those Jews, Christians, and Muslims who think that God's concern with humanity stops with their group, or those who think that God demands only the affirmation of the unity of God and not the unity of humanity.

When an Abrahamic religion is more a source of enmity than amity, then, as it were, God's reputation is tarnished. When, however, concern for God gets translated into concern for humanity, especially outsiders, then the name of God is sanctified. It is one thing to say my group comes first; it is another to say that my groups come first and last. Concern for my part of humanity is to pave the way for concern with the rest of humanity.

The history and contemporary expressions of the Abrahamic faiths show that both strains are alive and well. There is no shortage of Jews, Christians, and Muslims who make God over into their own image and limit God's purview to themselves. But as God is greater than all human understandings, so does God's concern exceed any group or religion. Such is the legacy of Abraham. This book shows how through interreligious communication we Jews, Christians, and Muslims can make ourselves more worthy of Abraham, realizing that none of us exhausts his legacy.

—Reuven Kimelman
Brandeis University

Muslim Preface

It is an honor and blessing for me to have been a participant in more than one interfaith peace initiative and dialog in the last several years. Such peace conferences contributed significantly to the promotion of better mutual understanding between representatives of the Abrahamic faith communities that are part of the mosaic of modern pluralistic societies in North America and elsewhere. They also afforded participants the opportunity to cultivate and enhance the bonds of friendship and brotherhood, thus modeling diversity within unity and unity within diversity. I was blessed to be a participant in many other interfaith activities in several countries around the world since 1963. The recent initiatives sponsored by the Rockefeller Brothers Fund stand out in terms of their welcoming and positive atmospheres. They duly focused on the faith-based common core values that resonated with the participants, such as justice, peace, mutual respect, and caring and acceptance of others in a way that is beyond the requisites of mere tolerance.

If we are to move to the next level, we need to understand each other's hermeneutics in more depth. Comparative hermeneutics can take us beyond understanding the stance or stances of each faith community on various peace-building issues to understand the methodology used by various faith communities to arrive at such stances. It is likely that there are some sound hermeneutical rules that resonate with more than one faith group. Learning from one another may help us identify those "common" methodologies and rules. The assumption here is that intrafaith hermeneutical variations do not obscure the commonality of the core methodology within each faith group. Likewise, comparative hermeneutics can help us understand the areas of differences or particularity, so as to avoid expecting other faith communities to follow what we consider to be "the right approach" according to our own traditions.

For example, mainstream Islamic scholarship since the Prophet's time upholds that the Qur'an is the verbatim divine revelation to Prophet Muhammad (*pbuh*) through Archangel Gabriel. This is a universal "belief" constituting an article of faith, defining who a Muslim is. There are also internal and other external historical and reasoned arguments that support this "belief." It is for that reason that the Qur'an is universally accepted as the ultimate and most authoritative primary source of Islamic teachings. It is, as Al-Qaradawi puts it, "the source of sources." It follows that the Qur'an is not subject to human editing by adding, removing, or modifying "the word of God," as this is tantamount to copyediting God's word or claiming greater wisdom than God's. This does not, however, preclude reflection on the meaning of the Qur'anic text. Nor does it preclude its reinterpretation. It should be noted that some Qur'anic texts are clearly definitive in meaning, *Qat`i al-Dalaalah*, while others are non-definitive texts, meaning that they allow for more than one valid and reasoned interpretation, *Dhanni al-Dalaalah*.

The above remarks are intended to give an example of hermeneutical particularity in understanding and interpreting the Qur'an. One reason I consider it as such is my understanding that there is no exact parallel to the notion of verbatim revelation applicable to the entire sacred text in mainstream Christianity.

Other aspects of Islamic hermeneutics include the role of hadith as the second primary source of Islam, and the grading of hadith in terms of authenticity based on the examination of the chain of narration as well as textual criticism. Other topics of interest include the textual and historical contexts of any sacred text, and they inform its interpretation. In fact, early Islamic scholars developed a highly sophisticated "science" that may be comparable to "legal theory" in law schools, as it deals with the methodology of interpretation, *usul al-fiqh*. That science was and continues to be instrumental in how Islamic teachings can respond to modernity without losing sight of their foundational hermeneutics or methodology of proper and authentic interpretation and reinterpretation of sacred texts.

Issues like those raised above can, in due time, be topics for a future equally informative and beneficial dialogue.

Finally, I wish to say a word of thanks to all contributors to this work. It is a significant boost to interfaith cooperation and collaboration in peacebuilding in a practical, action-oriented way.

—Jamal Badawi
Saint Mary's University (Halifax)

Acknowledgments

Every contributor to this volume must be acknowledged for her or his participation in the long-term work that led to the concept of the volume, as well as for each individual written section. It takes a high degree of commitment to the work of interfaith Just Peacemaking to sustain a group over a period of years, and the contributors to this volume have exhibited that profound commitment.

The group process was facilitated by a leadership team of two Christians, two Muslims, and two Jews. The Muslim leadership team consisted of Mohammed Abu-Nimer, Jamal Badawi and then Qamar ul-Huda; the Jewish leadership team was Robert Eisen and Reuven Kimelman; the Christian leadership team was Glen Stassen and Susan Thistlethwaite, and Susan oversaw whole editing process. In addition, group facilitation and help with final edits was provided by Steven Brion-Meisels. Steven provided incredible leadership in helping us design our process and then in facilitating our planning conference. Katherine Schofield was our able editorial assistant, group member, and ultimately contributor.

Every book of this nature is a group effort and warm acknowledgments go out to all of those who worked on this book.

In addition, we are all grateful to the Rockefeller Brothers Fund and their generous funding of our project, and for the use of the Pocantico Conference Center for our conference. It is entirely due to their support that the sustained work necessary to produce such a complex book with so many participants was made possible, and we are all thankful to the Rockefeller Brothers Fund for this assistance.

Notes

1. Guide for the Perplexed, 3.29.
2. "The Epistle to Obadiah the Proselyte," The Responsa of Maimonides, ed. L. Blau (Jerusalem, 1958-61), No. 293, 2:549. For this translation, see Lawrence Kaplan,"Maimonides on the Singularity of the Jewish People," Daat 15 (1985), V-XXVI, at XIX-XX.
3. Mishneh Torah, Book of Knowledge,"Laws of Idolatry," 1.3. See idem, Guide for the Perplexed, 2:13 (end), for those who go in the way of Abraham, namely, believe in the creator God.
4. Mishneh Torah, Book of Seeds, "Gifts to the Needy," 10.2.

Introduction

The twenty-first century is shaping up to become the century of the world's religions. Key religious elements are influencing most major conflicts and misunderstandings between peoples and nations around the world. Globalization has not only increased business connections, it has increased religious interactions. To date, these interactions have mostly been used as a means to instigate and inflate conflict. At least that is what has made news, since conflict grabs attention. But it is also true that the opening of the religious borders can reveal unprecedented religious opportunities for addressing conflicts in creative ways. Indeed, many are responding to current crises by demonstrating interreligious respect and by developing more peaceful relationships.

One important example is the Interfaith Just Peacemaking project, an ongoing effort by 30 Muslim, Jewish, and Christian religious leaders and scholars. The members of this group have worked together, year after year, to craft and refine a practical and inspiring interfaith model to address ongoing conflicts as well as to build sustainable peace.

Just Peacemaking theory is an emerging fourth paradigm or model beyond the historic ways of addressing peace and war: Pacifism, Just War, and Crusade. It was first articulated in a systematic way by a group of 23 Christian religious leaders and scholars from numerous Protestant denominations and the American Catholic Church who collaborated, on a volunteer basis, for five years. Through their efforts, the ten practices of Just Peacemaking were identified and elaborated. The paradigm has gained credence and recognition over the last ten years.[1] The prominence of the Just Peace paradigm and all ten practices of Just Peacemaking in President Barack Obama's Nobel Peace Prize acceptance speech[2] surprised many in the United States, but in fact Just Peace work has taken place over nearly three decades, and this consistency of effort is partly responsible for a foreign policy shift toward practices of Just Peacemaking.

The events of 9/11 and, even more, the reactions to 9/11, convinced many in the original Christian Just Peacemaking group that an Interfaith Just Peacemaking model was required, particularly between and among the Abrahamic faiths (Jews, Christians, and Muslims). They recognized the vital importance of highlighting the practices of peacemaking in all three traditions. They wanted to show how the three faith groups find support for these practices in their scriptures and have implemented them in their lives. A federal grant to Fuller Theological Seminary's Just Peacemaking Initiative supported their partnering with the Salaam Institute for Peace and Justice in Washington, DC, from 2003 to 2008 to produce *Resources for Peacemaking in Muslim-Christian Relations*[3] and *Peace-Building by, between, and beyond Muslims and Evangelical Christians.*[4] With the support of the Rockefeller Brothers Fund, the Islamic Society of North America, the Managing the Atom Project of the Kennedy School of Government of Harvard University, and the Churches' Center for Theology and Public Policy, several members of the original Christian group invited Muslim religious leaders and scholars to work with them at the Pocantico Conference Center of the Rockefeller Brothers Fund in May of 2005. They produced the document, "We Affirm Our Belief in the One God: A Statement Regarding Muslim-Christian Perspectives on the Nuclear Weapons Danger."

Following that successful work, the Muslim and Christian scholars invited an equal number of Jewish colleagues to participate in a larger project with the support of the United States Institute of Peace. Recognizing the need to develop a response to the ongoing destructive process of manipulating religious texts to justify violence in the name of religion in all three traditions, this group produced an initial comprehensive Abrahamic Statement on Jewish, Muslim, and Islamic approaches to practical peacemaking in a conference at Stoney Point, New York in 2007. The resulting monograph "Abrahamic Alternatives to War: Jewish, Christian, and Muslim Perspectives on Just Peacemaking" published by the USIP, outlined the commonalities and differences that needed to be addressed in a larger project.[5]

Two years later, in the spring of 2009, an interfaith leadership team assembled to begin laying the groundwork for the resultant Interfaith Just Peacemaking conference and book project. Participants in the earlier projects and additional scholars and religious leaders were invited to contribute to the endeavor. The structure of the book was laid out to include an introduction, conclusion, and ten chapters, each addressing a particular Just Peacemaking practice, with a Jewish, Christian, and Muslim author for each chapter. The project participants came together for the Just Peacemaking Conference in late January 2010. The goals of this three-day conference included community building among participants, the development of clear and mutually agreeable writing guidelines for the completion of the book chapters, and small-group collaboration among the three authors of each chapter. In addition to accomplishing these goals, a number of valuable insights emerged from the work done at the conference.

A particularly salient discussion focused on the issue of scriptural interpretation and use. As the Jewish and Muslim contributors in particular pointed out, "We are text-based faiths; we need to base our peacemaking practices on our scriptures."[6] Each of us has searched our scriptures for guidance in our peacemaking practices. We believe the revelation of God in our scriptures calls us to these specific practices.

In the days leading up to the earlier 2007 meeting at Stony Point, one participant suggested that contributors write a preparatory paper from each faith with three main points. The first point should identify problem passages in our own traditions—passages used historically to turn people against peace and for war. So we each began by acknowledging our own responsibility for some of the hostilities and killings that have happened. This made us each more honest. But more—it made us each less defensive and more open. Muslims and Jews did not have to say, "You Christians have used the New Testament to justify killing many of us"—the Christians had already said that. Christians did not have to accuse the others of justifying persecutions or attacks based on their holiest texts—Muslims and Jews had already said that. So we experienced a remarkably nondefensive spirit as we worked together.

Having described how some passages in our scriptures had been used to stimulate unjust violence, we then described ways that our traditions had found to interpret our scriptures that were better than using them to rile up hatred and violence. We each developed a hermeneutic—a method of interpreting scriptures—that showed respect for those problem passages but did not use them to cause harm. So again our focus was on interpreting our scriptures. And the truth is that each of our sets of scriptures does teach much more guidance for peacemaking than many have realized.

We were then able to focus our attention on the guidance for peacemaking practices that is found in our scriptures. We had been so used to reading the scriptures to ask whether some of them supported war making and some of them opposed war making that we had not paid enough attention to the main theme: the love of God and neighbor. We had not attended to the importance of practicing peacemaking. Once we focused on the specific teachings of practices of peacemaking in our scriptures, we discovered remarkable similarity.

How can that be? How can it be that these three different faiths, often at loggerheads with one another in history, can each have scriptures teaching similar practices of peacemaking?

Each of us has teachings that we believe God gives to guide people. Our scriptures teach us that God created all human persons. We believe we were all created by the same God. Each of us has teachings supporting the idea that conscience, or a moral sense, or a natural law, is in every person regardless of faith tradition. So it may not be totally surprising that when we grope toward defining practices of peacemaking, we each have some similar intuitions. Furthermore, each of our scriptures speaks of God's Spirit guiding us. We understand this somewhat differently in our respective theologies, but we all want to give credit for our shared understandings of these ten practices of peacemaking to the gift of guidance from God's spirit. We believe God got to these practices of peacemaking before we did, and God has given intuitions of them in people's moral sense as well as specific teachings about them in our scriptures.

And one more thing: we each believe in faiths that affirm life in this world. Judaism, Christianity, and Islam are not merely other worldly; we believe God has a will for what we do *in this life*. And we believe God's will affirms the sacred value of human life. So it is natural that we consult actual experience, as seen in history and in the social sciences, for what practices actually do prevent some wars and actually do work toward peace—in this life. Our affirmation of life in real history leads us to a practical-minded concern for what works to make peace. We notice that four practices of peacemaking initiatives—conflict transformation, nonviolent direct action, independent initiatives, and humbly acknowledging that we ourselves share in the wrong—are being enacted here and there in real life, and they are indeed working to decrease hostility and to find breakthroughs of peace.

We want to make as clear as possible that this book is not about "high ideals" that if only someone someday would try, then we could have peace. This book is about actual, real practices that people and groups and governments are already doing, and that are in fact working to prevent the killing of millions of people. In the first half of the twentieth century, an average of 3.5 million people were killed in war each year. But then there was a huge revulsion against war, especially after World War II. In the second half of the twentieth century, many got to work to develop and implement the practices of peacemaking to which we are pointing. And the surprisingly little-known consequence is that in the second half of the twentieth century, the number of people killed in war dropped to 0.8 million people per year. This is not heaven; this is not the arrival of the reign of God in its fullest. But for the 2.7 million people who were not killed each year, and for their families who were celebrating the presence of their loved ones rather than grieving their death, that four-fold drop in the number of killings in wars made a huge difference. Some of us who are writing this book have grieved the death of our fathers or mothers or sons or daughters or relatives in war. We know the difference between war and peace. We deeply want you, our reader, to know these practices, to know that they do work to save life and to prevent death, and to give your support to these practices. We hope you will be motivated to prod governments to support them too.

The first four practices of Just Peacemaking are nonviolent direct action, independent initiatives, cooperative conflict resolution, and acknowledging our own responsibility for conflict and injustice. Sometimes governments have practiced *conflict resolution*, as between Egypt and Israel at Camp David (1978); between Serbia, Bosnia, and Croatia at the Dayton Accords (1995); between the Irish and British in Northern Ireland (1994); between the Soviet Union and the United States at Reykjavik (1986–87), and the result was lasting peace where there had been ongoing war. At other times nations have refused to practice conflict resolution, as between the United States and North Korea, or the United States and Iran, and the result has been lasting conflict. Sometimes nations have respected *nonviolent direct action*, and the result has been peace between India and England, and the end of apartheid in South Africa. Other times they have not, and the result has been ongoing injustice and insecurity as in Palestine and Israel. Sometimes nations have practiced *independent initiatives*, as Mikhail Gorbachev and George H. W. Bush did in reducing nuclear weapons (1989), and the result has been increased security for both and an end to the Cold War. Other times they have not, or not effectively, and the result has been ongoing hostility as between Palestine and Israel. Sometimes nations have *apologized for their own responsibility* in massacres, as Germany did after World War II (1970) and the United States did after the massacres in Rwanda (1998), thereby lancing the boil of much resentment and bringing about much reconciliation.

Our faiths call us to do justice, and we have seen the empirical evidence that doing justice often prevents war. The fifth and sixth practices that we advocate respond to that calling in our faiths. And they often work to make peace and prevent war. "If you want peace, do justice." By justice, we do not mean—at least not mainly—punishment. We mean human rights and religious liberty, and we mean sustainable economic justice. Our scriptures proclaim that injustice leads to judgment, destruction, and war. Our experience points to many injustices that erupt into rebellion and war. But when we do justice, peace comes closer.

Our three faiths also call us to community. This became abundantly clear in the valuable space that was created by each of the Just Peacemaking conferences when participants from the three traditions had the opportunities to exchange views and build relationships. The hyperindividualism of most of our cultures in this economically globalizing world has formed many people to be more narcissistic, more "me first," more "my rights and let others fend for themselves," than our loyalty to God, who is love, calls us to be. So we advocate four practices that build community and decrease war. We cite empirical evidence that nations that participate in international networks and the checks and balances that come from respect for the wisdom of other nations make war less often and have war made against them less often.

You see what we mean: this book is about actual, real practices that people and groups and governments are already doing in reality, and that are in fact working to prevent the killing of millions of people. We believe this is God's will.

We share a hope: we hope that we can help awareness of these ten practices of Just Peacemaking to spread among Jews, Christians, and Muslims. And that then each of us can influence our fellow believers to practice these ways of peacemaking that are scriptural and that do work, and each of us can prod governments to practice them. We hope that Jews, Christians, and Muslims will become more articulate about the practices of peacemaking that are scripturally supported and that do actually decrease wars and make relative peace. Doing this together has already increased the interest of our fellow believers. When Christians learn that Muslims are affirming and adopting the new paradigm of Just Peacemaking, it causes those Christians to pay attention and to learn more about the practices of Just Peacemaking. Jews and Muslims likewise: when they learn that we are each working on Just Peacemaking practices, it arouses a glint of hope. Thus not only are we influencing those of our own faith, but we are strengthening each other's hands as we work among our own faith groups to make us more articulate about the real practices of peacemaking, more support-ive of them, and a little more peaceful ourselves.

Through this exchange of ideas we also find new directions for the work of Interfaith Just Peacemaking. For example, it is important to note that the Just Peacemaking paradigm originated from within the Christian tradition. Yet those original authors wrote, "We purposely fashioned the wording of the ten practices of Just Peacemaking so they could be adopted by persons of many faiths . . . We wrote chapters explaining each practice so its basis can be seen clearly in what is actually happening in our time to change the world. We appeal to all people of good will to adopt these practices and work for them, grounding themselves in a commitment to change our world . . . to peace rather than war and oppression. Each person can base these practices on his or her own faith."[7] During the 2010 conference there was also a great deal of discussion about the number of practice norms in the paradigm, whether some should be added, combined, or removed. It is clear that there is overlap between the practices, but for the purposes of this publication we all agreed to address the ten practices of the paradigm as they stand at present. Certainly, in the future the Just Peacemaking paradigm may shift to address additional topics and grapple more completely with the richness and complexity of our scriptures and religious practices.

The specific issue in play here is not the desirability of achieving resolu-tion of conflict and ending violence, self-evidently true and generally accepted whether on pragmatic or ideological grounds, but rather the role of religion in energizing this process and informing it with insights relevant to specific prac-tices of Just Peacemaking. People lack imagination about what does work to make peace. They debate whether war is right or wrong. They know our scrip-tures do affirm peacemaking. But they seem to have very little clue about what they would give their support to if they actually took seriously both our scriptures and our knowledge that war kills and devastates. For many people, being for peace simply means being opposed to war. And many believe sometimes war is needed. At the same time, they know something about how devastating war actually is. Some who have experienced war, including many veterans, have more intense awareness of how important it is to avoid war when we can. But we usually are as unimaginative about what can be done to heal the causes of war as we are about how to speak a foreign language—even though our own scriptures point to practices of peacemaking. Our purpose is to help people imagine what it actually means to work for peacemaking and to help us participate in the takeoff that is actually happening in visible ways around the world.

Notes

1. Glen Stassen, ed., *Just Peacemaking: The New Paradigm for the Ethics of Peace and War* (Cleveland: Pilgrim Press, 1998, 2003, 2008) is in its third edition at the time of this writing. It was preceded by Glen Stassen, *Just Peacemaking: Transforming Initiatives for Justice and Peace* (Philadelphia: Westminster John Knox Press, 1992), which was in turn preceded in the 1980s by book-length calls for a positive paradigm of peacemaking by Catholic, Presbyterian, United Church of Christ, and Methodist churches in the United States. The concluding chapter of *Just Peacemaking: Transforming Initiatives* analyzes and gives credit to those official church statements. Thus it has been a shared development over three decades.
2. Susan Brooks Thistlethwaite, "Obama's new 'Just War Peace' Policy," *The Washington Post*, December 11, 2009, http://onfaith.washingtonpost.com/onfaith/panelists/susan_brooks_thistlethwaite/2009/12/just_war_and_just_peace_the_emerging_obama_doctrine.html.
3. Dudley Woodbery, ed., *Resources for Peacemaking in Muslim-Christian Relations* (Pasadena, CA: Fuller Seminary Press, 2006).
4. Mohammed Abu-Nimer and David Augsburger, eds., *Peace-Building by, between, and beyond Muslims and Evangelical Christians* (Lanham, MD: Rowman & Littlefield, 2009).
5. Susan Thistlethwaite and Glen Stassen, "Abrahamic Alternatives to War: Jewish, Christian, and Muslim Perspectives on Just Peacemaking," United States Institute of Peace Special Report, October 2008, http://www.usip.org/pubs/specialreports/sr214.html.
6. Conference notes.
7. Stassen, ed., *Just Peacemaking: New Paradigm*, 17.

CHAPTER 1

Practice Norm 1
Support Nonviolent Direct Action

Definition

*E*xamples of nonviolent direct action include boycotts, strikes, marches, civil disobedience, public disclosure, accompaniment, and the creation of safe spaces. The last century attests to the ability of nonviolent direct action to transform a situation of conflict into a moment of constructive change. When we engage in actions that call us to stand with others in the face of injustice, we create a unified front against violence and oppression.

Introduction

In the hot sun and pouring rain, thousands of Muslim and Christian women sat side by side on the Monrovia airfield, clothed in sackcloth and covered in ashes to proclaim a message of peace. These women sat together, enduring harassment and beatings at the hands of the armed soldiers of Liberian president Charles Taylor. Driven by their faith and a desperate situation, they had come to protest against violence and government oppression.

For more than 15 years Liberia suffered the ravages of intense warfare. In 1990 two factions of the National Patriotic Front of Liberia, one led by Prince Johnson and the other by Charles Taylor, invaded the capital city of Monrovia. A bloody civil war resulted. Thousands of Liberian citizens were evacuated from their homes, and access to food, clean water, and adequate health care was nearly eliminated. Although a peace treaty was signed in 1995 violence continued. Murder, rape, and the use of child soldiers became commonplace, making living conditions unbearably dangerous, particularly for women.

By 2002, the women of Liberia had had enough. In that year Leymah Gbowee and Comfort Freeman, presidents of two different Lutheran

Churches, began to speak out. They organized the Women in Peacebuilding Network (WIPNET), a group that encouraged recognition of the important role women play in peacebuilding. Determined to change their circumstances, WIPNET issued a statement of intent: "In the past we were silent, but after being killed, raped, dehumanized, and infected with diseases, and watching our children and families destroyed, war has taught us that the future lies in saying NO to violence and YES to peace! We will not relent until peace prevails." Inspired by the work of WIPNET, Asatu Bah Kenneth, assistant minister for administration and public safety of the Liberian Ministry of Justice, formed the Liberian Muslim Women's Organization. These Christian and Muslim women soon joined together to create Women of Liberia Mass Action for Peace. Together they held peace vigils at churches and mosques, organized mass meetings at Monrovia's City Hall, and marched in the streets proclaiming, "We want peace. No more war."

Peace negotiations began in 2003, but the parties could not come to a peaceful resolution and violence once more began to escalate. After a missile landed in the American and Muslim compound where many displaced Liberians were living, the women staged a sit-in outside the presidential palace, determined that no one would come out until a peace treaty was signed. A tentative treaty was signed and the United Nations eventually charged Charles Taylor with crimes against humanity. The women of Liberia became a political force against violence and later helped bring to power the country's first female head of state, Ellen Johnson Sirleaf.

For the first time Liberian women of different religions had come together, motivated by their faith, to denounce violence and transform their society. But this is hardly the first chapter in the history of nonviolent direct action. For centuries people of faith, motivated by their understanding of human blessedness, their commitment to stand in solidarity with others, and their hope in the possibility of change, have participated in collective peaceful action to bring about social transformation.

Christian Reflection

James B. Burke

"You know what is wrong with the world?" Peter Maurin, the Catholic street philosopher, asked Dorothy Day when they first met in New York City in 1932.[1] "The people who act, do not think," Maurin answered, before Dorothy could, "and the people who think, do not act." Maurin's critique applies with modification to Christians who support nonviolent direct action today.

Christians who have engaged in nonviolent struggle have not failed to draw thinkers' attention to the power of nonviolent action, but Christian ethicists have failed to integrate nonviolent conflict coherently into the overarching Christian realism of the Just War tradition.[2]

This reflection identifies both milestones in pan-Christian practices of non-violent conflict since the massive wave of political unrest during the 1905 Russian Revolution and three twentieth-century Christian practitioner-thinkers who have most influenced Roman Catholic reassessment of nonviolent action. Then it lists post–Vatican II developments in teaching about nonviolent direct action. Lastly, this reflection names the central confusion Christian teaching retains about nonviolent conflict and shares related hope for the Interfaith Just Peacemaking collaboration. Roman Catholic Just Peace ethics, like Orthodox and Protestant ones, spring from the Bible. "For us as believers, the sacred scriptures provide the foundation for confronting war and peace today," the U.S. Catholic bishops write.[3] Even so, Catholic moral theology emphasizes scripture *and* tradition, employing in Just Peace dilemmas natural-law reasoning within a Just War framework.[4] However, despite these diverse approaches, Christian ethics is subject to the same fundamental confusion regarding nonviolent action.

Christian Teaching and Practice Milestones

By the twentieth century's end, tens of millions of people in popular movements each decade had battled "entrenched regimes or military forces with weapons very different from guns and bullets." The outcomes were historic at times. "Tyrants were toppled, governments were overthrown, occupying armies were impeded and political systems that withheld human rights were shattered. Entire societies were transformed, suddenly or gradually, by people using nonviolent resistance to destroy their opponents' ability to steer events."[5] Christians—first Orthodox, then Protestants, and later Roman Catholics—supported and joined other believers and unbelievers in these powerful nonviolent conflicts.

At times, Christians were among leaders of these public nonviolent conflicts or were a plurality of actionists in them. For example, Georgiy Apollonovich Gapon (1870–1906), a Russian Orthodox priest and popular working-class leader, organized 150,000 Russian workers in a Moscow nonviolent action that ignited nationwide protests in 1905. The action won "the country's first popularly elected national parliament" from the autocratic Tsar Nicholas II. From the 1920s through the 1930s, many British and American Protestants were entranced by Mohandas K. Gandhi's nonviolent experiments in India.[6] Some traveled to India to learn from Gandhi and participate. Gandhi's mass civil disobedience against the British during the 1930 to 1931 Salt March riveted worldwide attention. From 1940 on, Danish citizens refused nonviolently to aid the Nazi occupation. Churches were among those who helped rescue nearly all Denmark's eight thousand Jews. "Without picking up a single gun," Salvadorans forced long-time military dictator Maximiliano Hernández Martínez into exile in 1944.[7] Integrating Gandhi's teachings into his realist-pacifist theological ethic, the Baptist preacher Martin Luther King Jr. led the first globally televised nonviolent struggle, the U.S. civil rights movement (1955–68). A broad coalition of Jews and Christians joined the movement. Amid secular nonviolent actions, Christians were prominently represented among those who pressed forcefully for human rights without violence in Argentina (1977), Poland (1979), the Philippines (1986), and Serbia (1999). "Those who used nonviolent action . . . did not come to make peace," state Ackerman and DuVall. "They came to fight."[8]

Among twentieth-century Christians who used nonviolent action, three stand out for profoundly influencing Catholic social teaching: Dorothy Day, Martin Luther King Jr., and Karol Wojtyla. Dorothy Day, a single mother and journalist, who with Maurin founded Catholic Worker houses of hospitality and the *Catholic Worker* newspaper (1933), made nonviolent direct action a hallmark of her Catholic Worker protests, from defying 1950s civil defense drills to joining 1970s farm-worker pickets in California. Day grounded her Just Peacemaking in the scriptures, particularly in doing works of mercy (Matthew 25) and making "the Sermon on the Mount (Matt. 5–7) understandable and practical."[9] Day also traveled to the Second Vatican Council to pray, fast, and witness for the total condemnation of nuclear war. By her death in 1980, Day had introduced generations of Catholics to nonviolent action.

Worldwide coverage of Dr. King in the U.S. civil rights movement along with Pope Paul VI's personal endorsement of King's nonviolent movement after a 1964 Vatican meeting with King also exposed many of the 2,200 bishops at Vatican II's third session to nonviolent struggle. Day's and King's nonviolent actions would reach a wider audience two decades later through the three-year nationwide consultation to develop the U.S. bishops' peace pastoral (1980–83). Day's and King's nonviolent actions are explicitly hailed in the peace pastoral, *The Challenge of Peace: God's Promise and Our Response.*

As a university student in Krakow, Karol Wojtyla, the future Pope John Paul II, engaged in an underground theater group's nonviolent resistance against the Nazis. Later, Bishop Wojtyla employed a variety of nonviolent tactics to combat Poland's Communist regime.[10] The central theme in Wojtyla's moral teachings as Pope John Paul II, including his implicit realist Just Peacemaking ethic, was human dignity, rooted in the Genesis 1 and 2 accounts of human creation in God's image.[11] John Paul II deployed his papal authority and the Vatican diplomatic corps to stand with peoples' nonviolent struggles for justice around the world.

John Paul "tutor[ed] the Solidarity labor movement, contribut[ed] to the liberation of his native Poland and the end of communism in Eastern Europe, precipitat[ed] the fall of dictators . . . and utiliz[ed] interfaith prayer . . . to oppose outbreaks of religiously inspired violence and the notion of 'clash of civilizations.'"[12] History may prove none of John Paul's nonviolent praxis to be as globally pivotal as his three multiday pilgrimages to Poland between 1979 and 1989. Through them John Paul engaged dramatically in Solidarity's nonviolent struggle for the right to organize—kindling it in 1979, sustaining it under martial law, and staying in the background as Solidarity came to government power in 1989. Together with millions of people's ongoing nonviolent praxis throughout the last century, Day, King, and Wojtyla have propelled Catholic teaching on war and peace to the threshold of the totally new evaluation Vatican II hoped to initiate.

Teaching Developments

Catholic teaching's embrace of nonviolent conflict began with Vatican II's surprise praise of pacifists and those who use nonviolent means within Just War norms (1965).[13] In 1968, Paul VI inaugurated an annual World Day of Peace (WDP) message to all peoples and governments on New Year's Day.[14] In his 11 WDP messages (1968–78), Paul honored Gandhi and emphasized nonviolent action without naming it, showed little respect for pacifism, yet did not resort to customary papal Just War formulae. From the first of his 27 WDP messages, John Paul followed suit, honoring nonviolent struggle without name, not mentioning pacifism, rarely alluding to Just War reasoning. John Paul's experience with nonviolent action appeared increasingly as a WDP subtext and, ultimately, his WDP address explicitly praises the "luminous" witness of nonviolent practitioners in the events surrounding 1989 to 1991.

Peace day messages proved to be a major source for the U.S. bishops' peace pastoral (1983), which contains the most extensive treatment of nonviolent conflict in the modern Catholic social-teaching corpus. Drew Christiansen, former head of the United States Conference of Catholic Bishops Office of International Justice and Peace, points out that the peace pastoral "identified nonviolence as a legitimate part of the Christian tradition."[15] The pastoral "advanced the teaching by articulating a common presumption against the use of force in both nonviolent and Just War traditions." In the Soviet Union's waning days, John Paul wrote about lessons from the century's global nonviolent praxis in *Centesimus annus*, an encyclical celebrating one hundred years of modern Catholic social teaching (1991). The post–World War II European order, John Paul states, "has been overcome by the nonviolent commitment of people, who, while always refusing to yield to the force of power, succeeded time after time in finding effective ways of bearing witness to the truth." He hopes that "people learn to fight for justice without violence, renouncing class struggle in internal disputes, and war in international ones."[16] In their tenth anniversary statement on the peace pastoral, *The Harvest of Justice Is Sown in Peace* (1993), the U.S. bishops secure their embrace of nonviolent conflict. They assert that "nonviolence is the basic Christian response to injustice and that the legitimate use of force is only an exception—a last resort employed only when repeated attempts at nonviolent correction of injustice fail."[17] They declare that participation in nonviolent conflict has become a "*prima facie* public obligation of government officials and citizens," while not rejecting the pastoral's designation of pacifism, or in-principled nonviolence, as a personal calling.

Confusion and Hope

Nonetheless, whether twentieth-century Catholic teaching on nonviolent action has deepened an already "strong presupposition against violence" (Curran), or has developed from "a presumption of Just War to a priority of nonviolence and peacebuilding" (Christiansen), Christian ethics has not achieved a coherent integration of nonviolent conflict, pacifism, and Just War theory within twenty-first-century Just War tradition.[18] Celebrating global nonviolent praxis yet glossing over political science's definitions of nonviolent struggle, Christian teaching has continued to conflate public nonviolent conflict (pragmatic nonviolence technology) with Christian pacifism (in-principled nonviolence).[19] Since[0] Gandhi, Day, Wojtyla, and King "emerged from religious callings, non-violent action has been stereotyped as a moral preference rather than a pragmatic choice, obscuring its strategic value in conflicts."[20] This systemic confusion not only prevents society from seeing nonviolent conflict for what it is but also results in "the greatest misconception about conflict": "that violence is always the ultimate form of power, that no other method of advancing a just cause or defeating injustice can surpass it."

In his question to Dorothy Day, Peter Maurin sought[21] a kindred truth-seeker with whom to undertake the arduous weaving of lessons from his actions for justice into what he knew. Since its first ecumenical manifestation, the Just Peacemaking Initiative (JPI) has functioned providentially in much the same truth-seeking capacity for Catholic war and peace ethics. When the U.S. bishops finalized *Harvest of Justice* (1993), it contained both their decisive call for more than mere support of nonviolent action, and their otherwise prescient post–Cold War Just Peacemaking agenda without any prioritization of their support for nonviolent conflict.[22] Without Just War language stretched to differentiate nonviolent force from Christian pacifism and to morally evaluate nonviolent conflict as force, the bishops were stymied—trapped in Maurin's split between unreconciled action and thought. JPI has given Catholic ethics more time to wrestle with this integration of nonviolent conflict into Just War tradition in dialog with other Christians and scholars. JPI's emphasis on doing Just Peace practices has also reminded Catholic thinkers that responding to the cries of the poor takes precedence, for all Christians, even over achieving coherent theological ethics. The signs of our times require Catholics to support, develop, and experiment with nonviolent conflict in order to assure sustainable and equitable development, to secure human rights, to build cooperative security, and to mitigate global climate change. Simultaneously, actualizing JPI's Just Peace practices will drive self-critical reassessment of our tradition's ethics of war and peace.

One grace of today's Interfaith Just Peacemaking (IJP) collaboration is that it realizes Christian acting and thinking need Jewish and Muslim (and other) truth seekers to articulate an adequate, public Just Peacemaking ethic from within Christian tradition. IJP focuses the Abrahamic faiths in self-critical dialog on an ethic of working together for justice and human rights by means that build peace—whether these disparate Jews, Muslims, and Christians hold to an ethic of Pacifism or Just War pragmatic nonviolent conflict. Sidestepping Just Warrior and pacifist polarization, Just Peacemaking theory directs interdisciplinary and interfaith leaders into effective Just Peace praxis as a privileged source from which to construct realist Just Peace theologies and ethics for the twenty-first century.

Jewish Reflection

Peter S. Knobel

"Seek peace and pursue it" (Ps. 34:15). This passage provides the overall justification for nonviolent direct action, as well as conflict resolution, in the Jewish tradition. As the Midrash explains, we cannot remain passive when it comes to peacemaking. We are to pursue it actively. "Seek peace, and pursue it" (Ps. 34:15) means to seek it for your own place and follow it to another place.[23] While peace is an important value, Judaism does permit some wars, for example a defensive war, and permits violence to save one's own life or the life of another. However, there is also significant support for nonviolence in the faith tradition.[24]

Central to the concept of nonviolent direct action is protest and speaking truth to power. This is sometimes successful and sometimes unsuccessful. Different leadership styles are exhibited by Noah and Abraham. When God tells Noah that God is about to destroy the world Noah remains silent, but when

God informs Abraham that God is about to destroy Sodom and Gomorrah Abraham offers not only a strong protest, but also an appeal to God's nature as the Judge of All the World, demanding that he act justly (Gen. 18). Ultimately God decides to annihilate Sodom and Gomorrah because God concludes that there are no righteous people there. The forceful logical and emotional appeal that Abraham utilizes is paradigmatic. The appeal to those in power must speak not only to the logic of the situation, but also to the values they purport to embody. The peacemaker's role is to prevent violence.

A second example occurs in Exodus 39 following the incident of the golden calf, where God declares his intention to destroy the Israelites and is dissuaded by Moses's intervention. As one considers these incidents one is struck by the hubris of both Abraham and Moses in directly challenging what God proposes to do. In an attempt to thwart violence to be initiated by God they offer a direct and clear protest. What gives these examples the force of a paradigm, or model, is that the power being challenged is God. Inherent in these examples is the danger of challenging authority with the power not only to inflict violence on the intended victim, but also on the protestor. If God is not above reproach how much more so human authorities. In the face of violence, especially violence that will create injustice by harming the innocent along with the guilty, protest is mandatory.

These examples assume that violent action is both unjust and unnecessary. One may group this type of protest under the heading of speaking truth to power. An essential aspect of peacemaking is preventing violence in the first instance and therefore insisting that those with the power to inflict violence can justify it. While one can use this to encourage grassroots protests, it appears this applies most clearly to those with access to decision-making authority. Those in positions of power and influence have a special responsibility. There are also numerous examples of prophetic criticism of powerful establishments and elites that oppress their people. Protest is the most deeply ingrained of all the Jewish nonviolent direct-action peacemaking techniques.

Rabbi Jose b. Hanina (c. 280 BCE) and Rabbi Yo ḥanan bar Naf ḥa (d. 279 BCE) taught, "Whoever can protest to his household and does not, is accountable [for the sins] of his household; if he could protest to his townspeople, he is accountable for their sins; if he could protest to the whole world, he is accountable for the whole world" (Mishnah *Shabbat* 54b). The Maharal of Prague (c. 1525–1609) also explained, "While a person may be individually pious, such good will pale in the face of the sin of not protesting against an emerging communal evil . . . such a pious person will be accountable for having been able to prevent it and did not."[25] A classic example of such civil disobedience is the story of Shifrah and Pual, the two Egyptian midwives who refused Pharaoh's order to kill all the Hebrew male babies. When confronted by Pharaoh they said, "Because the Hebrew women are not like the Egyptian women: they are vigorous. Before the midwife can come to them, they have given birth" (Exod. 1:19).

David Golinkin, in his article "The Jewish Attitude Towards Nonviolent Protest and Civil Disobedience,"[26] tells the story of a mass protest against Emperor Gaius Caligula, who sent Petronius to Israel to put a statue of the emperor in the Temple in Jerusalem. According to Josephus's account, Petronius was confronted by tens of thousands of Jews who expressed their resolve to become martyrs if necessary in order to prevent the installation of the statue.[27] The nonviolent anti–Vietnam War movement owed much to Martin Luther King Jr. and twentieth-century theologian and activist Abraham Joshua Heschel. In an essay, "The Reasons for My Involvement in the Peace Movement," Heschel wrote, "Although Jewish tradition enjoins her people to obey scrupulously the decrees issued by the government of the land, whenever a decree is unambiguously an immoral one nevertheless has a duty to disobey it."[28] Heschel's prominence in the civil rights movement and the antiwar movement became an encouragement for other religious leaders to join. Heschel felt compelled by his understanding of *halacha* (Jewish law) and his reading of the prophets that speaking out and encouraging nonviolent protest were essential to stopping an unJust War. His own views were rooted in the description of the creation of humankind as being created in the image of God and the Mishnaic teaching that to kill a single individual is equivalent to killing the entire world and saving a single life is equivalent to saving the entire world. He understood the challenge was to move to a broad concept of the supreme value of every human life. The anti–Vietnam War movement had the effect of undermining national support for continuing the war. Without grassroots support a democratic government is unable to pursue certain policies. The power of the antiwar movement rested on its ability to create mass nonviolent confrontations.[29] The willingness of religious leaders to publicly engage in acts of civil disobedience, often at the risk of losing their jobs, was important in creating legitimate protests and suggests an important role for religious leaders in direct acts of nonviolence. Religion, which is often seen as the problem, must come to be seen as the solution.

An important discussion of nonviolence in Jewish tradition is Reuven Kimelman's classic article "Non-violence in the Talmud." Two examples of the many cited by Kimelman are important. In discussing the encounter between Jacob and Esau upon Jacob's return, Kimelman challenges the concept that violence in pursuit of self-defense is permissible. The first example is as follows: "'Then Jacob was greatly afraid' (Gen. 32:9). Do you think that Jacob really feared Esau, that he could not overcome him? It is not so. Rather, why did he fear him? That he would not stumble into the shedding of blood. Jacob thought, 'Any way you want, if I kill him I will transgress [the command] "Thou shalt not murder."'"

The second example is the encounter between Saul and David. Saul is pursuing David, his arch rival, with the intent to kill him. David is hiding in a cave when Saul enters the cave to relieve himself. "Now David and his men were sitting in the innermost parts of the cave. And the men of David said to him, 'Here is the day of which the Lord said to you, "Behold, I will give your enemy into your hand, and you shall do to him as it shall seem good to you."' Then David arose and stealthily cut off the skirt of Saul's robe. And afterward David's heart smote him" (1 Sam. 24:3–5).

The midrash goes on to make clear that not only could he have killed Saul, and it would have been certainly justified from the perspective of self-defense, but he had to make a difficult affirmative decision to resist the natural temptation to kill Saul.

"Rabbi Samuel b. Nahman said: 'His urge appeared and said "If you fell into his hand he would have no mercy for you and would kill you. And from the Torah it is permissible to kill him, for he is a pursuer." Accordingly, he [David] leaped and swore twice, "By god, I won't kill him!"'"[30]

These examples are part of a broader tradition that rejects violence. David's action has the potential to change the relationship between himself and Saul. When one has both the power and the opportunity to kill one's enemy and one resists the temptation, there is the possibility to create an opportunity for future conflict resolution. Returning violence for violence simple perpetuates violence.

"If a man returns evil for good, evil will not depart from his house" (Prov. 17:13). "Rabbi Simeon b. Abba said: 'Not only he who returns evil for good, but even he who returns evil for evil. "evil will not depart from his house."' Rabbi Alexandri commented on the verse, "He who returns evil for good": 'Now the Torah said, "If you see the ass of one who hates you lying under its burden you shall refrain from leaving it him with it, you shall lift it up" (Exod. 23:5) of such scripture says, "He who returns evil for good, evil shall not depart."'"[31]

The line between direct nonviolent action and conflict resolution is often blurred. To pave the way for conflict resolution, it is necessary to break the cycle of violence. This reflection, and especially the work of Kimelman and Golinkin, point toward a tradition of nonviolence that can serve as a model of Jewish Just Peacemaking.

Muslim Reflection

Mohammed Abu-Nimer

There is an assumption held by many researchers, writers, and policymakers (both Muslim and non-Muslim) that the concept of nonviolence is either strange or contradictory to Islamic religious beliefs. Most of them have based their argument on Qur'anic sources or on the Prophet's tradition (*hadith*). However, while the majority of Islamic studies that address the question of war and peace have focused on justifying the defensive use of violence in Islamic scripture, few have reviewed and emphasized the great potential for nonviolence in Islam. Such studies have identified values and principles such as basic belief in unity, supreme love of the creator, mercy, subjection of passion, and accountability for all actions.

However, prior to identifying Islamic sources of nonviolence, it is important to clarify the misperception associated with nonviolence and pacifism that is often cited by scholars who reject the hypothesis of an Islamic nonviolence framework. An example of this confusion is reflected in Abdulaziz Sachedina's statement, "Pacifist silence in the face of continuous violation of justice amounted to being an accomplice of those unjust forces, and that was regarded as a major sin of associating other beings to God."[32]

The feature of "passive silence and pacifism" was mischaracterized with nonviolent resistance, which is an effective set of activities that have been utilized by many Muslims around the world in fighting against occupation, colonial powers, or other forms of aggression and oppression. Another classic mischaracterization of the concept of peace and nonviolence is often reflected in the pressure to choose between peace and nonviolence on one side and justice, freedom, and equality on the other side. Such an equation has been utilized especially when the call for peace and nonviolence was issued by dominant majorities and oppressing regimes in dealing with militant oppositions (Israel, Northern Ireland, South Africa, Turkey, etc.).

Theorists and practitioners of nonviolence have maintained the position that nonviolence is a viable and effective way to accomplish justice, freedom, pride, and empowerment. These are certain outcomes when applying nonviolent resistance.[33] Thus, when examining the relationship between Islam and nonviolent resistance, it is important to define the meaning of nonviolent resistance principles and strategies. To what extent are those values and strategies reflected in Islamic religion and tradition? How and in what contexts were those values expressed?

Islamic Sources of Nonviolent Resistance

Islamic values are identified by scholars and connected to active rather than passive nonviolence. These include *aadl* (justice), *ihasn* (benevolence), *rahma*[34] (compassion), and *hikmah* (wisdom). The very spirit of these key concepts would be injured by violence.[35] *Amal, yakeen,* and *muhabat* (service, faith, and love) form another set of Islamic values or principles that have been identified by Abdul Ghaffar Khan[36] in an attempt to make the connection between Islam and nonviolence more obvious than the stereotypical violent characterization of Islam.

Nonviolent direct action (NVDA) principles and strategies are an integral component of Islamic religious sources, and therefore they have been integrated in many Muslim societies, movements, and communities (see current political movements in the Philippines, Palestine, Pakistan, Iran, Egypt, etc.). In addition to the practical examples in Muslim societies, in the last two decades scholars have made major efforts to develop a theoretical framework for Islamic nonviolence. Such scholars refer to Qur'anic and *hadith* interpretation and attempt to contextualize principles of peace and nonviolence in Islamic tradition and religion.[37]

Among the writings of these scholars, it is possible to find some who justify the use of restricted violence under strict conditions. However, overall their focus and perspective are entirely based on, or in some cases devoted to, nonviolent resistance and even to the potential pacifist nature and characteristics of Islamic religion and tradition.

When explaining the reasons and motivation for their research and hypothesis, scholars in this group rely on several arguments:

1. The historical period has changed, and therefore the use of violence as a means to resolve differences or to spread the religion is not religiously permissible. Whatever Muslims used to create, establish, or spread their faith 1,400 years ago is not valid for today's reality. Therefore, if Muslim culture and tradition would thrive and prosper again, both Muslim leaders and Muslim people have to adopt a nonviolent approach to address their differences and conduct their lives.

2. The status of the Muslim community in the global system and in local communities has changed enormously, and it does not permit the use of violence. Many Muslim communities live as minorities in the world; their economic, social, and political status is different than six or seven centuries ago, when they were the majority or the dominant force in their regions and outside. In addition, the types of global economic and political systems that have developed in the last century prohibit the use

of violence, particularly mass destruction weapons, in settling conflicts. The use of such weapons will bring total destruction for all Muslims.

3. The use of violence as a means to address conflict was a minor aspect in the life of the Prophet and in the scripture, therefore, it should not occupy as much attention or importance today. The *hadith*, the Islamic tradition, and history and culture are all rich in examples of nonviolence and peacebuilding.

Searching for scriptural proofs that legitimize shunning violence in all its forms has been another primary focus of scholars of nonviolent direct action. They highlight all Islamic sources that condemn violence and war in any context, such as these Qur'anic verses: "Whenever they kindle the fire of war, God extinguishes it. They strive to create disorder on earth and God loves not those who create disorder" (Qur'an 5:64).

Tolerance and kindness to other people are also emphasized as a base of nonviolent approach, dealing with all people in such manner with no exception: "God commands you to treat (everyone) justly, generously and with kindness" (Qur'an 16:90). "Repel evil (not with evil) but something that is better (*ahsan*)—that is, with forgiveness and amnesty."[38]

Jawdat Said (b. 1931) provides a famous *hadith* that is widely quoted in Islamic literature and, as he describes, one often sees it hung as a calligraphic adornment in people's homes: "Whenever violence enters into something it disgraces it, and whenever 'gentle-civility' enters into something it graces it. Truly, God bestows on account of gentle conduct what he does not bestow on account of violent conduct."[39] Supporters of the nonviolent Islam hypothesis often rely on the Meccan period of the Prophet's life (610–622 CE) during which, for 13 years, the Prophet showed no inclination toward the use of violence in any form, even for self-defense. Despite the torture, accusation of blasphemy, humiliation, and ostracization of his family and supporters, he did not curse, or encourage violence. On the contrary, his teachings were centered around prayer and hope for enlightenment and peace. He conducted a nonviolent resistance campaign that was reflected in all of his instructions and teachings during that period when Muslims were a minority. The Prophet's teachings were focused on the values of patience and steadfastness in facing the oppression.

In responding to the argument in support of using force, scholars of Islamic nonviolence argue that although the use of force is prescribed in the Qur'an under specific and strict conditions, believers are instructed to adopt patience and forgiveness as the preferred path: "The requital of evil is an evil similar to it: hence, whoever pardons (his enemy) and makes peace, his reward rests with God—for verily, He does not love evil-doers. Yet indeed, as for any who defend themselves after having been wronged—no blame whatever attaches to them: blame attaches but to those who oppress (other) people and behave out-rageously on earth, offending against all right: for them is grievous suffering in store! But if one is patient in adversity and forgives, this is indeed the best resolution of affairs" (Qur'an 42:40–43).

Active nonviolent resistance and open defiance of persecution is the proper Muslim response according to these verses, and was in fact, the Prophet's own practice during this period. There is no call for war or use of violence, but there is a clear call for active resistance. It establishes the higher moral ground of for-giveness and not revenge. In addition, the migration of the Prophet to Medina is viewed as a strategic act of nonviolence. It enabled the Prophet to construct a powerful center of Islam in that city. A similar teaching on migration and avoid-ance of confrontation took place when the Prophet instructed the poor family of former slaves to take refuge in the Christian kingdom of Abyssinia.

Many *hadiths* have been identified by proponents of nonviolence to illus-trate the importance of patience. Jawdat Said best summarizes several of those sayings in an attempt to prove the pacifist nature of Islam, particularly when the dispute involves two Muslims:

> I don't see anyone in this world who clearly explained when it is incumbent upon a Muslim to behave like (Able) the son of Adam! Nor does anyone teach the Mus-lims that the Messenger of God said to his companion Sa'd Ibn Abi Waqqas, "Kun Ka-Ibni Adam/Be as the son of Adam!" at the time when Muslims turn to fight one another. The prophet (s) said to his companion Abu Dharr al Ghifari in a similar situation, when Abu Dharr Asked him, "But what if someone entered into my home (to kill me)?" The Prophet replied: "if you fear to look upon the gleam of the sword raised (to strike you), then cover your face with your robe.—thus will he bear the sin of killing you as well as his own sin." And for the same situa-tion, the Prophet (s) told his companion Abu Musa al-Asha'ri: "Break your bows, sever your strings, beat stones on your swords (to break the blades); and when infringed upon by one of the perpetrators, Be as the best of Adam's two sons." . . . once he [the Prophet] said concerning a person who wished to revenge the killing of his brother, "if he kills him, he will be the same as him."

Muslims already have the values and principles in both their religion and their daily practice to adopt nonviolent action as tools to fight injustice. The values that underlie the five pillars of Islam are foundational for Muslim non-violent action: to obey God and the Prophet only and disobey others if neces-sary; to practice discipline through prayers; solidarity and support of the poor through Zakat tax; self-sacrifice, suffering, and patience through fasting; unity and brotherhood through pilgrimage.[40]

Islamic Principles and Values of Nonviolent Direct Action

In an Islamic context, there are many specific principles and values that directly relate and allow the implementation of an effective nonviolent resistance strategy. The following section will explore only some of them.

Steadfastness (somud): There is no doubt *somud* and its associated values are derived from Muslim cultural and religious context. Often the life of the Prophet and his early followers is alluded to as an example of *somud*. Suffering for one's faith and rights is a quality that Muslims are brought up to respect and accept. In practice, this is a concept largely introduced by Palestinian national activists and political activists and movements in the Arab world. Steadfastness referred to the ability of Palestinians to stand up to and face the various oppressive Israeli policies after 1967.

Justice and empowerment: Belief in a sense of justice and the importance of fighting injustice is a central objective and a unifying value for Muslims when opposing oppression. An abundance of proofs and evidences support the duty of Muslims to achieve justice and pursue it in their daily lives. The stories of the Prophet opposing and defeating the powerful enemies during his early period were constantly repeated among people and by preachers in mosques.

A main call of Islamic religion is to establish a just social reality. In Islam acting for the cause of God is synonymous with pursuing *adl*, justice. Islam calls for action whether you are strong or weak. It is the Muslim's duty to work for justice and reject oppression and injustice on interpersonal and structural levels.[41]

There is a consistent message to resist and correct conditions of injustice, which can be accomplished through both activism and third-party intervention and through divine intervention. Justice and peace are interconnected and interdependent. In addition, the Prophet has called Muslims to mobilize and stand steadfast against injustice, even if the injustice is originated by a Muslim: "O, Ye who believe, be steadfast in service of God's truth and bear witness for justice and let not hatred of a people seduce you so that you deal with them unjustly. Act justly for that is what piety demands." "He who support a tyrant or oppressor knowing he is a tyrant casts himself outside the pale of Islam."[42]

The concern for justice, as ascribed by Islamic principles and teachings, is compatible with approaches of nonviolence that mobilize communities to resist injustice in society. Thus this approach does not mean submission or passivity to aggression and injustice, contrary to the popular misperceptions among opponents of this method of resolving conflicts. For example, in several conflict areas, such as Palestine, Northern Ireland, and South Africa, political militant opponents have argued that the nonviolent form of resistance is a source of submission to the majority or the occupying forces. However, when examining the various strategies and techniques supported not only by great leaders such as Gandhi, Martin Luther King Jr., and others, but also by local community leaders or student groups on campuses, submissiveness and compromise of their sense of justice cannot be found or validated in the actions of the leader or their opponents.

Sacredness of human life: Nonviolence and peacebuilding approaches assume that human life is valuable and must be saved and protected, and resources should be utilized to preserve life and prevent violence. The Qur'an clearly suggests the sacredness of human life: "And if any one saved a life, it would be as if he saved the life of the whole people" (Qur'an 5:32). "And do not take a life which Allah has forbidden save in the course of justice. This he enjoins on you so that you may understand" (Qur'an 6:15). A person's life has meaning. It is an integral part of the great cosmic purpose. Consequently, what a person does matters profoundly. "Lord, Thou has not created all this in vain!"[43]

Thus destroying and wasting resources that serve human life is prohibited. Even when Muslims in the early period launched an armed conflict, their rulers instructed them to avoid destruction and restrict their wars. A well-known speech made in the early seventh century by the first caliphate, Abu Bakr, when he dispatched his army on an expedition to the Syrian borders, states, "Stop, O people, that I may give you ten rules for your guidance in the battlefield. Do not commit treachery or deviate from the right path. You must not mutilate dead bodies. Neither kill a child, nor a woman or an aged man. Bring no harm to the trees, nor burn them with fire, especially those which are fruitful. Slay not any of the enemy's flock, save for your food. You are likely to pass by people who have devoted their lives to monastic services, leave them alone."[44]

In a similar context Caliph Imam Ali (c. 599–661 CE), reacting to his people's pressure to go to war, was forced to utter the following words: "If I order you to march on them on warm days, you say 'this is the fire of summer. Give us time until the heat is over.' If I ask you to march on them in winter, you say 'this is the bite of the frost. Give us the time until the cold is over.' All this and you fleeing from the heat and the cold, but, by God, you are more in flight from the sword."[45] Saving lives, exhibiting patience, and avoiding violence are the main values conveyed by the imam.

Patience (sabr): Muslims are encouraged to be patient and to wait on the judgment of others, whether they are Muslims or non-Muslims. Also, patience is a virtue of the believers who can endure enormous difficulties and still maintain strong belief in God. This value is very appropriate to implementing any of the nonviolent direct action strategies. Interveners need a great deal of patience to carry it out. Patience is an important quality of believers—as agents of change— in Islam.

Ummah and solidarity: Nonviolent direct action is based on a strong sense of solidarity among those who resist. Expressing sympathy and solidarity in support of the just cause is a core Islamic principle that can be clearly reflected in the principle of *ummah*. A well-known *hadith* in Islam, "God's hand with the Jama'a (group)," is often used to motivate disputants to reach an agreement and achieve unity, gain strength, and be empowered by working together. It also contains the meaning of reducing cost and damage that might occur to individuals if they stand alone in a conflict. It is used to mobilize unity and support against the outside enemy, and to motivate people to avoid political and social splits or rivalries (*fitna*) too. Nevertheless, the saying encourages the collaborative approach to challenges. Such a concept has been easily utilized as a base for social and political mobilization, and it can be employed for nonviolent resistance in a social or economic development context.

Solidarity among Muslims is a central value too. There is a well-known traditional saying, "Help your brother (Muslim) whether he is an aggressor or a victim of aggression." When the Prophet was asked how can we assist our brother when he is the aggressor, he replied, "By doing your best to stop him from aggression."[46] This is a clear message to avoid the use of violence and prevent aggression by Muslims against other Muslims and non-Muslims. Solidarity in this context is the opposite of tribal solidarity (*assabiyyah*—assisting members of the same tribe or clan or family against outsiders regardless of the conditions).[47]

The concept of *ummah* has functioned as a base for collective action since the Prophet's period. During the early period of Islam in Mecca, where the Prophet lived for 13 years, he utilized the values of collaboration and collectivism to mobilize his followers and respond nonviolently to the accusation and force of those who did not follow his prophecy. The Prophet instructed his followers on many occasions of the importance of unity and solidarity among the believers and Muslims. He would compare their relationship to the organs of the body that communicate pain if one part is ill, or like a building that is strengthened by the strength of its various parts.

It is clear that the *ummah* as a principle and value can be a powerful mobilizing frame for various communities to pursue nonviolent direct action and systematically organize to resist structurally unjust arrangements.

Rituals and religious symbols: Many Islamic religious symbols and rituals have been deployed in nonviolent resistance campaigns. For example, the mosques are often used as places for those who seek protection from assault. The use of the local mosques for the purpose of nonviolent resistance has been widespread among Muslim communities (Palestine, Pakistan, Afghanistan, Egypt, etc.).[48] It is part of the Islamic faith that Muslims should congregate in the mosque not only for prayers, but also to discuss the affairs of their religion and their states.[49]

As mentioned above, many other values in Islam support nonviolent direct action, such as commitment and discipline, and self-sacrifice for justice. However, it is essential to explore their application in the daily lives of Muslims too.[50]

Islam as a religion and tradition has a set of values, beliefs, and strategies that facilitate nonviolent resistance and peacebuilding. It is up to scholars, policy makers, and activists to utilize or practice these principles and strategies when dealing with intracommunity and intercommunity conflicts. Obviously there are forces, conditions, and factors that will obstruct and challenge any agent of change from applying these principles to resolve concrete problems (poverty, state-sponsored terrorism, domestic violence, basic human rights violations) in Muslim societies. Nevertheless, there are microlevel examples and cases of success (interpersonal and small community) that can inspire wider applications and dissemination.

Conclusion

The power of nonviolent direct action has been testified to by the real, positive social transformation that has been brought about by millions of people throughout the world. At the heart of such movements for change is a recognition of the harmful cycle that violence perpetuates and an affirmation of the blessedness of all humanity. While Christians, Jews, and Muslims have, at different times and in different circumstances, turned to their sacred traditions to support the choice of war making, as this chapter shows, these religions also include scriptural references that encourage nonviolence and rich historical examples of peacebuilding activities.

It is vital that nonviolence not be considered synonymous with pacifism. If nonviolence becomes associated with nonaction, violence is framed as the ultimate form of power and therefore can no longer be overcome by any other form of action. Nonviolence must be active in the pursuit of justice. Movements that engage in nonviolent direct action can draw strength from the historical example of individuals and faith communities that, driven by their convictions, have spoken truth to power and stood in steadfast solidarity with the oppressed. When these examples come from the religious traditions of others, they serve to affirm the notion that interfaith dialog and cooperation can enrich our own faith understandings and drive us to more fully live out our commitments to compassion, patience, and hope.

Notes

1. This quotation is taken from a scene in John Wells, *Entertaining Angels: The Dorothy Day Story*, directed by Michael Ray Rhodes (Worcester, PA: Gateway Films; Burbank, CA: Warner Home Video, 1996), DVD. It may be historical fiction.
2. In this piece *nonviolent direct action* means the pragmatic nonviolent technology used by millions throughout the twentieth century. The following synonyms for nonviolent direct action will also be used: *nonviolent conflict*, *nonviolent struggle*, *strategic nonviolent conflict*, and *nonviolent action*. This is different from a principled commitment to pacifism. See Gene Sharp, *Waging Nonviolent Struggle: 20th Century Practice and 21st Century Potential* (Boston: Porter Sargent, 2005), 20–21. Sharp says, "The use of the term 'nonviolence' is especially unfortunate, because it confuses these forms of mass action with beliefs in religious or ethical nonviolence (principled nonviolence)."
3. National Conference of Catholic Bishops, *The Challenge of Peace: God's Promise and Our Response* (Washington, DC: United States Catholic Conference, 1983), no. 27.
4. Utilizing the *hermeneutical* or *pastoral circle*, Catholic social thinking employs a four-step method: (1) insertion into the social reality to gather data; (2) critical analysis of the data to uncover causes of injustice and to propose solutions; (3) theological reflection on the problem; and (4) planning Just Peace actions, congruent with Christian values. In its social analysis method, Catholic social teaching tends to stay at the level of universal principles in teaching in order to allow local communities to actualize social teaching in very different cultures. This means that grassroots Christian communities will have lead roles in supporting nonviolent direct action via steps 1, 2, and 4 in any given conflict. Thomas J. Massaro, *Living Justice: Catholic Social Teaching in Action* (Lanham, MD: Rowman & Littlefield, 2008), 55–78.
5. Peter Ackerman and Jack DuVall, *A Force More Powerful: A Century of Non-Violent Conflict* (Hampshire, UK: Palgrave Macmillan, 2001), 2.
6. Gandhi's reprehensible advice to Jews of Germany near *Kristallnacht* in November 1938 has raised serious questions about Gandhi's judgment and the effectiveness of nonviolent conflict outside a Just Peacemaking framework—that is, one in which strategic nonviolent conflict, Just War theory, and pacifism are dynamically integrated and work together to prevent, reduce, or transform violent conflicts.
7. Ackerman and DuVall, *Force*, 3.
8. Ibid., 5.
9. William G. Storey, *Novenas: Prayers of Intercession and Devotion* (Chicago: Loyola Press, 2005), 168.
10. The best account of John Paul's participation in nonviolent action is Jonathan Kwitny, *Man of the Century: The Life and Times of John Paul II* (New York: Henry Holt, 1997).
11. Charles E. Curran, "Sources of Moral Truth in the Teaching of John Paul II," in *The Vision of John Paul II: Assessing His Thought and Influence*, ed. Gerard Manion (Collegeville, MN: Liturgical Press, 2008), 132.
12. Drew Christiansen, "Catholic Peacemaking, 1991–2005: The Legacy of Pope John Paul II," *The Review of Faith and International Affairs* 4, no. 2 (Fall 2006): 115.

13. Austin Flannery, ed., *Vatican Council II: Constitutions, Decrees and Declarations* (Northport, NY: Costello, 1996), no. 78.
14. In *Catholic Social Teaching, 1891–Present: A Historical, Theological, and Ethical Analysis* (Washington, DC: Georgetown University Press, 2002), Charles Curran directs researchers to the World Day of Peace messages corpus as the best means of understanding developments in Catholic ethics on war and peace.
15. Christiansen, "Catholic Peacemaking," 116.
16. John Paul II, *Centesimus annus*, no. 23.2, in *The Encyclicals of John Paul II*, ed. J. Michael Miller, CSB (Huntington, IN: Our Sunday Visitor Publishing Division, 1996), 611.
17. Christiansen, "Catholic Peacemaking," 116. These are Christiansen's assessments, not direct quotes from *The Harvest of Justice Is Sown in Peace*. *The Harvest of Justice Is Sown in Peace* also contributes morally imaginative additions to Just Peace thinking. The bishops present a post–Cold War agenda for peacemaking and their own presentation of renewed Just War schema, which is the most comprehensive presentation of Just War theory in the modern Catholic social teaching corpus documents (and perhaps in all magisterial documents). The bishops also admit weaknesses in Just War reasoning. United States Conference of Catholic Bishops, *The Harvest of Justice Is Sown in Peace: A Reflection of the National Conference of Catholic Bishops on the Tenth Anniversary of The Challenge of Peace: God's Promise and Our Response* (Washington, DC: United States Catholic Conference, 1994).
18. Curran, *Catholic Social Teaching*, 167–68. Curran summarizes today's Catholic teaching on war and peace in this way: "Individuals may support pacifism or a limited Just War approach. All people are called to work for peace that involves a change of heart as well as a change of political and international structures. . . . A strong presupposition against violence has become even stronger in the past half-century. In this imperfect world, however, nations—as a last resort—can use limited violence in defense against aggression. Nations and people today too readily and quickly resort to war and violence, however." Christiansen ("Catholic Peacemaking," 117) speaks of a "trend from a presumption of Just War to a priority of nonviolence and peacebuilding."
    Lisa Sowle Cahill reports on Kenneth R. Himes and J. Bryan Hehir's inquiry into "whether the allowance, made by *The Challenge of Peace* for both pacifism and Just War as individual vocational choices . . . can be translated into a coherent overarching theory." Cahill writes, "Himes, like Hehir, doubts it." Cahill says Himes holds that "merely having roots in the Catholic tradition, as many conflicting positions do, is no guarantee of complementarity. Although he grants to the Just War position the stronger support of the church, Himes concludes that there is genuine moral ambiguity in the problem of war, and suggests that allowing pluralism on the matter in theory as well as in fact may be the most adequate present alternative." Lisa Sowle Cahill, *Love Your Enemies: Discipleship, Pacifism, and Just War Theory* (Minneapolis: Fortress Press, 1994), 211–12.
19. James B. Burke, "Crafting a Just Peacebuilding Ethic from Just War Theory and Strategic Nonviolent Conflict" (dissertation, Loyola University Chicago, 2007). Sharp, *Waging Nonviolent Struggle*, 547, defines nonviolent action: "A general technique of conducting protest, resistance, and intervention without physical violence.

The term nonviolent struggle can be used as a synonym. Such action may be conducted by (a) acts of omission—that is, the participants refuse to perform acts that they usually perform, are expected by custom to perform, or are required by law or regulation to perform; (b) acts of commission—that is the participants perform acts that they usually do not perform, are not expected by custom to perform, or are forbidden by law or regulation from performing; or (c) a combination of both. The technique includes a multitude of specific methods that are grouped into three main classes: nonviolent protest and persuasion, noncooperation, and nonviolent intervention."

20. Ackerman and DuVall, *Force*, 7. What they say society is not seeing in nonviolent conflict is that it has been "more frequent and widespread than supposed"; "effective against all types of oppressive opponents"; more likely to fail if it incorporates any violence; linked to "strengthening a civil society and establishing or sustaining a democracy"; effective when it is "less spontaneous than intentional, less theatrical than technical"; and essentially focused on "separating governments from their means of control."

21. Ibid, 9.

22. The bishops list six global priorities that otherwise parallel the Just Peacemaking practices: ensure sustainable and equitable development, secure human rights, build cooperative security, end religious violence and reduce nationalism, strengthen global institutions, reenvision U.S. leadership. From their document, either of these priorities could have been proposed—"experiment with nonviolent struggle" or "research and develop strategic nonviolent conflict."

23. Midrash *Leviticus Rabbah* 9:9.

24. Reuven Kimelman, "Non-Violence in the Talmud," *Judaism* 17 (1968): 316–34.

25. Reuven Kimelman, trans., *Netivot Olam, Netiv Hatochecha*, in "The Rabbinic Ethics of Protest," *Judaism* 19, no. 1 (Winter 1970): 41.

26. David Golinkin, "The Jewish Attitude towards Nonviolent Protest and Civil Disobedience" *Insight Israel*, http://judaism.about.com/library/3_askrabbi_sijs/bl_47_protest.htm. Golinkin provides numerous examples of protest and civil disobedience in Jewish texts.

27. Josephus, "Jewish Antiquities," trans. Louis H. Feldman, Loeb Classical Library, vol. 12, bk. 18, ch. 8 (Cambridge, MA: Harvard University Press, 1912), 153; and Philo, "The Embassy to Gaius," trans. F. H. Colson, Loeb Classical Library, vol. 10, para. 232.

28. Abraham Joshua Heschel, *Moral Grandeur and Spiritual Audacity*, ed. Susannah Heschel (New York: Farrar, Straus and Giroux, 1996), 226.

29. In addition I suspect that there was an element of self-interest among the protestors because at the time there was a still a draft in the United States. Both those eligible for the draft and their parents had a personal stake in the nature of the conflict. Therefore, they were willing to protest and commit acts of civil disobedience not only on the moral ground that war was unjust but on the grounds of self-interest that their own lives were in jeopardy.

30. Tanhuma *B'ha·a lot'kha* 10; see *Berakhot* 62b.

31. Midrash *Genesis Rabbah* 38; Midrash *Yalkut Shimoni* 956.

32. Abdulaziz A. Sachedina, "Justification for Violence in Islam," in *War and Its Discontents: Pacifism and Quietism in the Abrahamic Traditions*, ed. J. Patout Burns (Washington, DC: Georgetown University Press, 1996), 148.

33. Gene Sharp, *The Politics of Nonviolent Action* (Boston: P. Sargent, 1973); and Gene Sharp, "The Intifada and Nonviolent Struggle," *Journal of Palestine Studies* 19, no. 1 (1989): 3–13. The legacy of Martin Luther King Jr., Ghandi, and others is too obvious to be ignored.

34. "He who does not show compassion to his fellow men is undeserving of God's compassion." K. G. Saiyidain, *Islam: The Religion of Peace* (New Delhi: Har-Anand Publishing, 1994), based on *Sunan al-Tirmidhi* 34 and al-Bukhari, *al-Adab al-Mufrad* 53.

35. Michael Nagler, "Is There a Tradition of Nonviolence in Islam?" in *War and Its Discontents: Pacifism and Quietism in Abrahamic Traditions*, ed. J. Patout Burns (Washington, DC: Georgetown University Press, 1996), 165. Based on Ashgar Ali Engineer, "Sources of Nonviolence in Islam," *Gandhi Marge* 14 (1994): 98–106.

36. A Muslim leader who created a nonviolent social and political movement to fight the British colonial forces in Pakistan, before independence.

37. See Chaiwat Satha-Anand, "The Non-violent Crescent: Eight Theses on Muslim Non-violent Actions," in *Islam and Nonviolence*, ed. C. Satha-Anand, G. Paige, and S. Gilliat (Honolulu: University of Hawaii, 1993), 7–26; Eknath Easwaran, *A Man to Match His Mountains: Badshah Khan, Nonviolent Soldier of Islam* (Tomales, CA: Nilgiri Press, 1984); Khalid Kishtainy, *Sabah al-khayr* (Jiddah, Saudi Arabia: al-Sharikah al-Sa'udiyah lil-Abhath wa-al-Nashr, 1994); Wahiduddin Khan, *Principles of Islam* (New Delhi: Goodword Books, 1998); Jawdat Said, *Al-Din wa-al-qanun: Ruyah Quraniyah* (Damascus, Syria: Dar al-Fikr, 1998); Abudul Aziz Said, Mohammed Abu-Nimer, and Meena Sharify-Funk, eds., *Contemporary Islam: Dynamic, Not Static* (New York: Routledge, 2006); Mohammed Abu-Nimer, *Nonviolence and Peace Building in Islam: Theory and Practice* (Gainesville: University Press of Florida, 2003).

38. Saiyidain, *Islam*, 164.

39. Jawdat Said, *Peace and Nonviolence in History and with the Prophets*, trans. Abdudhu Hammud al-Sharif and Karim D. Crow (Damascus: Conference on "Islamic Values for Peaceful Change," 1997).

40. Chaiwat Satha-Anand, "Non-violent Crescent," 7–26.

41. Such belief is supported by the following Qur'anic verses: 4:58, 135; 5:8; 16:90.

42. Based on this hadith and others, Saiyidain (*Islam*) argues that refusal to support wrongdoing by one's country is a proof of patriotism or an act of virtue.

43. Saiyidain, *Islam*, 29.

44. Abdul Hamid Siddiqi, trans., *Sahih Muslim*, vol. 3 (Lahore, Pakistan: Kazi Publications, 1976), 838; cited in Satha-Anand, "Non-violent Crescent," 11. Also in Muhammad ibn Jarir al-Tabari, *Kitab al-Umam wal-Muluk*, vol. 3 (Cairo: Darul Maarif, 1969), 226–27.

45. Al-Sharif al-Radhay, *Nahj al-Blagha*, vol. 1 (Beirut, 1978), 77; Khalid Kishtainy, "Violent and Nonviolent Struggle in Arab History," in *Arab Nonviolent Political Struggle in the Middle East*, ed. Ralph E. Crow, Philip Grant, and Saad E. Ibrahim (Boulder, CO: Lynne Rienner Publishers, 1990), 12.

46. Muhammed Khawli, *Al-Adab al-Nabawi* (Cairo: al-Maktabah al-Tijariyah al-Kubra, 1961), 66. Al-Bukhari, *Kitab al-Mazalim* 22, no. 1–2; also *Sahih Muslim* 34 (cited in Saiyidain, *Islam*, 159).
47. Islam attempted to abolish such value of tribal solidarity; however, it remains a strong norm among many Arab and non-Arab Muslims.
48. The mosques were used for mass mobilization during the first and second Palestinian Intifada. The weekly Friday prayer functioned as a meeting place for many activists.
49. Kishtainy, "Violent and Nonviolent," 23.
50. Abu-Nimer, *Nonviolence and Peacebuilding in Islam: Theory and Practice* (Gainsville, Florida: University Press of Florida, 2003).

CHAPTER 2

Practice Norm 2
Take Independent Initiatives to Reduce Threat

Definition

*E*ffective independent initiatives are highly visible and surprising actions, outside of the frustratingly slow process of negotiation, which stimulate a climate where negotiation can be truly transformative and successful. Independent initiatives should be designed to decrease the threat to the other side without compromising the strength of the initiator. The purpose should be made clear and should always aim toward de-escalation and invite reciprocation. For these initiatives to be truly successful they should be undertaken in a series so that, whether the other side reciprocates or not, the sequence of initiatives continues. Independent initiatives differ from concessions in that they are not coerced or negotiated responses and are executed graciously on an announced schedule.

Introduction

Social psychologist Charles Osgood first introduced the concept of independent initiatives as a strategy on the level of international relations in 1962.[1] In situations of conflict and distrust between nations and international actors, this practice seeks to decrease the threat perception of one's adversary and lower the level of distrust in the relationship. One side takes initiatives that are independent of the slow process of negotiations (although they are designed to elicit comparable initiatives in response from the other side). Independent initiatives need to be publicly announced and verified to show that they are not a ploy, but a genuine effort to work toward a peaceful settlement. They also ideally should not leave the initiator in a weaker position, but serve as concessions that enhance the security and well-being of the opposition without greatly compromising one's own position. Independent initiatives have been successful in establishing a climate of greater trust that can lead to a series of initiatives from both sides that can break out of the cycle of distrust and escalation of violence.

One example of an independent initiative occurred when President Dwight D. Eisenhower announced a one-year halt to test-exploding nuclear weapons, and said that if the Soviet Union would also halt, the United States would continue the halt in testing year by year. President John F. Kennedy resumed the halt in testing, the Soviet Union again reciprocated, and these actions led to the treaty that halted nuclear testing above ground, under water, and in outer space. That in turn halted the spread of nuclear radiation from the tests, which had been quietly causing deaths of babies downwind. And eventually it led to the Comprehensive Nuclear Test-Ban Treaty—a major breakthrough for stopping the spread of nuclear weapons to other nations.

An interfaith example occurred during the war in Bosnia. Muslim students had been driven from their homes and their colleges, not only by Serbs fighting against Muslims in Bosnia itself, but also by Catholic Croats in Croatia. They had no way to continue their education. They were victims of enormous ethnic and religious hatred and war. The U.S. Fellowship of Reconciliation (FOR) learned of their plight and decided to take an independent initiative. But there were many obstacles. They had to get the students visas and passage out of the war zones. They had to persuade mostly Christian colleges in the United States to accept the students without documents and without charging tuition. They had to find families who would provide lodging and emotional support for the students thousands of miles away from home.

The FOR succeeded in getting 150 Bosnian students to safety. They were not only able to continue their education, they were introduced to a dramatic and deeply felt reconciliation between young Muslims terribly persecuted by "Christian" armies, and caring Christians, as well as some Jews and Muslims scattered throughout the United States. It made a huge impact on these students and on the host families and colleges. Doug Hostetter of FOR describes the project and the impact:

> The project not only saved the lives of scores of excellent students, it also gave Americans something positive to do in the face of an overwhelming tragedy . . . [It] offered American Christians an opportunity to distance themselves from the triumphalist tradition of the "Christian" armies of the [Crusades in the] Middle Ages and enabled them to identify with a much older Judea-Christian tradition of hospitality, compassion, and love as practiced by the Patriarchs, Christ, and the apostolic church. It was a great shock to many students who had been driven from their homes by "Christian" armies in Bosnia to see that the families and schools that gave them love, shelter, and education in the U.S. were also Christian.[2]

After four years, Hostetter went to Bosnia to visit families of the students. He brought photos of the children they had not seen for four years, and took photos of the families for their homesick children in the United States. Hostetter continues, "The tears of joy and pain on both sides of the Atlantic were almost too much to absorb. One mother explained, 'You have been the face of God to us at a time when the whole world seems to have turned its back on the Bosnian people.'"[3]

The actions undertaken by Doug Hostetter and the FOR were done not merely to be opposed to violence and not only to pressure governments to negotiate a peace treaty; they were to take an initiative of Just Peacemaking independent of the slow process of negotiations. This independent initiative may have turned out to be more effective in opposing violence and supporting peacemaking negotiations than anything else they could have done. And it made a huge difference for 150 Bosnian students and their families, and for thousands of Americans who got to know the Bosnian students and their personal drama in the midst of a history of terrible tragedy.

Independent initiatives, as these examples show, can work both on the individual level as with the FOR initiative with the Bosnian Muslim students, and on the governmental level in relations between nations, as in the process that led to the nuclear ban treaty Eisenhower example.

Christian Reflection

Matthew Hamsher

Taking independent initiatives to reduce threat does not necessarily depend upon a religious rationale but nevertheless can be rooted in a Christian understanding of scripture. It has been affirmed by a number of Christian denominations, including Roman Catholics, United Methodists, Presbyterians, and the United Church of Christ,[4] and is therefore not dependent upon a pacifist interpretation of scripture, although this rationale might be strengthened by the pacifist commitments of the historic peace churches (Quakers, Mennonites, and the Church of the Brethren).

The New Testament Exhorts Believers to Take Independent Initiatives toward Enemies

It should not be surprising to find support for independent initiatives among many different followers of Jesus because the life and mission of Jesus can be understood as an independent initiative on God's part toward a sinful and rebellious humanity. God did not wait for human beings to live up to their end of the bargain since, as the Apostle Paul writes, "all have sinned and fall short of the glory of God" (Rom. 3:23), but rather took the initiative to send Jesus into the world to demonstrate the love of God to a rebellious world. In Paul's words, again, "God proves his love for us in that while we were still sinners Christ died for us . . . While we were still enemies, we were reconciled to God through the death of his Son" (Rom. 5:8, 10). God acted independently in order to demonstrate the depth of God's love and commitment to reconciliation with the world (2 Cor. 5:18–21).[5] And even though God's initiative resulted in the crucifixion of Jesus, God's sovereignty was not put into question, as Christians believe that God was able to resurrect Jesus to eternal life.

God's independent initiative here forms the background for understanding biblical instructions for Christians to take independent initiatives of their own toward their enemies. In his Epistle to the Romans, for example, Paul exhorts his Christian readers not to become trapped in a cycle of violence and revenge, but to break out of this human pattern by repaying evil with good.

> Bless those who persecute you; bless and do not curse them. Rejoice with those who rejoice, weep with those who weep. Live in harmony with one another; do not be haughty, but associate with the lowly; do not claim to be wiser than you are. Do not repay anyone evil for evil, but take thought for what is noble in the sight of all. If it is possible, so far as it depends on you, live peaceably with all. Beloved, never avenge yourselves, but leave room for the vengeance of God; for it is written, "Vengeance is mine, I will repay, says the Lord." No, "if your enemies are hungry, feed them; if they are thirsty, give them something to drink; for by doing this you will heap burning coals upon their heads." Do not be overcome by evil, but overcome evil with good. (Rom. 12:14–21)[6]

The reference to blessing echoes the Christian understanding of God's blessing the world through Abraham in Genesis 12:3 (something to which Paul also alludes in Gal. 3:8). Blessing is tied to witness, both in the sense of sharing something that will benefit others and of living one's life in such a way that others will see and want to experience similar blessings themselves. Abraham and Israel (and Christians) are to live in such a way that the nations will come to know God through their lives and their relationship to God. This evangelistic logic explains Paul's pairing of not repaying evil for evil with taking account of how one's actions appear in the eyes of others in verse 17. Similarly, in Matthew 5:43–48, Jesus teaches his disciples to love their enemies and pray for their persecutors as a demonstration of the love of God; a love that is perfect, or complete, in God's providence of sunshine and rain for both the evil and the good, the righteous and the unrighteous—another example of God's independent initiatives toward humankind.

Although many persons have been tempted to assume the role of agents of the vengeance of God, it is clear in Paul's usage that this action should be left to God alone. In fact, Christians do not need to take vengeance if God can be trusted to repay what is due and vindicate God's people. This is also true in this quotation's earlier context of Moses's farewell song in Deuteronomy 32:35, which envisions not only a time of exile as punishment for human unfaithfulness, but a restoration of Israel so that the nations will know God's power and God's plan.[7]

Paul also inserts a saying from Proverbs 25:21–22, calling for the care of one's enemies by giving food and water as a way of overcoming evil with good: "To heap coals of fire on his head" does not mean "burn a hole in his brain." It means "bring him to repentance," bring him to put on sackcloth and ashes. For by so doing, one might shame one's enemies into recognizing the evil they are perpetrating and restore the dignity and identity of opponents as fellow children of God.

Paul's teaching here also parallels that of Jesus in Matthew 5:38–42, where Jesus diagnoses the vicious cycle of retaliation, in which both sides get stuck in mutually retaliatory action—an eye for an eye and a tooth for a tooth. Each of the actions in Matthew 5:38–42 (turning the other cheek, giving your cloak to one who is suing you, going the extra mile) is designed to reclaim dignity in the face of enforced servitude, insult, and injustice, shaming the oppressor or the offender into recognizing one's own humanity. None of them says simply to comply with what you are forced to do. Each of them is an initiative, on your own turf. Each is an initiative designed to confront the injustice and to call for a transformation of the relationship. Each is a transformation of one's own self and one's relationship with the other, and each hopes for a transformation of the other as well.

In that culture, a Roman soldier could demand that you carry his pack one mile. Jesus says we should take the independent initiative of offering to carry it a second mile. In that culture, when you are slapped on the right cheek, it is a degrading insult. Jesus says we should take the independent initiative of nonviolently turning the cheek of equal dignity, the left cheek. In that culture, to be sued for your coat is a greedy injustice; Jesus advocates the nonviolent initiative of giving your cloak as well, which means you will be standing in the law court naked. This reveals the greed of the creditor for all to see, with embarrassing humor. And if someone begs of you, take the independent initiative of offering a loan as well. All of these are independent initiatives, not mere compliance with what is being forced on us.[8]

When Glen Stassen first developed this understanding of transforming initiatives in Matthew 5:38–42 in 1967, and then read Charles Osgood's advocacy of the practice of independent initiatives while Stassen was thinking of how to stop the escalation of the nuclear arms race, the light dawned for him that we need a new ethic of Just Peacemaking—based on proactive initiatives, not merely prohibitions. And then he saw how Matthew 5:38–42 connected with the practice of nonviolent direct action during the U.S. civil rights movement, in which he was much involved. Thus Matthew 5:38–42 may be seen as the pivotal passage from which much that we are doing in Just Peacemaking has emerged—at least from the Christian side.

Independent Initiatives Can Work Today

The Just Peacemaking practice of independent initiatives can be understood as an application of this theme in Christian scripture: an attempt to break out of a downward spiral of violence and vengeance by overcoming evil with good. Taking steps to demonstrate goodwill and a desire to move past the conflict to a mutually beneficial future makes it harder and harder for nations and other international groups to demonize their opponents. Independent initiatives are designed to offer an opportunity to gain a more realistic assessment of the goals and intent of the opposition, and a chance for both sides to choose other ways of resolving conflict. Too often, the negotiation process is disrupted by those who accuse the other side of not negotiating in good faith or maintain that the other side will gladly choose war (or terror) rather than accept any kind of compromise in the interest of peace and security. Opponents of negotiation often maintain that the other side will not accept anything less than worldwide domination or eradication of our side. Independent initiatives can increase trust and make actual motives clearer if they cannot be seen or interpreted as a ruse or ploy to increase one side's advantage over the other.

Furthermore, in a Christian understanding, independent initiatives need not entail capitulation to the enemy. What is called for is not the end of resistance, but an opportunity to resolve conflict in a different manner. Independent initiatives have the best chance to gain public and governmental acceptance when they do not weaken the position of the side taking the initiative. It is not necessarily a pacifist response.[9] It is consistent with the Just War criterion of just cause, recognizing that one may need to continue to resist evil with force to protect innocent life, but also rejecting any actions that do not serve this principle (such as revenge, economic benefit, or punitive actions). Independent initiatives alleviate opponents' fears that such motivations are driving the conflict. Thus they promote a greater willingness to seek a just resolution of the conflict.

Bridging Pacifism and Just War Theory

Writing as a Mennonite and a pacifist, I completely agree with James Burke, who writes as a Catholic and a Just War theorist, that Just Peacemaking practices can be supported by Just War theorists and by those committed to consistent nonviolence.[10] Pacifism is not just a principled rejection of violence, but commitment to Pacifism may also have strategic, practical effects, such as support for Just Peacemaking practices that do in fact prevent many wars. Both Pacifists and Just War theorists are obligated to support Just Peacemaking practices if they understand the need to overcome injustice while seeking not to cause war. Both support them if they understand the horror of war in our time and the need to seek realistic and empirically verifiable practices that can prevent many wars and pursue practical peace. Both support these practices if they understand God's call to peacemaking. Just Peacemaking brings both pacifists and Just War theorists together in supporting these practices. As Burke writes, this is the genius of Just Peacemaking.

Just Peacemaking does not attempt to settle the debate between Pacifism and Just War as to whether violence can ever be justified in any specific instances. Rather, it is a proactive approach that calls adherents of both traditions to faithfulness in obeying Jesus' command to be peacemakers. It is important not to abandon the debate between Pacifism and Just War, even though Just Peacemaking does do much to "clear the ground" in terms of future rapprochement between the two in linking peace with justice as both necessary and obligatory aspects of following Jesus.

Furthermore, Burke's argument on the basis of Catholic social teaching and teachings by recent Popes and my argument on the basis of Paul's and Jesus's teachings support both practices--nonviolent direct action and independent initiatives. Both practices may be understood as implementations of the Apostle Paul's and Jesus's teaching of transforming initiatives of peacemaking toward enemies as well as friends: (1) They are not simply passive withdrawal, but proactive ways of grace that empower us to take peacemaking initiatives, as Paul and Jesus call us to do. (2) They acknowledge the log in our own eye and take our own responsibility for peacemaking rather than simply judging the other, as both Paul and Jesus teach. (3) They affirm the dignity and interests of the enemy, even while rejecting an enemy's wrong practices. (4) They confront the other with an invitation to peacemaking and justice. (5) They invite into community in a way that includes, rather than excludes, former enemies and outcasts. Furthermore, both are empirically validated—they are making a significant difference in international relations and domestic conflict.

Jewish Reflection

Robert Eisen

Jewish thought has less to say about dramatic gestures designed to de-escalate international conflicts between adversaries simply because most of the major texts in Judaism were written when Jews did not have political power. There is, therefore, relatively little material in the Jewish tradition that deals with conflicts between Jews as a people and other nations. Yet there is much in Judaism about conflicts between individuals, and that tradition can shed a great deal of light on this practice norm. There are certainly precedents in the Jewish tradition in which one of two parties in a conflict takes action to transform the relationship between them into a more peaceful one by means of an independent and unexpected action.

Dramatic Gestures for Reducing or Resolving Conflicts

It is not only necessary to acknowledge that most of the major texts in Judaism were written when Jews did not have political power, it is also necessary to note that the one major text written when Jews did have political power and were involved in conflicts with other nations was the Hebrew Bible. In consulting that text, one is hard-pressed to find instances of dramatic gestures of the kind that interest us in biblical narratives describing these conflicts.

There are, however, numerous Jewish texts that deal with conflicts between individuals, and here one does find material that clearly supports the practice of making dramatic gestures to one's adversaries in the interest of peace. The most significant biblical source to this effect is Exodus 23:4–5 where we have the following law: "When you encounter your enemy's ox or ass wandering, you must take it back to him. When you see the ass of your enemy lying under its burden and would refrain from raising it, you must nevertheless raise it with him." In this passage, we are instructed to help an enemy either by returning his lost animal to him or by helping him raise the load on his animal when it has collapsed under its burden. A number of rabbinic commentators attempt to explain the meaning of these laws. In one midrashic source, we find the following: "When your enemy sees that you came and you helped, he will say to himself, 'I thought that he is my enemy. God forbid! If he was my enemy he would not have helped me, but if he is my friend, then I am his enemy in vain. I will go and pacify him.' He went to him and made peace. Accordingly, it says, 'And all her paths are peace'" (Prov. 3:17).[11]

Here the transformative nature of the action of helping one's enemy is clearly spelled out. When a person comes to the aid of an enemy in a time of need, the action inspires the enemy to completely rethink his feelings toward that person.[12]

We can also find support for dramatic peacemaking gestures in a number of places in the biblical narrative. Most significant in this regard is Jacob's reunion with his brother Esau in Genesis 32–33. Jacob had fled the land of Canaan to live with his uncle Laban for 14 years because he incurred Esau's wrath by "stealing" the blessing from their father Isaac, and Esau intended to kill Jacob in revenge. As Jacob returns to the land of Canaan, he is told by his messengers that Esau is coming toward him with four hundred men. Before Jacob meets up with Esau, there is the famous scene of Jacob wrestling with the angel. But what interests us most is the actual meeting between Jacob and Esau. When the two finally encounter each other, Jacob offers Esau a large quantity of livestock as a gift, and he tells Esau, "Please accept my present which has been brought to you, for God has favored me with plenty" (Gen. 33:11). What is significant is that the Hebrew term for "present" here is *berakhah*, which also means "blessing." That is, the text is suggesting that Jacob is, in effect, giving back to Esau the blessing that he stole. Moreover, the term *berakhah* is a pun on the word *bekhorah*, which means "birthright." The two words contain the same letters, and their difference is in the transposition of two of those letters. Therefore, the text hints that Jacob, in giving back the blessing to Esau, is attempting to give the birthright back to him as well.[13] Most important for our purposes is that Jacob's actions constitute a dramatic gesture to Esau to settle the long-standing conflict between them. Jacob is implicitly admitting his wrongdoing and trying to make amends.

One may object that Jacob's actions do not reflect generosity but fear. The biblical narrative informs us that Jacob is indeed frightened by the prospect of meeting his brother, fearing the latter still holds a grudge against him. The fact that Esau has four hundred men with him, as Jacob's messengers report, was also cause for worry. However, one can question whether dramatic gestures lose their value because they are initiated by fear. After all, fear is often felt by those in conflict situations, particularly those involving nations in our own era when heavy weaponry can wreak such havoc. What is most important is that conflicts be de-escalated by dramatic gestures, and Jacob's actions provide us with a model for such gestures.

Furthermore, Jacob is not the only person who makes a dramatic gesture here for the sake of peace. Even more dramatic are the gestures made by Esau. Esau, after all, is the one who was wronged, and one can sympathize with Esau's anger at his younger brother. Yet when the two finally meet, Esau runs to greet Jacob with a hug and tears. Just as significant is that Esau initially refuses to accept Jacob's gifts, telling him, "Let what you have remain yours" (Gen. 33:9).

Esau takes them only after Jacob insists. Esau also offers to escort Jacob and his entourage to their destination. With these actions, Esau indicates to Jacob that he forgives him. He does not need the blessing or the birthright. Jews often find it difficult to see any virtue in Esau because in later Jewish tradition Esau's descendants would be associated with their worst enemies: the Edomites, the Romans, and the Christians. And yet the real hero of the narrative from a moral standpoint is Esau, who lets go of the past and wants peace with his brother.[14]

Let us note a brief statement that appears in the Talmud and is also relevant to our inquiry. The statement appears in a discussion about Korah and his followers who rebel against Moses in the book of Numbers. Just after the rebellion has erupted, we are told that "Moses rose and went to Dathan and Abiram," two of Korah's supporters, in order to address the Israelites (Num. 16:25). One rabbi, Resh Lakish, comments on Moses's action as follows: "This teaches that one must not be obdurate in a quarrel."[15] That is, Resh Lakish sees great significance in the fact that it is Moses who initiates communication with the rebels by coming over to them rather than waiting for them to come to him. According to Resh Lakish, Moses forgoes his dignity for the sake of ending the dispute, and his actions become a paradigm for all of us to follow. Resh Lakish's statement is exceedingly brief, yet it is frequently cited by later Jewish commentators as support for dramatic gestures in order to bring an end to conflict. Moses, the greatest prophet in Israel, swallowed his pride to make peace with a group of wicked rebels; thus, this practice norm has impressive Jewish credentials.[16]

Today, one can cite examples of any number of Jewish groups that have used independent initiatives to reduce conflict both in Israel and in the Diaspora. In Israel, for instance, Rabbis for Human Rights (RHR), founded in 1988, has taken a prominent role in easing the plight of Palestinians in Israel, the West Bank, and Gaza, and it has often done so with highly public gestures to dramatize its cause. When extremist Jewish settlers have forced Palestinians to abandon their villages, RHR has worked to bring the Palestinians back to their homes. When the settlers have cut down Palestinian olive trees, an important source of Palestinian livelihood, RHR has organized Jews to replant those trees.[17]

An individual who has become particularly well known in Israel for organizing his followers to reach out to Palestinians is Rabbi Menachem Froman (or Fruman), the chief rabbi of the West Bank settlement of Tekoa. Froman has been unique among West Bank rabbis in his ability to forge dialog and create friendships among government figures and clerics in the Palestinian Authority and Hamas. Like RHR, Froman has frequently organized public initiatives to build bridges with Palestinians when they have come under attack by settlers. For instance, in October of 2010, when a mosque was set afire in the Palestinian village of Beit Fajjar and was seriously damaged in what seems to have been an arson attack by settlers, Froman organized his followers to come to the village with a stack of Qur'ans to replace those that had been destroyed in the fire.[18]

In the United States, one can also find examples of dramatic gestures for the reduction of conflict. For instance, in the 2010 controversy surrounding the construction of a mosque in proximity to the site of the 9/11 attacks, most mainstream Jewish organizations opposed the project. However, a number of Jewish groups came out in support of the construction of the mosque and staged public demonstrations in order to make their views known.[19]

Muslim Reflection

Zeki Saritoprak

Our recent history has witnessed the unprecedented devastation of two world wars. The number of people killed in the two world wars of the past century is more than the number of people killed throughout human history. These destructive wars, on one hand, may have led some to claim that there will be an inevitable clash of civilizations. On the other hand, some have said working for justice and peace will prevent future clashes so that catastrophic atrocities should never be seen again. The possibility of another war in this age of nuclear weapons has resulted in an urgent need to unite all possible efforts to make Just Peace on Earth. The Qur'an, the example of the Prophet Muhammad, and the practice of Muslims contain many instructions on the promotion of peace and harmony on our planet. One contemporary example of this effort that is particularly applicable to this practice norm of independent initiatives to reduce threat is the example of the Gülen movement and its founder Fethullah Gülen.

Qur'anic Support for Independent Initiatives

The Islamic support for this practice norm is rooted in the principle of peace and harmony that comes from the Qur'anic statement, "Peace is better" (Qur'an 4:128). Although the occasion of this revelation is family dispute, with such a broad statement the Qur'an indicates that in all circumstances peace is preferable. Even in the midst of war, on the battlefield, if there is an opportunity for peace, the Qur'anic injunction is "if the enemy inclines towards peace, you should incline towards it too" (Qur'an 8:61). As the Qur'an speaks of peace it also speaks of justice. Both the Peace (al-Salam) and the Just (al-Adl) are considered among the most beautiful names of God. And both words are among the most frequently mentioned in the Qur'an.

The Qur'an strongly suggests that one should overcome evil with good and states that one should ward off evil with good deeds. The Qur'an asks, "Do not incline towards those who practice oppression. Fire may touch you. There is no protector for you other than God and you will not be helped [if you incline toward wrongdoers]. Be steadfast in prayer in the beginning and in the end of the day, and in some part of the night. Surely, good deeds are washing away bad deeds. This is a reminder for the mindful. O Muhammad, have patience. Surely God does not forget to reward those who do good deeds" (Qur'an 11:113–115).

Again the Qur'an praises those who repel evil with good: "Those people will take their reward twice; that is because they had patience and they repelled evil with good and they gave away from what We have given to them" (Qur'an 28:54). Another Qur'anic verse advises that repelling evil with good and beautiful actions eliminates animosity and results in friendship (Qur'an 41:34). Many Muslim scholars who comment on this verse suggest that seeking vengeance is a wrong principle and not compatible with the overall teaching of the Qur'an. Historically speaking there is no record that the Prophet Muhammad ever suggested revenge against those who persecuted him. In fact, the opposite is true; the Prophet forgave the people of Mecca, who tortured him for a period of time at the beginning of his prophethood.

It should be noted that the Prophet Muhammad is the best example for Muslims and the first addressee of the Qur'an. The Qur'an, in the personality of the Prophet, commands people to initiate good actions. For example, one of the early commands of the Qur'an to the Prophet asks him to rise and warn his community patiently (Qur'an 74:1–7). Another verse commands the Prophet to convey the divine message with no fear and no hesitation and grants divine protection for him. The verse says, "O Messenger, convey what is revealed to you from your Lord. If you do not do that it means you do not fulfill your duty. Surely God will protect you from people" (Qur'an 5:67). It can be argued that the entire message of the Qur'an is based on the principle of taking initiatives despite hardships. The verse "For a human being there is nothing except the result of his work" (Qur'an 53:39) praises human beings who are taking initiatives and doing good actions. One interesting figure of the Qur'an, Luqman the Wise (c. 1100 BCE), addresses his son and asks him to initiate beautiful and good actions. In fact, in the personality of Luqman, the Qur'an gives instructions to the entire realm of humanity to follow those principles. Luqman commands his son to do the following:

> O my dear son! God will bring all things to light, be they as small as the grain of a mustard seed; be they hidden inside a rock, or the heavens, or the earth. God is the most gracious and the most knowing. O my son, be steadfast in prayer. Enjoin justice and forbid evil and have patience on whatever befalls you. Surely all of that is among greatly meritorious things requiring great resolution to fulfill. My son, do not turn away your face from people. Do not walk on earth arrogantly. Surely

God does not love any arrogant and boaster. Be modest in your walking and lower your voice. Certainly the most repugnant of voices is the braying of the ass. (Qur'an 31:16–19)

In this verse, in order to create a harmony in society, the Qur'an gives instructions through the story of Luqman, including the promotion of righteousness, patience, and merit, as well as the prohibition of negative qualities such as arrogance and boastfulness.

As a commentator of the Qur'an, the Prophet of Islam, in one of his famous sayings, says, "Anyone who establishes a good tradition will get reward of all those who follow the tradition without decreasing anything from their reward. Similarly, anyone who establishes a bad tradition will get his burden and the burden of those who follow that tradition without decreasing anything from their burden."[20]

The famous story of the two sons of Adam, Cain and Abel, is given as an example of this. Cain kills Abel and thereby establishes a bad tradition, the tradition of murder. Therefore, according to this prophetic tradition, throughout history until the end of time when anyone commits murder, due to Cain's evil initiative a full burden of murdering falls on Cain without any decrease in the burden of the murderer. The Islamic principle of "the one who initiates some good or bad traditions is as if he or she does it" is rooted in the abovementioned saying of the Prophet. Again, a part of initiating the idea of good is related to the Prophet's saying on two individuals with animosity toward one another. The Prophet suggests that the best of them is the one who starts with a greeting of peace. The Prophet states, "It is not allowed for a man to abandon his brother more than three nights in a way that they meet and one turns to one direction and the other turns to the other direction. The best of both is the one who starts with a greeting of peace."[21]

One of the principles of the Qur'an is to bring an end to conflicts and to make all efforts to de-escalate tensions and possible clashes. In early Islam when the Prophet was persecuted by idol worshippers of Mecca, he preferred migration to clashing with his opponents. Following the teaching of the Qur'an and the way of the Prophet, Muslims throughout history anxiously practiced this principle. An example from recent history is the case of a prominent Islamic scholar in Turkey, Beduizzaman Said Nursi (1878–1960), who protected Armenian children during World War I and de-escalated conflict between Muslims and Armenians. In response to this gesture, Armenians also protected Muslim children. Nursi's initiative saved the lives of thousands of children. A more contemporary example is the practice that Fethullah Gülen followed when Israeli soldiers attacked a Turkish ship carrying aid to Gaza on May 31, 2010. While eight Turkish activists were killed and tensions in the country were high, which could have caused a wave of revenge on all Jews in the country, Gülen advocated for calmness and expressed his condolences to the families of the victims but also criticized the leadership of the aid flotilla because they did not get proper permission from the Israeli authorities. This public criticism and invitation to calmness de-escalated the tension in the country, and in fact many demonstrations stopped after this public statement. This action serves as an example of taking an initiative to de-escalate conflicts between majorities and minorities, or between two states.

The Example of the Gülen Movement

The Gülen movement started in the beginning of the 1970s as a small group and with only a humble contribution from the community. Fethullah Gülen, an official preacher appointed by the Directorate of Religious Affairs in Turkey, was a humble but passionate member of this governmental religious institution. Even at the very beginning of his preaching, his way of addressing the issues was remarkably different from that of the regular preachers. He was not only a preacher at the mosque, but an active member of his community as well. Therefore hundreds of community problems came to him, and he would wisely solve these problems. Like many great founders, Gülen did not intend to establish a movement and even today when people relate this particular movement to his name, he rejects the association and says that this is a community of volunteers of which he is only a member. He repeatedly states that people mistakenly relate this movement to him. In the past three decades the movement has become a large and influential community that promotes initiatives such as education, health, relief aid, and interfaith dialog, which contribute greatly to the building of peace both in Turkey and around the world. The movement remained peaceful during the time of conflicts in the country and in fact worked ardently to prevent young people from involvement in the armed conflict between the leftists and the nationalists in the 1970s, which caused the military coup of September 12, 1980.

The movement follows the principle stated in the saying of the Prophet, "A Muslim is the one from whose hands and whose tongue believers are safe."[22] The movement has used this saying of the Prophet as a reference for its behaviors and educational system. One can argue that through this understanding the movement is able to form a generation of character, and probably this understanding is the secret of the movement's success throughout the world. As indicated in Gülen's writings, the movement uses the love-force, or *satyagraha*, because love is the essence of his teachings. If we use the genre of the contemporary world and make a parable of weapons, for Gülen and for his movement there is no weapon greater than love. Love cannot be defeated. This is evident in his definition of religion: "Religion is the title of a deep relationship and love towards all creation in His [God's] name."[23] Love and compassion are considered the foundation of the teaching of the Gülen movement. Without these two components a Just Peace cannot be achieved thoroughly. Gülen says, "Close the doors of greed, abhorrence, and hatred. Otherwise, they may be a small seed, but by opening the door they could grow and become a huge tree of evil."[24] If this door is not closed and the seeds of hatred grow, the social environment will be ready for Samuel Huntington's idea of the alleged "clash of civilizations."[25] As a Sunni Muslim scholar Gülen showed a great openness to Shiites, known as Alavis in Turkey. He strongly emphasized dialog and understanding among the two groups and particularly encouraged the government to give more freedom to the Alavis, which will eventually contribute to the building of peace between Sunnis and Alavis.

Another practical example can be given from an educational institution that was established by admirers of the Gülen movement. Father Thomas Michel, former executive secretary for the Office of Interreligious and Ecumenical Affairs, speaks of his visit to this institution in the southern Philippines in 1995. A sign caught his attention: "The Philippine-Turkish School of Tolerance." He then visited the school and found out that it contributed to a peaceful coexistence between Muslim and Christian students.[26] These examples of Gülen's educational institutions that contribute to peaceful coexistence can be found in Northern Iraq, the Balkans, and Nigeria.

In conclusion, the overall teaching of the Qur'an and the sayings of the Prophet strongly encourage the building of peace, the prevention of conflict, and the de-escalating of tensions. Taking reference from the holy sources of Islam, a considerable number of civic, social, and religious movements and initiatives in the Muslim world have contributed to the building of peace. There is no doubt that one of the greatest of these initiatives, the Gülen movement, which grew so rapidly in the span of 40 years, promises a great hope for the future of peace on our planet.

Conclusion

The concept of independent initiatives in international relations came from a psychologist, Charles Osgood, but it is echoed in Christian and Muslim thought and scripture. As Robert Eisen points out, this is less the case with the Jewish scriptures regarding conflicts with other nations. As with all three traditions, however, using Just Peace norms today may involve generalizing from the sacred text and its injunction to individuals to the political level. Just Peacemaking does involve pushing forward on new initiatives in interfaith perspective, while using sacred texts to inform the direction and provide guidance for new work.

Notes

1. Charles E. Osgood, *An Alternative to War or Surrender* (Urbana: University of Illinois Press, 1962).

2. Doug Hostetter, "Neighbors in the Bosnian Tragedy," in *Transforming Violence: Linking Local and Global Peacemaking*, ed. Robert Herr and Judy Zimmerman Herr (Waterloo, ON: Herald Press, 1998), 105–6, 109.

3. Ibid., 117.

4. See, for example, the National Council of Catholic Bishops, *The Challenge of Peace: God's Promise and Our Response* (Washington, DC: United States Conference of Catholic Bishops, 1983), par. 204–6; United Methodist Council of Bishops, *In Defense of Creation: The Nuclear Crisis and a Just Peace* (Nashville, TN: Graded Press, 1986), 77; Susan Thistlethwaite, ed., *A Just Peace Church* (New York: United Church Press, 1986), 75, 136–37, 142–43; 216th General Assembly of Presbyterian Church USA, *Resolution on Violence, Religion, and Terrorism* (Louisville, KY: Advisory Committee on Social Witness Policy, 2004), 6, 29.

5. "All this is from God, who reconciled us to himself through Christ, and has given us the ministry of reconciliation; that is, in Christ God was reconciling the world to himself, not counting their trespasses against them, and entrusting the message of reconciliation to us. So we are ambassadors for Christ, since God is making his appeal through us; we entreat you on behalf of Christ, be reconciled to God. For our sake he made him to be sin who knew no sin, so that in him we might become the righteousness of God."

6. New Revised Standard Version.

7. See also Ezekiel 36:22–28.

8. See Glen Stassen, *Living the Sermon on the Mount* (New York: Jossey-Bass, 2006), 89–98.

9. At least some pacifist Christians might argue that this logic also entails a commitment to nonviolence as the highest expression of trust in God, choosing to bless others (even enemies) and to promote recognition of human dignity.

10. See James Burke's reflections in chapter 1 of this book.

11. Midrash *Aggadah*, ed. Solomon Buber (Vienna: A. Fanto, 1894) on Exodus 23:5. See also Midrash *Lekah Tov* (Jerusalem: Zikhron Aharon, 2006) on the same verse.

12. Reuven Kimelman, "Non-Violence in the Talmud," *Judaism* 17 (1968): 318–19; Marc Gopin, *Between Eden and Armageddon: The Future of Religions, Violence and Peacemaking* (New York: Oxford University Press, 2000), 178.

13. See the comments of Nahum Sarna on Genesis 33:11 in his commentary on Genesis in *The JPS Commentary on the Torah: Genesis* (Philadelphia: Jewish Publication Society of America, 1989), 230; and Jon D. Levenson's comments on the same verse in his commentary on Genesis in *The Jewish Study Bible*, ed. Adele Berlin and Marc Zvi Brettler (New York: Oxford University Press, 1999), 68–69.

14. I would like to thank my brother, Daniel Eisen, for inspiring these insights on Esau's actions.

15. Babylonian Talmud, *Sanhedrin* 110a.

16. See, for instance, the remarks of Rabbi Israel Meir Kagan in *Sefer Hafets Hayyim: Shemirat ha-Lashon* (Jerusalem: Merkaz ha-Sefer, 1999), *Sha'ar ha-Zekhirah*, ch. 17, p. 68. See also the discussion of Daniel Z. Feldman, *The Right and the Good:*

Halakhah and Human Relations (Brooklyn: Yashar Books, 2005), ch. 4, especially p. 42, who notes several other figures who cite this source for its moral lesson as peacemaking.

17. Information about RHR can be found on their Web site: http://www.rhr.org.il.

18. The Global Oneness Project, "Rabbi Menachem Froman," http://www.global onenessproject.org/interviewee/rabbi-menachem-froman.

19. See, for instance, the demonstration led by the Shalom Center in "Voz Is Neias? Manhattan, NY: Jewish Leaders Rally in Support of WTC Mosque." August 5, 2010, http://www.vosizneias.com/61619/2010/08/05/manhattan-ny-jewish-leaders -rally-in-support-of-wtc-mosque.

20. *Sunan al-Tirmidhi* 15, in Abu Isa Muhammad bin Isa bin Sawra al-Tirmidhi, *al-Jami' al-Sahih*, ed. Ibrahim Atwa Awad (Cairo: Maktabah Mustafa al-Babi al-Halabi, 1975).

21. Sahih al-Bukhari, *Al-Adab al-Mufrad*, 62.

22. Sahih al-Bukhari, *Iman*, 4; *Riqaq*, 26.

23. Fethullah Gülen, *Olcu Veya Yoldaki Isiklar* (A Criteria or Roadsigns) (Istanbul: Nil Yayanlari, 2001), 27.

24. Ibid.

25. Samuel P. Huntington, *Clash of Civilizations and the Remaking of World Order* (New York: Touchstone, 1997).

26. Thomas Michel, "Fethullah Gülen as Educator," in *Turkish Islam and the Secular State: The Gülen Movement*, ed. M. Hakan Yavuz and John L. Esposito (Syracuse, NY: Syracuse University Press, 2003), 69–84.

CHAPTER 3

Practice Norm 3
Use Cooperative Conflict Resolution

Definition

*C*ooperative conflict resolution encourages the active collaboration of parties in conflict toward the development of creative solutions that each can affirm and support. Cooperative conflict resolution becomes a shared enterprise, where former adversaries begin to see each other as partners and recognize multiple possibilities for the transformation of the situation. They pay respectful attention to the religious and cultural loyalties of the other side, seeing them as possibly contributing to ways of seeking solutions rather than disrespecting them because they are "different." This transparent strategy requires self-critical honesty and is nonjudgmental. As such, cooperative conflict resolution involves risk taking and cultural and spiritual awareness. To truly engage in this kind of initiative, participants must be willing to listen carefully, understand the perspectives of their adversaries, and suspend judgment, even though they may personally disagree.

Introduction

Violent conflicts are the result of a degenerating relationship of injustice and attack that is mutually cultivated, complex, and interwoven in space and time. The longer these conflicts drag on, the more protracted they become, and the more all are drawn into fueling their sustenance: not just people but their economic, political, and social institutions. As political and economic engines drive continued war, communities at conflict with each other become divided spiritually, psychologically, and physically. Bias and stereotypes about the dignity and intention of the other side proliferate, and trust erodes and with it faith in the possibility of finding a conflict settlement through cooperative negotiated means. Military victory becomes the only option. You can't, after all, negotiate with an enemy you've deemed irrational, untrustworthy, uncommitted to peace, and bent on your destruction. And so the bombs continue, flung across the divide.

In the midst of this reality, it might seem idealistic to promote cooperative conflict resolution as a viable means to address conflict. As the practice norms concept illustrates, however, it is eminently practical to reduce conflict through bringing about negotiated settlements. Wars are very costly in terms of civilian livelihood, and the total defeat of one side leaves grievances that can fuel future violence. Negotiated ends of conflict, beyond reducing the potential cost of human life and livelihood, can often do more to address directly the root drivers of conflict and thereby establish a lasting Just Peace.

The biggest barrier to cooperative conflict resolution, however, is the lack of trust between adversaries. Hence the process of collaborative conflict resolution as a modern practice of problem-solving workshops, facilitated dialog, and conflict analysis training for adversaries in conflict focuses on establishing enough trust and relationship building to set the stage for formal negotiations. These processes seek to move adversaries from a relationship of mutual aggression to a relationship in which they can work together—even if tentatively—to address their common problem.

There are many examples of such cooperative conflict resolution taking place throughout the world. Although in May 2009 the government of Sri Lanka officially announced its defeat of the separatist group the Liberation Tigers of Tamil Eelam, ending a 26-year civil war, Sri Lankans continue to experience significant tensions and conflict between their multiple ethnic and religious groups. Many experts argue that a sustainable peace will not take hold on the island until a political settlement is reached and a reconciliation process initiated, whereby the grievances of Sri Lanka's minority Tamil and Muslim communities are addressed and the root causes of conflict are acknowledged. Interfaith and intercommunal cooperation and dialog must be at the center of this work. Religious leaders from the four main faith traditions that call Sri Lanka home—Buddhism, Hinduism, Islam, and Christianity—are often called upon when local violence and intercommunal tensions arise. In 2008 the United States Institute of Peace, in partnership with the Colombo-based Centre for Peace-Building and Reconciliation, established a project to train over a hundred clergy and professionals from these faith communities in peacemaking principles, conflict transformation theory, and peace program development. Following the implementation of locally based peace projects, these religious clergy and professionals, who work across lines of religious, cultural, and ethnic difference to promote reconciliation, prevent violence, and advocate for justice, have seen strong positive results. A future of sustained peace in Sri Lanka requires a foundation of trust and reconciliation. Interfaith cooperation is an effective means by which to promote conflict resolution in this deeply faithful nation.

Christian Reflection

Susan Hayward

Scripture

In the gospels, Jesus is portrayed as consistently seeking to transform understandings of those considered to be traditional adversaries in first-century Palestine. In telling the Good Samaritan parable (Luke 10:25–37), Jesus argued against considering any person to be inferior or suspect because of tribal or ethnic identity, and instead encouraged recognition of the dignity of all and the capability of every person to act with compassion. He consistently sought to expand the capacity for empathy among his followers and extend that empathy toward those of other economic, ethnic, and political classes. In this, he sought to undo ideologies that served one individual or group at the expense of others, and to upturn traditional social dividing lines that sometimes became battle lines in the midst of political and economic insecurity. In so doing, he promoted relationship building between traditional adversaries; he promoted collaborative work to live out God's will.

Second, Jesus extended compassion to those who attacked him. While being arrested, imprisoned, and then executed by the Roman Empire, Jesus did not verbally or physically attack his adversaries. In fact, when his disciple sought to defend him with the sword, Jesus told him to put it away (Matt. 26:52). In his dying moments, he pleaded with God to forgive his executioners and their supporters (Luke 23:34). In so doing, he recognized and affirmed the dignity of his adversaries and resisted actions that might have escalated a violent conflict and caused more destruction. He also, presumably, was able to awaken the compassion of his enemies and so challenge their attempt to perceive him as a threat seeking their destruction. He sought to transform an interaction of competition and aggression into a relationship of mutually recognized dignity.

We can also turn to the epistles of the New Testament, which offer a great deal of advice to church communities facing conflict. These were not violent conflicts in the sense we are discussing in this study, but the ethics and practice of interpersonal conflict resolution Paul and other epistle authors preached can certainly be extended to intercommunal or interstate violent conflict. These letters encourage members of the Jesus-follower community to be quick to listen and slow to speak and get angry, thereby striving to understand the other in moments of conflict (James 1:19).[1] They call for a nondefensive or non-reactive response to conflict, avoiding name-calling and threats (Rom. 2:1–4; Gal. 5:22–26).[2] They also encourage followers to work through disagreements constructively, seeking to understand the interests of others (Phil. 2:1–11).[3] Finally, the letters, particularly Paul's, continued Jesus's practice of redefining traditional definitions of in-group and out-group by encouraging followers to reach out to those of other nations and to recognize and seek to deepen feelings of brotherhood and sisterhood with all.

Christian History

How have Christian communities sought to extend these foundational teachings in their work to address conflict?[4] During the conquistador destruction of the fifteenth century, several formative theologians sought to challenge the holy war ideology and genocidal practices of the Spanish Army (operating in collusion with the Church), by defending indigenous communities and seeking to encourage political, military, and religious leaders to understand their needs and concerns. Francisco de Vitoria (c. 1492–1546), Bartolomé de Las Casas (c. 1484–1566), and others defended the dignity of the indigenous people, seeking, as Jesus did, to extend the empathic awareness of the conquistadors across traditional boundaries. Vitoria and other early Just War theologians also put a great deal of emphasis on conciliation and engagement with adversaries as the better means to address conflict.

In more contemporary times, the historic peace churches, particularly the Mennonites, have taken collaborative conflict-resolution practices into conflict zones in attempts to help traditional adversaries find alternative means to address their mutual grievances. Many Catholic and other Protestant communities have developed faith-based organizations and international ministries that seek to support local efforts at collaborative conflict resolution. In their work, they have contributed to, built off, and strengthened concepts and practices of academic social scientists of the 1960s.

These initiatives have largely been grouped under the term *interactive problem solving*, which is used to describe facilitated face-to-face nonviolent contact between adversaries, including consultations, trainings, dialogs, and problem-solving workshops.[5] The goal of these sessions is to promote collaborative approaches to address the conflict by recognizing the human needs and interests of both sides and the costs of continuing to use violence to address the problem. The ultimate objective is to build enough trust between the parties that they become convinced a negotiated end to the conflict is achievable and in their best interests and, in some cases, to help them begin to formulate that agreement in an informal setting.

As a technique, interactive conflict resolution was born from an academic experiment by an Australian diplomat turned scholar at University College London, John Burton, in the 1960s. His experiment to bring together adversaries from both sides of the Malaysian-Indonesian conflict for a series of five meetings to analyze the conflict jointly resulted in a framework for settlement that helped set the stage for the Jakarta Peace Accord (1966).[6] According to one of Burton's colleagues, the sessions "allowed the parties to correct misperceptions, redefine the conflict, reassess its costs, and develop options to resolve it."[7] These particular sorts of problem-solving workshops were mostly a Western academic enterprise but have been picked up by peace practitioners around the world as well. They have shaped the evolution of work they had been doing previously and continue to do, in addition to the more traditional civil resistance, community-mobilizing advocacy work. A conviction that peace is achieved through person-to-person contact across lines of conflict is key to interactive conflict resolution peacemaking philosophy.[8]

Examples of the success of collaborative conflict resolution abound. Take for example the work of the Catholic lay organization the Community of Sant'Egidio. Approached in the 1990s by rebels and the government, this community was able to serve as a third party to facilitate face-to-face engagement that ultimately led to the negotiations that ended Mozambique's civil war. In Guatemala, Lutheran and Catholic religious leaders were able to serve as facilitators of a dialog process between government officials and an alliance of rebels that led to an agreement to search for peace through political means, launching a six-year process that led to the signing of peace accords in 1996.[9] In Northern Ireland, Mennonites partnered with local Protestants and Catholics in the 1980s and 1990s, as conflict raged, in order to build ecumenical connections and impart peace skills such as mediation. This intercession led to the creation of The Mediation Network (1987), an organization that sought to proliferate skills in mediation to civil society, the security sector, and political actors, and that directly mediated in many instances to address escalating tensions before violence broke out.[10] In each of these examples, the work found success in part due to the Christian peacebuilders' long-term commitment and engagement with their communities. Because these actors were living and working within the conflict, providing support to local communities in an unbiased manner, they were trusted by various communities to guide these delicate processes over a series of years and with respect for local culture and tradition. The first two examples above highlight work with political elites and senior-level armed actors. But Christian and other religious peacebuilders often put just as much focus on involving community members from the grassroots in processes of collaborative conflict resolution, believing that building Just Peace societies requires transformation at all levels of society.

In conflict environments in which the divide is across a religious identity, interfaith dialog is cited as a way to build cooperative relationships and to transform religious commitments to violence or exclusion. Interfaith dialog and engagement is a facilitated process whereby those of different religious communities come together seeking to understand the other's perspective, to find common ground, and, oftentimes, to initiate collaborative efforts to address injustice and bring peace. Christians are involved in interfaith dialog in many global conflicts, including Sri Lanka, Israel and Palestine, Sudan, and Nigeria. The World Council of Churches launched an interfaith initiative in 1997 that includes regular thematic focuses on issues that have historically driven conflict between religious traditions, such as religious violence and conversion. The Catholic Church has increased its involvement in interfaith engagement over the last century, creating the Pontifical Council for Interreligious Dialogue in 1964. Pope John Paul II regularly affirmed interfaith dialog as a tool for building peace, and Catholic Relief Services supports interfaith engagement in many contexts of interreligious tension and violence, including India and the Philippines.[11] These interfaith encounters are crucial for building peace not only as a means to challenge religious biases that fuel conflict, but also for creating larger and more representative mobilizations for Just Peace.

Those committed to the realist paradigm of international relations and conflict may not be convinced of the worth of these sorts of initiatives. But time and again the work of Christian and other religious and secular peacemakers who have engaged in these activities has proven their effectiveness in stemming war and opening the door to negotiations.

Jewish Reflection

Reuven Firestone

Judaism offers some interesting examples that resonate with the model of cooperative conflict resolution originally considered in relation to Christianity. Because of the particularly self-critical nature of Jewish tradition, some helpful examples are articulated through illustrations of failure to resolve conflict adequately. In the following, all of which treat conflict resolution but not always cooperatively and not always successfully, four paradigms or stories found in Jewish religious texts illustrate the complexity of the problem and provide some lessons.

Scripture

The first example suggests that conflict should be managed through words rather than physical actions. This is indicated in the very beginning of Genesis when God creates the universe by words: "God said, 'Let there be . . .' and there was . . ." (Genesis 1). God speaks the universe into being through a series of verbs that are formulated grammatically to express the divine will: "Let the water be gathered," "Let there be lights in the sky," "Let the earth bring forth every kind of living creature," and so forth. All these things are "spoken" into their createdness. The last "Let . . ." in the series of verbs results in the creation of humanity in Genesis 1:26: "Let us make humanity in our image," immediately after which God creates human beings.

Humanity is the last of creations and is uniquely created in the "image" of God (Gen. 1:26–27), a notion that has been a conundrum for commentators throughout the centuries. In literally the same breath of God's willing human creation, God wills that humanity "rule the fish of the sea, the birds of the sky, and all the living things that creep on the earth" (Gen. 1:26).[12] It can be argued, therefore, that God's design is for humanity to emulate the Creator by overseeing and governing through the creative word, through language. While the divine command just mentioned does not specifically address human inter-relations, it soon provides examples of how human failure to manage conflict through speech results in disaster. The earliest occurs in Genesis 4, when Cain and Abel experience conflict but are unable to resolve it with words. The text is puzzling and immediately invites speculation and analysis: "Cain said to his brother Abel—and when they were in the field, Cain set upon his brother Abel and killed him" (Gen. 4:8). The text mentions that "Cain said—" but does not include the words, if any, that were exchanged. Perhaps none were. Perhaps they were inadequate. The result is the first homicide. When words are inadequate or break down, violence ensues.

Schools of Law

The second paradigm shows how two conflicting schools of Jewish law (*hala-cha*) articulated and taught their differences. These are the schools of Hillel and Shammai, which arrived at different conclusions to ethical and ritual questions throughout rabbinic literature. In almost all cases, it was the opinion of the school of Hillel (*beit hillel*) that was favored by later rabbis and became established as law. The reason for the preference of the school of Hillel is provided by the Talmud in the following words:

> For three years there was a dispute between Beit Shammai and Beit Hillel, one
> asserting "The *halakhah* is in agreement with our views," and the other asserting,

"The *halakhah* is in agreement with our views." Then a heavenly voice was issued that said, "These and these are [both] the words of the living God, but the *halakhah* is in agreement with the rulings of Beit Hillel." But since both are words of the living God, why did Beit Hillel merit to have the *halakhah* established according to their rulings? Because they were kindly and modest, they studied their own rulings and those of Beit Shammai. Not only that, but they even mentioned the words of Beit Shammai before their own. (Babylonian Talmud *Eruvin* 13b)

It may seem surprising that the importance of finding "truth" is outweighed by establishing "process," and process includes the need for the parties in dispute to be civil and modest in their argument. It teaches the value of learning from the opponent's point of view, even when only one can be codified into Law. It is even possible to understand the text as teaching that it is only when the teachings of both schools are considered in relation to one another that they are in fact "words of the living God."

Mishnah

The third paradigm occurs in a section that is said to be the physical center of the Torah. Some scholars argue that in a biblical chiasm—a structure in which text is mirrored (e.g., ABCCBA)—the material in the center of the chiasmic structure is stressed, suggesting that the section in which this verse lies has special importance. Whatever the truth to this assumption, the verse is a biblical injunction to verbally rebuke one's fellow when one is wronged or witnesses transgression: "You shall not hate your kinsfolk in your heart. Reprove your kinsman but incur no guilt because of him" (Lev. 19:17). The verse is universally interpreted in Judaism to command responding to conflict through words rather than physical action. The purpose is to prevent engaging in revenge or carrying a grudge, either of which extends the conflict rather than resolving it.

Interpretation of this verse is developed in some detail in rabbinic literature and then synopsized by Maimonides (1135–1204) in his code of law. The law requires that one admonish one's fellow who transgresses, without shaming or being cruel. If the transgressor repents, then he or she must be forgiven, but if no remorse is shown he or she must be admonished until the point where he or she threatens physical violence.[13] This set of rules regarding the responsibility to admonish one's fellow, with all of its details (which extend beyond the items mentioned here[14]) applies to fellow Israelites—that is, to fellow Jews. The Torah verse couches the requirement to act properly in relation to kinfolk, literally "brothers." The responsibility as contextualized in scripture does not apply to non-Jews (Mishnah *De'ot* 6:3–4).

The fourth paradigm treats a situation highlighting the conflict between "truth" and "process" (Babylonian Talmud *Bava Metzi'a* 59b). As in the second case, process trumps truth in the sight of God. The paradigm revolves around the need to determine whether or not an oven is ritually fit ("pure") to be used. The actual issue of whether or not it is pure is irrelevant to the discussion, which centers rather on the resolution of conflict within the community of religious sages.

One rabbi by the name of Eliezer knew the answer to the query, was absolutely confident that he did so, and was actually correct as proven by another issuance of a divine voice that said, "Rabbi Eliezer is right!" The other rabbis would not accept his ruling, however. They insisted on holding to the majority position even though it was actually proven wrong, and the story confirms that the procedure of following the majority is accepted. This story, called "The Oven of Akhnai" because that particular oven was being discussed, is often cited by Jews who wish to point to what they consider to be the inherent democratic nature of Jewish religious tradition. Whether Judaism is inherently democratic or not is not considered here, but the continuation of the story is often ignored by those who cite it.

After the majority of rabbis overruled the correct view of Rabbi Eliezer, they destroyed the record of all his rulings and threw him out of the academy (or court), presumably for not going along with the majority when he was so confident that they were wrong. Rabbi Eliezer was thus excommunicated by the rabbinic leadership under the leadership of one Rabban Gamliel, who, incidentally, was married to Eliezer's sister. In response, Rabbi Eliezer destroyed much of the world through his rage, which, because of the power associated with knowing the truth, naturally harnessed extraordinary energy and strength (Mishnah *Rosh HaShanah* 2:8).

Rabban Gamliel proved to be acting cruelly and is depicted elsewhere as embarrassing rabbinic sages in public (Mishnah *Berakot* 27b). As a result he was removed from office by his rabbinic colleagues. He was eventually killed by the power of Rabbi Eliezer's prayer despite the attempt of his wife, Rabban Gamliel's sister, to prevent that dour end to the great Rabban Gamliel (Mishnah *Bava Metzi'a* 59b).

The story is complex and includes a number of additional issues that are not directly relevant to our discussion. As is common in such stories, there is no clear solution to the many problems or issues raised. Nevertheless, a number of items present themselves for discussion. They include the following:

• What does it mean to be "right" or to have "the truth?"
• God ultimately confirmed the incorrect ruling of the majority against the correct ruling of Rabbi Eliezer. What might be the purpose of this result in the story?

- The story depicts a classic example of the "tyranny of the majority" wherein the conflict was not really resolved.
- Despite the rightness of both positions (for different reasons), or perhaps because of them, the conflict between Rabbi Eliezer and the rabbis was never resolved and the lack of resolution was extremely bitter. Terrible damage resulted.
- What might have been better ways to resolve the conflict between Rabbi Eliezer and the majority?

These examples provide both positive and negative paradigms for conflict resolution. It is not uncommon for Jewish tradition to teach ethics through models of human failure. Even the greatest biblical heroes are flawed, for example, and in fact there is not a single biblical protagonist who is without failing or blemish. The four examples cited here contain aspects that are ambiguous and perhaps even confusing. All would invite discussion about the issues as they are laid out for the reader or student. In the case of the "Oven of Akhnai," for example, the story conveys the possibility that a person may actually know the absolute truth and would therefore naturally insist that everyone must go along with it. God even confirms the truth claim of the person through the issuance of a divine voice. The answer to the question of the fitness of the oven, however, is ultimately decided according to a group of rabbis persuading one another on the basis of evidence and logic. This would appear to convey the lesson that group consultation is the proper strategy for conflict resolution even if the decision is not technically "correct." Yet the final result is tragic. The tragedy may have been caused by the resultant tyranny of the majority in its decision to expel the person holding the minority opinion, perhaps because he would not give in to majority rule but insisted uncompromisingly that only his position was correct (and it actually was!). Or perhaps the tragedy was caused by the autocratic behavior of the leader and the fact that the community of rabbis went along with him.

The complexity of this as well as other stories allows for—indeed encourages—discussion. The question nevertheless arises as to how one would cite Jewish tradition to support cooperative conflict resolution in a general setting that extends beyond the community of Jews. Because Jews were isolated from the larger community in which they lived—often against their will but sometimes also willfully—Jewish religious ethical tradition tended to develop in relation to problem solving within the Jewish community and less significantly in relation to the community at large. While such writings certainly exist (often organized around the Talmudic notion "for the sake of peace"—*mipney darkei shalom*), much work still needs to be devoted to developing this field of study.

Muslim Reflection

Zainab Alwani

As Muslims, we regard the Qur'an as the last divine Speech revealed by God. It came with a message that is universal and to an audience that comprises all of humanity. Islam yields a set of peace-building values that, if constantly and systematically applied, can transcend all levels of conflicts. These values include justice (*'adl*), beneficence (*ihsān*), and wisdom (*hikmah*), which constitute core principles in peacemaking strategies and conflict resolution.

The Qur'an and Its Preventive Approach toward Conflict Resolution

Qur'anic guidelines construct a preventive model for conflict resolution by providing a framework for healthy interpersonal relationships. Divine laws foster values, establish clear boundaries, and identify priorities in relationships. Divine laws guide human action and encompass every facet of human life including *'ibā*da (the code of worship), *sulūk* (a system of ethics), spirituality, and *mu'*āmalāt (human interactions). Muslims believe that the function of divine laws is not hardship, but rather mercy and ease.[15] The objective of divine law is to preserve one's worldly and cosmic (afterlife) welfare by establishing peace, happiness, justice, equity, and piety on earth through the good behavior and actions of people.

In regard to the field of conflict resolution, Islam presents (a) a preventive model, (b) a nonviolent and ethical model toward enemies, (c) a prophetic model of preempting conflicts, and (d) general principles and practical methods for building the nonviolence moral model.

A Preventive Model

The preventive model is embedded in different verses starting with: "O mankind! Behold, We have created you all out of a male and a female, and have made you into nations and tribes, so that you might come to know one another. Verily, the noblest of you in the sight of God is the one who is most deeply conscious of Him [*atqākum*—a derivative of *taqwa*[16]]. Behold, God is all-knowing, all-aware."[17]

This verse outlines the Islamic philosophy of human relations on all levels. First, it acknowledges the equality of all human beings, as we all originate from the same source and are created in the same fashion; second, it establishes human diversity as a product of divine wisdom ("so that you might come to know one another"), as reflected in this verse; third, by establishing that "coming to know one another" is one of God's objectives for diversifying his creation, human beings are then ordained with responsibility to learn about the other;[18] and finally, the Qur'an creates a new standard for measuring the merit of human beings. Rather than looking to people's financial status, race, religion, or gender, God establishes that "God-consciousness" (*taqwa*) is the true indicator of nobility and human merit.

A Nonviolent and Ethical Model toward Enemies: Concepts and Attitude

Islam encourages an attitude toward one's enemies of forgiveness and empathy, not retribution. Through strategies like dialog, kind words, and the return of evil with goodness, the Qur'an argues that one can transform an enemy into a friend, even a close friend: "The idea is to eliminate enmity and not the enemy."[19]

"Good and evil are not alike. Requite evil with what is best. Then truly he between whom and you there was enmity, will become your dearest friend"(Qur'an 41:34).

There is a clearly articulated preference in Islam for nonviolence over violence and for forgiveness (*'afu*) over retribution.[20] The Qur'an aims to regulate the commonplace, retributive responses of people to conflict and violence. Forgiveness is consistently held out as the preferred option for humanity in responding to clear injustice or crime. "The recompense of an injury is an injury the like thereof; but whoever forgives and thereby brings about a reestablishment of harmony, his reward is with God; and God loves not the wrongdoers"(Qur'an 42:40).

Neither naïve pardon nor a mechanical retribution is urged; what is sought is the reformation of the guilty party, which is accomplished through the example of moral goodness and sincere forgiveness. As Islam emphasizes individuals' free will to act and believe, it also underscores the human potential for both good and evil. No individual is expected to be a perfect angel. The Qur'an acknowledges that every human being will commit a sin or make mistakes in his or her lifetime. "And those who, having done something to be ashamed of, or wronged their own souls, earnestly bring Allah to mind, and ask for forgiveness for their sins—and who can forgive sins except Allah?—and are never obstinate in persisting knowingly in *the wrong* they have done" (Qur'an 3:135).

The Qur'anic approach, therefore, is not to expect perfection from others or ourselves, but to expect and encourage sincere repentance. There are four important conditions to repentance in Islam, which are relevant to our subject of conflict resolution: The first is to acknowledge that one has done wrong. Repentance is first contingent upon a person's ability to reflect inwards and confess his/her sin to him/herself.

The second important condition of repentance that one hopes is sincere and acceptable to God is that one never intends to return to that act of sin or evil. When one repents, one must sincerely intend to never commit that act of sin again.

The third condition of repentance is that one must begin to transform his or her lifestyle. This is not a superficial type of change, but one that emanates from internal reflection, character building, and self-discipline. While the *intention* to change (the second condition mentioned above) is a positive step toward change, it is not enough. One must begin to take concrete actions internally and externally to change one's thought process and behavior.

A fourth condition is to rectify the wrong that was done, whether by restoring the rights of the person wronged, paying reparations or compensation for harm inflicted, or negotiating an agreeable settlement with the wronged party.

The Qur'an explains, as part of the process of *sulh* (reconciliation), that it is important to fulfill all the contracts, settlements, and agreements that were signed by the parties. *Sulh* is a Qur'anic concept that may be translated as *reconciliation*. It derives from the root *sa la ha*, from which are also derived words for righteousness, goodness, making amends, compensation, restitution, reform, and setting things right. The word *islāh,* from the same root, is also used for peace, reconciliation, and reform. "O People who Believe! Fulfill your words" (agreements; Qur'an 5:1). "And fulfill the promise; indeed the promise will be asked about" (Qur'an 17:34).

The process that Islam outlines for sincere repentance and reconciliation is useful and practical for our topic of conflict resolution. It acknowledges that human beings will inevitably commit mistakes, which creates an atmosphere and environment whereby people find it easier to admit their mistakes. The Qur'anic process for repentance also emphasizes that intention and internal reflection are key to behavioral reform. Reform must first emanate from within. Reform does not stop there, however, as the Qur'an demands behavioral change by (1) not going back to the sin, and (2) rectifying the wrong that was done through restoration and good works.

The Prophetic Model for Preempting and Resolving Conflicts

The implementation of the *sulh* process was developed by the Prophet. As a messenger of God, he illustrated through his actions how to implement the divine teachings. He was known for his mediation and arbitration competency when he prevented bloodshed in Mecca during the rebuilding of the Kaaba (600 CE) even before he received the revelation and became a Prophet.[21] When he migrated to Medina, he attempted to transform the tribal system into a civil society that provides inner protection for both the individual and the community. In emergency situations, such as war and the absence of government, the community should be able to govern itself and resolve any conflict peacefully and properly.

In order to understand the practicality of the prophetic model, today, for example, in Western cultural contexts, successful conflict resolution usually involves fostering communication among disputants, undertaking problem-solving strategies, and drafting agreements that meet their underlying needs. In these situations, conflict resolvers often talk about finding the win-win solution, or mutually satisfying scenario, for everyone involved.[22] That model was applied by the Prophet Muhammad in at least two different situations:

> First, when he entered *Madinah,* he drafted the Constitution of Medina; the historical authenticity of this document has been proven and attested to by historians. This document regulates relations between all the significant families, tribes and religious minorities living at the time in Yathrib (the pre-modern name for Medina). It guaranteed the security of all its residents regardless of their religious orientation. It guaranteed equal political, cultural and religious rights for non-Muslims living in Yathrib. By specifying the rights and responsibilities of Yathrib's diverse tribal and religious groups, the Medina Constitution attempted to prevent disputes before they occurred. Further, the Constitution established peaceful methods of conflict resolution "among diverse groups living as one people but without assimilating into one religion, language, or culture."[23]

Welch in *Encyclopedia of Islam* states, "The constitution reveals his [Muhammad's] great diplomatic skills, for it allows the ideal that he cherished of an *ummah* (community) based clearly on a religious outlook to sink temporarily into the background and is shaped essentially by practical considerations."[24]

Another example of the Prophet's skills in arbitration is the drafting of the Treaty of Hudaibiya (600 CE), which prevented imminent bloodshed between the Meccans and the Muslims of Medina. By signing this treaty, despite the unreasonable concessions it imposed upon Muslims[25] and despite his companions' opposition to it, the Prophet demonstrated his unequivocal position to choose peace over war. In this case, the Prophet defused the situation by signing the *Hudaibiya* treaty by unilaterally accepting all of the enemy's conditions. This policy of conciliation proved productive as the atmosphere was more relaxed for dialog and is described in the Qur'an as a "manifest victory" (Qur'an 48:29).

A Modern Model

Islamic sources and culture-based Muslim responses can make a significant contribution to move conflict resolution toward a global heritage, shaping and implementing peace-building strategies. Today, in the United States, the American Muslim community usually faces different challenges at the family and community levels. The role of the imams as religious leaders of the American Muslim community is crucial. They often find themselves synthesizing secular, Western, Islamic, and cultural techniques in dealing with disputes in their communities.

One specific example that may prove to be a successful model for other American Muslim communities is the model of conflict resolution established at the All-Dulles Area Muslim Society (ADAMS) in northern Virginia. The imam of ADAMS, Imam Muhammad Magid, and a professional family counselor, Salma Abugideiri, work hand in hand to resolve conflicts among members by utilizing techniques derived from both Western and non-Western models. Many cases require professional counseling, a Western-based technique. Abugideiri, a professionally trained Muslim counselor, was invited to deal with a couple or a family based on approaches and techniques from the secular, Western model. With other parties who may be involved in the same case, such as in-laws or other relatives (especially in the case of immigrant families), the imam will use mediation or arbitration techniques, which derive from customary Muslim techniques, as well as Qur'anic processes of conflict resolution. Therefore, in a single case of conflict resolution, the imam creates a synthesis between customary and cultural practices of *sulh* as well as professional strategies of conflict resolution.

Islamic principles and values provide a relevant and constructive framework—among others—for promoting Just Peacemaking in a way that fulfills the modern needs of conflict resolution. This framework opens great opportunities for the community of peacemakers to address current global challenges in the field.

Conclusion

Cooperative conflict resolution is a shared endeavor, one that demands trust, patience, and forgiveness on the part of all involved. Honest self-criticism, facilitated dialog, conflict analysis, and problem-solving sessions can go a long way to help adversaries recognize humanity in the face of the other. To truly engage in this work involves a high level of risk taking and cultural and spiritual awareness, but such efforts can serve to expand and strengthen one's own sense of purpose. It is clear that interpersonal relationship development and cooperation across lines of difference are key to nurturing peace in areas of conflict.

Whereas, in the past, religious division has been a significant source of conflict in the world, a shift has emerged. Faith communities and religious leaders are now taking up the task of establishing relationships across lines of difference to promote reconciliation and peace. Our religious differences must not be minimized in this process, for our faith commitments are deep resources that can provide support and guidance for the work of conflict resolution and Just Peacemaking.

Notes

1. "You must understand this, my beloved: let everyone be quick to listen, slow to speak, slow to anger."
2. "Let us not become conceited, competing against one another, envying one another" (Gal. 5:26).
3. "Let each of you look not to your own interests, but to the interests of others," says v. 4 in this passage.
4. I will leave aside discussion of how Christians have fallen short of these teachings by wielding the sword against other communities, contributing to ghastly levels of death and destruction—especially to indigenous communities around the world, but also to those of other religions (the Holocaust being a prime example). Instead, I will point to what I consider positive and constructive examples of collaborative conflict-resolution practices by Christian communities.
5. R. J. Fisher, "Reflections on the Practice of Interactive Conflict Resolution Thirty Years Out. Twelfth Annual Lynch Lecture," Institute for Conflict Analysis and Resolution (Fairfax, VA: George Mason University, 1999).
6. Ibid., 3.
7. Ibid.
8. See David Smock, *Catholic Contributions to International Peace* (Washington, DC: U.S. Institute of Peace, 2001), 11.
9. U.S. Institute of Peace, "Certificate Course in Interfaith Conflict Resolution," http://www.usip.org/education-training/courses/certificate-course-in-interfaith -conflict-resolution (accessed June 10, 2010).
10. Cynthia Sampson and John Paul Lederach, eds., *From the Ground Up: Mennonite Contributions to International Peacebuilding* (Oxford: Oxford University Press, 2000), 77–103.
11. See Mark Rogers, Tom Bamat, and Julie Ideh, eds., *Pursuing Just Peace: An Overview and Case Studies for Faith-Based Peacebuilders* (Baltimore: Catholic Relief Services, 2008), 99–132.
12. There is some question whether or not the next verb, *veyirdū*, is in the same jussive mood.
13. Mishnah *Hilkhot De`ot* 6.
14. For example, the founder of Hassidism (the Baal Shem Tov) is said to have taught the following regarding Leviticus 19:17b: *Reprove your kinsman but incur no guilt because of him* (the Hebrew of the Torah verse is, literally, *but do not lift up sin over him*): "First rebuke yourself, and only afterwards, your kinsman, for it will become clear that you have a part in his transgression. *Do not lift up sin over him*—do not load the sin only upon him." A. H. Greenberg, *The Eloquence of Torah* (`iturey torah*) 6 vols. (Tel Aviv: Yavneh, 1977), 4:112.
15. The Qur'an describes the main characteristics of the divine law in 7:157: "Those who follow the Messenger, the unlettered prophet, whom they find mentioned in their own scriptures in the Law and the Gospel, for He commands them what is Just and forbids them what is evil; He allows them as lawful what is good and pure and prohibits them from what is bad and impure, He releases them from their heavy burdens and from the yokes that are upon them."

16. *Taqwa* is at the heart of traits cultivated by the good deeds that serve to build up the moral character of both the individual and the community.

17. Qur'an 49:13, Muhammad Asad's translation, Muhammad Asad, and Ahmed Moustafa, *The Message of the Quran: The Full Account of the Revealed Arabic Text Accompanied by Parallel Transliteration* (Bitton, England: Book Foundation, 2003).

18. Irani is a modern example of the first Western scholars whose work was a very effective method in the field of conflict resolution. George Irani, "Islamic Mediation Techniques for Middle East Conflicts," *Middle East Review of International Affairs (MERIA) Journal* 3, no. 2 (1999).

19. Zeenat Shaukat Ali, "Non-Violence and Peace-Building in Islam: The Concept of Non-Violence in Islam," *World Council of Churches Current Dialogue* 48 (2006), http://www.wcc-coe.org/wcc/what/interreligious/cd48–08.html.

20. Marc Gopin shows some concerns regarding the Abrahamic faith's perspective on forgiveness, especially on the issue of jeopardizing justice: "In particular, forgiveness as a means of peacemaking, depending on how it is realized, brings into sharp relief the perennial challenge of balancing peace and justice in the pursuit of conflict resolution. Often, at least on the surface, it appears that forgiveness is at odds with the demands of justice, at least as justice is perceived by either side of a conflict." In the case of Islam, justice is highly emphasized and forgiveness is more on the part of the victim as a psychological remedy, and of course it will positively influence the community and then the society. Read and contemplate Qur'an 42:36–43. See Marc Gopin, "Forgiveness as an Element of Conflict Resolution in Religious Cultures: Walking the Tightrope of Reconciliation and Justice," in *Reconciliation, Coexistence, and Justice in Interethnic Conflicts: Theory and Practice*, ed. Mohammed Abu-Nimer (Lanham, MD: Lexington Books, 2001), 87–99.

21. Karen Armstrong, *Muhammad: A Biography of the Prophet* (New York: Harper Collins, 1992).

22. See Roger Fisher, William Ury, and Bruce Patton, *Getting to Yes* (New York: Houghton Mifflin, 1981).

23. Hisham M. Ramadan, *Understanding Islamic Law: From Classical to Contemporary* (Lanham, MD: Rowman & Littlefield, 2006).

24. Ford Welch, "Muhammad," in *Encyclopedia of Islam*, ed. P. J. Bearman et. al. (Leiden: Brill, 1993).

25. It denied them the right to perform the pilgrimage for that year; it also demanded that the Muslims return any pagans who convert to Islam back to Mecca, while the Meccans were not obliged to allow Muslims to leave to Medina.

CHAPTER 4

Practice Norm 4

Acknowledge Responsibility for Conflict and Injustice and Seek Repentance and Forgiveness

Definition

*T*he capacity for empathy is vital when working toward peace. Empathy requires that a person look past his or her own interests and perspective and come to an understanding of the other side. Peacemaking also calls us to move beyond our desire for retaliation and revenge, and focus instead on the possibilities for future reconciliation. Before we are able to accomplish these aims, we must acknowledge our wrongs and the ways in which we have been complicit in injustices and our responsibility for righting them. Further, in the act of forgiving, we experience empathy, a capacity for forbearance from revenge, and a transformed sense of the future possibilities for Just Peace.

Introduction

There is an increasing interest around the world in apology, pardon, mercy, repentance, responsibility, forgiveness, and reconciliation, not only in theology, but also in literature, political science, sociology, and psychology. What was once dismissed as the dream of undoing the wrongs of the past has now become the indisputable practice of changing the context of the past and with it the way in which the past enters the present and the future. This practice norm can challenge the power of appalling histories to sabotage the present; it holds out the promise that the future can be tamed and turned toward greater peace and justice, though only with extraordinary effort and, of course, not all the time.

While forgiveness and reconciliation are no longer the exclusive province of religion, one of the elements that helps to make forgiveness and reconciliation methods successful is support from religious ideas and religious communities.

The practical power of this practice norm can be seen in this interfaith example: Several years ago a dispute erupted between a group of Muslim leaders in Boston and a number of individuals and groups in the Jewish community. At issue was the initiative undertaken by the Muslim community to build an Islamic cultural center in Roxbury, Massachusetts, on land acquired from the city of Boston. At issue were the terms under which the land was acquired from the city, the sources of funds for the construction of the cultural center, and the backgrounds of some of the early supporters of the Muslim initiative. A lawsuit alleging defamation was initiated in 2002 by the cultural center's proponents, and a countersuit was initiated by *their* opponents. The Interreligious Center on Public Life, a Boston-based interfaith not-for-profit, undertook to meet with both sides, to allow their competing narratives to be shared and to lower the "temperature" of the prevailing discourse. While there continues to be controversy, the efforts led to developing significant relationships among Jews, Christians, and Muslims, and the very beautiful Islamic Cultural Center that was built has hosted important interreligious and intergroup events and programs. Not coincidentally, the legal actions on both sides were dropped in 2007. This chapter illustrates the need to be able to hear narratives alternative to one's own, and to find ways of resolving disputes utilizing Just Peacemaking techniques.

Jewish Reflection

David Gordis

In terms of the specific practices of acknowledging responsibility for conflict and injustice, and seeking repentance and forgiveness, the Jewish tradition's paradigm for human reconciliation is the reconciliation of human beings with God.

Tradition: The Process of "Return"

The reconciliation of human beings with God, the process of *teshuvah* (return) embodies some interesting insights into conciliation that are relevant to human reconciliation as well. Sources for the process of *teshuvah* include biblical, rabbinic, and medieval texts, and there is a prevailing link between human and divine reconciliation. Underlying the process is the fact that conflict and violence represent a cosmic distortion and disruption that requires repair and correction. This distortion or *shever,* a breaking apart, requires healing to bring about *shalom* (reintegration), and this is accomplished both on the cosmic level and on the personal level by the process of *teshuvah*.

One classic and instructive formulation of *teshuvah* is that of the towering twelfth-century philosopher and legist Moses Maimonides (1135–1204). Following earlier authorities, Maimonides suggested that *teshuvah* requires three steps: *harata* (remorse), *vidui* (confession), and *teshuvah* (the actual accomplishment of the "return").

The process cannot begin without the motivation to correct that which requires correction. Satisfaction with the status quo implies that no change is called for and that therefore none will materialize. The first step in the process is remorse—regret over one's present condition and one's role in it. Only the realization that a change in the self is required can lead a person to change and to work toward change in the world. This means accepting responsibility for oneself, one's attitudes, and one's behaviors as a first step to effecting change. We might characterize this first step of *teshuvah* as emotional and motivational.

The process of *teshuvah* will be stillborn unless it goes beyond the emotional and motivational, however. It requires *vidui* (confession), which is a confrontation with the specifics of the behaviors and attitudes requiring correction. Jewish tradition requires no confessional booth or human confessor for *vidui*; confession is an act of verbal articulation of specifics on the part of the individual. If *harata* is emotional and motivational, *vidui* is intellectual and verbal. It implies that a generalized feeling of remorse is not sufficient to effect change; specification and confrontation with the specific are required.

But the process of reconciliation is not accomplished without the translation of the emotional and intellectual into the world of the practical and applied. If another person has been the object of one's errant behavior, conciliation must be effected with that person before *teshuvah* is accomplished. And the test of true change is its durability: the individual must find himself or herself in circumstances similar to those that elicited the original aberrant behavior and overcome the inclination to repeat it. Only then is *teshuvah* achieved. The applicability of *teshuvah* to contemporary practices of conciliation is, I believe, clear and self-evident. The reader of the classical Jewish sources on *teshuvah* will easily comprehend the significance of this Just Peacemaking practice.

These reflections raise a corollary question: are there characteristics of Jewish discourse that in and of themselves define it and that might be relevant to Just Peacemaking and its practices? In the nature of Jewish discourse, in the minds of many readers, there exists a resource that attunes the reader to the ability to hear alternative narratives. This description applies to the biblical narrative as well as to postbiblical literature including even liturgical texts, as I shall attempt to demonstrate. A key to Just Peacemaking generally, and to acknowledging responsibility and seeking forgiveness and reconciliation specifically, lies in the ability to hear alternative narratives to one's own. Jewish discourse conditions one to nurture that ability.[1]

Scripture

Beginning with scripture, it should be noted that the narratives of the Hebrew Bible contain no unflawed ideal types. The comment was once made by a scholar of the Hebrew Bible that the Bible does not describe a single personality that you would want a child of yours to grow up resembling. Rather, the personalities in the biblical narrative struggle, sometimes with success and sometimes failing, to apply values *in vivo*, in real-life situations. In so doing, they invite reaction and response from the reader of the narrative. They do not elicit utter admiration and expectation of emulation. Put another way, the narrative invites the reader to enter into conversation with the text. This is part of a characteristic "ambivalence" toward texts that characterize the Jewish exegetical tradition. On the one hand, the text is "at the center"; on the other, the text is challenged, even subverted.

There are many examples of this ambivalence from Hebrew biblical narratives. The most characteristic genre of classical Jewish discourse, however, is the Talmudic pericope. A brief and of necessity highly schematic overview of Jewish literary development in the postbiblical period may be helpful. Following the canonization of Hebrew scripture probably in the fourth to third century BCE, there developed two exegetical directions, the legal (*halachic*), and the ethical (*aggadic*). In time, the accumulating oral traditions were shaped into literary texts, initially in an interpretive, or *midrashic*, style. The legal tradition developed substantially during the latter part of the first century CE and especially during the second century CE by scholarly authorities known as *Tannaim*. The capstone of their work was a legal compilation known as the Mishnah, assembled by Rabbi Judah the Nassi at about the turn of the second century. Along with other Tannaitic material that continued to circulate, including a collection structured similarly to the Mishnah, known as the *Tosefta*, the Mishnah became the principal text studied in rabbinical academies in Palestine and Babylonia and served as the primary legal reference as well. The text was central in both Palestinian and Babylonian academies for several hundred years, and the end products of the circulating oral traditions were transformed into literary texts first in Palestine in a somewhat laconic and disjointed text, the Palestinian Talmud, or Talmud of Jerusalem (actually produced in Galilean centers and not in Jerusalem), compiled about 400 CE, and some 50 years later in a much larger and more highly structured literary text, the Babylonian Talmud. Common references to the Talmud are to the Babylonian Talmud, and it is principally to its discourse that I refer here.

The Babylonian Talmud is an idiosyncratic text and can be described without exaggeration as *sui generis*, entirely unique. While it is filled with discussions of legal matters, and these materials are incorporated under relevant paragraphs of the Mishnah, the Talmud contains extensive theological, folkloristic, interpretive, historical, and other types of material as well. Moreover, its legal discussions are of an unusual nature. By and large, Talmudic legal discourse is inconclusive; it is not preoccupied with resolving legal issues, often, in fact, shying away from formulating conclusions at all. Though sometimes referred to as a legal code, and certainly relevant to later legal codifiers, the Talmud itself is certainly not a legal code. Further, it should be noted significantly that the Talmud consistently preserves minority views, even those that have been refuted in the discourse. The text is composed in a mixture of Hebrew and Aramaic, is concise in style, and is often challenging to understand in argumentation. Maimonides, whom we cited in his formulation of the process of *teshuvah*, in his introduction to his own elegant literary code, the *Mishneh Torah*, comments that he is writing his code to save the student the tedium of entering the world of Talmudic discourse and argumentation. But in this effort Maimonides failed. The Talmudic text above any other defines the status of the literate Jew. The knowledgeable Jew is one who can find his or her way in a page of Talmudic discourse, who can successfully "swim in the sea of the Talmud."

How then does this most characteristic of Jewish literary genres address the reader? It invites, in fact it requires the reader to enter into conversation with the text. The student or reader enters into the process of argumentation, considers conflicting views, weighs relative strengths and weaknesses of alternative positions, and along with the redactors themselves comes to appreciate the centrality of the process of *shakla vetarya*, of give and take, as even more significant than the bottom line.

The reference to biblical and rabbinic literature is meant to suggest the flavor of Jewish discourse as dialogical in nature and contributing to an enhanced ability to hear alternative narratives. This characterization of Jewish discourse as dialogical applies not only to biblical narrative and the rabbinic legal canon, but also to theological formulations and liturgical texts.

How do our texts and traditions enter into resolving conflict? For a world in which religious beliefs and behaviors so frequently contribute to the pathology of human interrelationships, provoking conflict and generating violence, is it possible to uncover resources within religious traditions in general and in Jewish tradition specifically that can generate beliefs and behavior that enhance healing relationships and attitudes toward the other? Moreover, can one do so in a way that is faithful to one's religious tradition and not do violence to it? Adopting an approach to textual meaning that locates it in the intersection of text and reader, and also that one most often can and will find in the text that one seeks, one can uncover resources relevant to acknowledging responsibility and encouraging forgiveness and reconciliation out of Jewish tradition. Some texts are inspiring and helpful, and others are problematical. Problematical texts need to be removed from privileged status and dealt with in some way. A productive approach is rooted in the assertion that texts that are destructive and contribute to the pathology of interrelationships must not be considered authoritative. Through some process of historical contextualization, creative exegesis, or even radical emendation, their claims must be rejected.

It is impossible to ignore the text question, however. First, we have no alternative, since the Jewish people are heirs and custodians of their tradition, accept it as central in their lives, and at the same time consider as a central imperative that they should engage in the process of repair of the world. This mode of selective reading is internally derived, however. These criteria emerge from reading and the very immersion in this dialogical tradition and culture. The nurture of the tradition causes reading as an insider, rather than as an outsider looking in.

Jews who seek resources for a respectful and tolerant stance toward the other and toward alternative narratives can find them within this tradition. Beyond the specifics of *teshuva* and the motivating power of inspirational texts, there are characteristics of Jewish discourse, objectively studied, that condition the reader and participant to the ability to hear and value alternative narratives and to respect those who bring with them alternative narratives and formulations. This is the critical requirement for Just Peacemaking in general and for the acknowledgment of responsibility for conflict and violence and fostering forgiveness and reconciliation.

Furthermore, these characteristics might have some usefulness across particularistic lines in two ways. First, some of these texts that are shared by our Abrahamic religions can contribute not only to shaping Jewish attitudes and behaviors, but to those of other faith communities as well. Moreover, this inquiry suggests a way of motivating us to realize Just Peacemaking through the affirmation of the values of diverse religious and cultural traditions, while at the same time nurturing a sense of appreciation of the other as a resource for enhancement of one's self rather than as a challenge and a problem. That is both the starting point for Just Peacemaking and its ultimate objective.

Muslim Reflection

Muhammad Shafiq

Repentance and forgiveness are fundamental principles of Qur'anic theology and worldview. In the Islamic tradition, God is the most forgiving. When people forgive, they join the world of God.

The Qur'anic Paradigm

The story of Prophet Joseph (Yusuf in Arabic) son of Jacob is narrated in detail in chapter 12 of the Qur'an. The story is similar to but not identical with the biblical story in Genesis 37–50, and the atmosphere is wholly different. Growing in the house of Prophet Jacob, Joseph is wise and smart and dear to his father. His brothers become jealous of him. He has a dream in his young age of 11 stars, the sun, and the moon together prostrating to him. When he tells his dream to his father, Jacob admonishes him to keep his dream secret. The father knows that his son will become a future prophet and a great man.

Joseph's brothers plot to kill him. One day they take him on a trip and decide to throw him to the bottom of a deep well. On returning home, they tell their father that a wolf devoured Joseph and show him Joseph's shirt covered with blood. A caravan passing by the well goes to get water and finds the boy there in its depths. He is taken out and sold in Egypt to a great Egyptian court dignitary who adopts him. He grows in the house of this dignitary and becomes a handsome man. One day the dignitary's wife seeks, in vain, to attract Joseph to the delights of earthly love. His resistance brings him disgrace and imprisonment. As usual, Joseph remains kind and friendly to his fellow prisoners and interprets their dreams.

The king has a vision of seven fat cows that are devoured by seven lean cows, and seven green ears of corns and seven others that were withered. The king asks for interpretation of the dream. All are helpless and point to Joseph to interpret the dream. Joseph insists that he will not interpret the dream until he is cleared of the earlier scandal. Once he is honorably released he explains the dream to the king, saying that the first seven years will bring rain and richness, and the next seven years will be times of drought and famine. The king appoints Joseph to manage the storage facilities.

The famine brings Joseph's brothers to Egypt where they request assistance and, surprisingly, encounter their brother. The brothers accept their guilt with repentance and seek his forgiveness. Joseph accepts his brothers' repentance and tells them, "This day let no reproach be (cast) on you. Allah will forgive and He is the most merciful of those who show mercy" (Qur'an 12:92).[2] Later the entire family shifts to Egypt and lives together in peace and harmony (Qur'an 12:99)

Another example is the battle of Uhud (625). When the Prophet heard that the Makkans were attacking at Medina, he consulted his followers and the majority decided to defend Medina in its borders. The Prophet himself wanted to defend the city, staying inside and not going out. Following the majority opinion, about a thousand people left the city for Uhud, a few kilometers from Medina. On their way out some three hundred people acted hypocritically and abandoned them. This was a great disaster and demoralization for the rest. The Makkans' army was of about three thousand, with all sorts of equipment. The Muslims incurred heavy losses. Some 70 were martyred. The Prophet received injuries and lost his front teeth. After the war, people thought that the Prophet would punish the defecting people. The Qur'an admonished the Prophet not only to forgive them but to keep them in counsel: "And it was by God's grace that thou [O Prophet] didst deal gently with thy followers: for if thou hadst been harsh and hard of heart, they would indeed have broken away from thee. Pardon them, then, and pray that they be forgiven. And take counsel with them in all matters of public concern; then, when thou hast decided upon a course of action, place thy trust in God: for, verily, God loves those who place their trust in Him" (Qur'an 3:159). This shows a general amnesty without acknowledging guilt in public.

In chapter 24 of the Qur'an, 'Aisha, the wife of the Prophet and the daughter of Abu Bakr, the first caliph in Muslim history, was accused of adultery and one of the accusers was Abu Bakr's relative. He was poor and Abu Bakr supported him and his family with a stipend. When 'Aisha was cleared of any wrongdoing, Abu Bakr stopped his stipend as an act of punishment. The Qur'an admonished the community to investigate to find the truth and to stay away from rumors and character assassination. Abu Bakr was asked to overlook his relative's sins and continue to support him. "Hence, [even if they have been wronged by slander,] let not those of you who have been graced with God's favor and ease of life ever become remiss in helping [the erring ones among] their near of kin, and the needy, and those who have forsaken the domain of evil for the sake of God, but let them pardon and forbear. [For,] do you not desire that God should forgive you your sins, seeing that God is much-forgiving, a dispenser of grace?" (Qur'an 24:22).[3]

The Qur'an is a book of justice, not of revenge. Justice must be established, and peace without justice is a dream. These and other examples in the Qur'an clearly demonstrate that justice shall be followed with forgiveness—not revenge—to have a positive impact on society.

The Prophetic Paradigm

In the Qur'an the Prophet is called a man of high moral character,[4] a messenger of mercy for the whole universe,[5] and his life is presented as a model for humanity to emulate.[6]

Muhammad and his followers were persecuted at Mecca. The suffering reached such an extent that Muhammad asked his followers to migrate to Ethiopia. Later the Makkans plotted to kill Muhammad, yet God saved him and allowed him to migrate to Medina. The Makkans attacked Medina and fought several battles against Muhammad. Finally the Makkans were defeated, and Muhammad and his followers entered Mecca in victory. The Makkans were fearful of revenge. Muhammad declared a total amnesty and used the same words that Prophet Joseph had used for his brothers, accepting their repentance and forgiving them. Some criminals went into hiding and could not face Muhammad. One after another was brought to Muhammad. Each one would confess his or her guilt and he would forgive. Finally, Hinda, a wife of Abu Sufyan, came before Muhammad, hiding her identity. She had hired a slave to kill Hamza, the uncle of the Prophet, and she mutilated his body after the killing. When she came before Muhammad, he recognized her. She confessed her crime and was forgiven. Muhammad not only forgave his Makkan enemies, but later blessed them with gifts and money to win their hearts and repair relations in peace.[7] This model shows the extension of a general amnesty to the public, but some leaders were made to confess their crime before they were forgiven.

Another example is the incident of Ta'if, a hilly station at the outskirts of Mecca. Muhammad in his last years at Mecca lost his wife Khadijah and his uncle Abu Talib. Facing increased persecution with little support, he looked for new places to live. He went to Ta'if with Zaid, his adopted son, to find a shelter. He had some relatives there too. No one gave him any support, but the leaders of Ta'if asked their children to stone Muhammad. He received many bloody injuries and fell down very weak and unconscious. As he regained consciousness, an angel was standing facing him and asking his permission to destroy the twin cities. Muhammad humbly said no, noting that God had sent him as a messenger of mercy, not a destroyer of the world. He told the angel that he would rather see someone from their loins who would worship Allah. When Muhammad migrated to Medina in 622, Islam started to spread. 'Abd Yalail, a leader of Ta'if who was also Muhammad's relative—the one who instigated the children to throw stones at him—brought a delegation to Medina to meet with Muhammad. Seeing him entering the Mosque of the Prophet, Muhammad stood up, welcomed and embraced him and made him sit next to him. Muhammad honored him and his delegation and did not say anything about the torture in Ta'if. He then talked to the delegation about Islam.[8]

There are several examples of the Prophet in which he dealt in forgiveness with individuals who treated him very harshly. It is noted in Muslim history that the Prophet never took revenge on anyone for his personal injuries, but tolerated respectfully and forgave everyone. On one occasion someone came to meet with the Prophet and stayed overnight. The Prophet offered him his own bed. The man urinated in his bed and left it filthy. He departed but forgot his sword in the Prophet's house. On his return, he found the Prophet washing the bed. The Prophet gave him his sword and did not say anything to him about his filth.[9]

A Contemporary Paradigm

The Jirga system, as practiced in some areas of Afghanistan and Pakistan, is an important part of the tribal life system where people live together in peace. It is a sort of restorative justice system that resolves individual and community conflicts. Tribal feuds and offenses are judged through this system. Jirga members are selected from among known religious and tribal leaders from the nearby area in consultation with both parties. The Jirga then goes from place to place consulting people, collecting data to find the truth and reach the roots of the conflict. After the members reach some conclusion, they sit with both parties and take them into confidence before the conditions for *sulh* (peacemaking) are announced. The Jirga system is based on the following Qur'anic principle: "If two parties among the believers fall into a quarrel, make ye peace between them. But if one of them transgresses beyond bounds against the other, then fight ye (all) against the one that transgresses until it complies with the command of Allah. But if it complies, then make peace between them with justice, and be fair. For Allah loves those who are fair (and just)" (Qur'an 49:9).

The procedure for Just Peacemaking is discussed in detail in the *Shari'ah* (Islamic Jurisprudence) as the right to *Qissas* (Law of Equality), *diyat* (monetary compensation), and *maghfirah* (forgiveness). *Justice* (*'adl*) must be established before the victims are asked for forgiveness. In case the victims are poor, monetary compensation could be a better way to heal the wounds. *Qissas*—eye for an eye, tooth for a tooth—is the last option in the Qur'an. Forgiveness is preferred and highly commended in the Qur'an: "The recompense for an injury is an injury equal thereto (in degree): but if a person forgives and makes reconciliation, his reward is due from Allah. For [Allah] loveth not those who do wrong." Another verse says, "But indeed if any show patience and forgive, that would truly be an exercise of courageous will and resolution in the conduct of affairs" (Qur'an 42:40, 43).

The Qur'an repeats these words: "But let them pardon and forbear. [For,] do you not desire that God should forgive you your sins, seeing that God is much-forgiving, a dispenser of grace" (Qur'an 24:22). Here the forgiveness of the offenders and criminals is linked with the forgiveness of God. In some cases, and especially in individual cases, it is not necessary that an offender acknowledge the crime and repent and ask for forgiveness from the victims. The command in the Qur'an is to do well toward such people and to return their evil with goodness: "But [since] good and evil cannot be equal, repel thou [evil] with something that is better and lo! he between whom and thyself was enmity [may then become] as though he had [always] been close [unto thee], a true friend" (Qur'an 41:34).

The words *taubah* (repentance), *istighfar* (to seek forgiveness), and *'maghfira* (forgiveness) appear frequently in the Qur'an. To receive forgiveness from God the following steps are to be taken:

- Make ablution (a cleansing act) and perform two units of prayers.
- Facing Qibla (direction to the House of God at Mecca), acknowledge the sin and its admission before God.
- Make a commitment not to repeat the sin.
- Supplicate for forgiveness from God.

If the sin or guilt was committed against another person, do the following before praying to God for forgiveness:

- Take a step and go to the house of the one against whom the sin was committed.
- Acknowledge the guilt; repent before the victim.
- Do whatever is necessary for the remedy of the guilt in a reasonable way and ask for forgiveness from the victims.
- Supplicate to God for forgiveness.

The Qur'an asks the powerful to be forgiving and merciful toward the weak and remove their deprivation by helping them to become an integrated part of the society. In the case of conflict between two parties, justice must be restored followed by acknowledging responsibility for conflict and injustice with repentance and the asking of forgiveness. Support for the Jirga system in the tribal areas of Afghanistan and Pakistan is the best way to bring peace to the region, to avoid warfare, and to bring an end to violence and terrorism. The system resembles the South African model of the Truth and Reconciliation Commission.

Christian Reflection

Susan Brooks Thistlethwaite

Hannah Arendt famously claimed, "The discoverer of the role of forgiveness in human affairs was Jesus of Nazareth."[10] This is inaccurate by any historical measure. As is clear from this chapter, both Judaism and Islam, in addition to Christianity, have important sacred texts and practices that support the idea of forgiveness. Yet forgiveness does play an enormous role in the Christian faith, and this cannot be overlooked. It is also the case that Christian practices have not followed Christian belief in terms of the role of forgiveness and reconciliation in human life. The disconnect between Christian texts and Christian practice is also instructive and demonstrates the fundamental shift in Just Peace thinking—practice, and not just theory, even when that theory is found in sacred texts, must guide efforts to transform violence into nonviolence, war into peace, conflict into justice.

Christian Scripture

There is no question that Jesus's teaching is the basis of a radical Christian emphasis on forgiveness, and rightly so, as he is emphatic that believers must "love your enemies and do good . . . judge not . . . ; forgive, and you will be forgiven" (Luke 6:27–37).[11] In fact, four times Jesus says that if we forgive, we shall be forgiven, but if we do not forgive, we shall not be forgiven.

Jesus's central proclamation of the good news that the reign of God is at hand comes with a direct call for our own repentance: "The kingdom of God has come near; repent, and believe in the good news" (Mark 1:15). "Repent, for the kingdom of Heaven has come near" (Matt. 4:17). One of Jesus's best-known teachings is "Do not judge, so that you may not be judged . . . Why do you see the speck in your neighbor's eye, but do not notice the log in your own eye? . . . You hypocrite, first take the log out of your own eye, and then you will see clearly to take the speck out of your neighbor's eye" (Luke 6:37–42).

The relationship among the practices in this norm can also be found in Jesus's teaching. Jesus advises that we should actively seek reconciliation, even when someone in our community "has something against" us. If we are at the altar, about to offer a gift, and remember that there is an unresolved conflict with another person, we are advised to leave the gift at the altar "and go; first be reconciled" to that one, and "then come and make your gift" (Matt. 5:23–24). The implication is that the divine-human relationship in repentance and forgiveness is correlated with the human-human need to resolve conflict and seek reconciliation as a part of the dynamic of forgiveness and reconciliation with God.

Forgiveness, in the teaching of Jesus, does not eliminate human responsibility for doing harm to others. Jesus may tell the paralytic "your sins are forgiven" and cure his paralysis (Mk. 2), but he also harshly judges those who reject the kingdom of God and who harm God's children. In the parables, Jesus teaches that those who beat and kill the servants of the owner of the vineyard will have to answer for their deeds, and the vineyard be given to others (Mark 12:1–12). Forgiveness is not a "get out of jail free" card in the view of Jesus, and those who do not repent will be judged. Forgiveness and reconciliation can come about when parties to conflict are willing to acknowledge responsibility.

Christian History

As the Christian movement became the official religion of the Roman Empire under Constantine (272–337), the nature of forgiveness and the role of forgiveness as a cornerstone of faith practice became subordinated to the power of the church and the state as they worked together. The institutionalized Christian Church in Europe, through the doctrine of penance, took control of forgiveness and used it to shore up the power of the Church to control not only a believer's ecclesial[12] and social status in this life, but also in the next. Even worse, violent expansions of European power in the Crusades of the twelfth and thirteenth centuries carried the Pope's promise of forgiveness of sins for participating in these wars.

The Reformers attacked the Roman Church's ecclesial and social power, especially indulgences (paying one's way out of eternal punishment), but did not necessarily restore the centrality of forgiveness in the practice of faith. Instead, John Calvin, for example, emphasized the doctrine of divine providence. Some people were regarded as destined to be saved, while others were destined to be damned. This narrows the gate for salvation, though being in good standing in your church membership was a sign you were a chosen one and thus destined to be saved. While Lutherans did not go so far as to claim that some people are predestined to damnation, church membership did effectively become a sign of being one of the "elect," that is, the saved. In these Reformers, the divine-human axis of forgiveness is overemphasized, and the human-human axis is often ignored. In the "left wing" of the Reformation, of course, the work of forgiveness was, and is, more central to faith practice. The evolution of Catholic doctrine since the Reformation has also moved far beyond the medieval views of penance.

Calvinism came to the American continent on the *Mayflower* along with the Pilgrims in 1620. These Calvinists brought with them their sense of being led by divine providence to these shores, and a sense of religious entitlement due to God's favor. That attitude has persisted to this day, and it often makes it very difficult for the American people to engage the concept of acknowledging responsibility and seeking repentance and forgiveness.

In the United States at this time, a self-styled "Christian nation" continues to hold on to a strong myth of its exceptionalism, considering itself, as theologian Reinhold Niebuhr so accurately said, "the darling of Divine Providence." This conviction of God's blessing upon this nation above all nations leads to an almost impenetrable conviction of national innocence. This has not been good for the national soul, nor for the national practice. As Niebuhr concluded, "Nations, as individuals, who are completely innocent in their own esteem, are insufferable in their human contacts."[13] The United States' international reputation (and ability to broker resolutions to international conflicts without resorting to war) has been damaged—and it is not yet fully repaired—in large part due to the fact that other nations have considered us insufferable in recent years.

It is ironic that while New Testament texts strongly support the norm of acknowledging responsibility and seeking repentance and forgiveness, Christian theology, especially in the doctrine of divine providence, undercuts the biblical text. The power of the Christian idea of forgiveness cannot "get off the ground," so to speak if Americans persist in believing that "God blesses America" no matter what. The ethical effort it takes to engage the power of forgiveness in national and international affairs is stymied at the outset if a nation, or an individual, believes God's providence protects its innocence. As André Trocmé of the International Fellowship of Reconciliation (and the Huguenot pastor of Le Chambon, a village in France that saved 3,500 Jews from the Nazis) so wisely observed, "People convinced of their own innocence cannot be reconciled."[14]

Practice: Acknowledge Responsibility

Thus the first step in engaging this practice norm is to break through the capacity of individuals and nations to hide their worst deeds from themselves, as well as from others, and thus fail to even see the wrongs of the past, let alone acknowledge them. The Truth and Reconciliation Commission (TRC) in South Africa is widely acknowledged as an extraordinary action, given that country's violent history under apartheid. One of the most effective things that happened in the TRC process was that the hidden past became visible. "After two years of a daily barrage of media stories generated by TRC hearings, it is no longer possible for the average South African credibly to deny the nature and extent of the gross human rights violations that took place under the old regime and during the country's transition to democracy."[15]

Breaking through the denial of abuse is the first step in engaging this practice norm, and it gives rise to acknowledging responsibility. People and nations have to see the wrongs of the past in order even to start to acknowledge responsibility. *Confronting the Truth: Truth Commissions and Societies in Transition*[16] is a documentary on the work of truth commissions. Since 1983, there have been truth commissions in 20 countries. The film documents the work of truth commissions in South Africa, Peru, East Timor, and Morocco. These kinds of commissions take testimony from victims and perpetrators; conduct detailed investigations; and identify patterns of abuse, historical records of often hidden abuses, and structural problems (cultural, societal, legal) that failed to stop or even facilitated violations.

This kind of work helps model the role of truth telling in this norm. The United States Institute of Peace (USIP) has distributed more than 440 Arabic and Kurdish language copies of this documentary in Iraq. In addition, USIP premiered an Arabic language version of another documentary film, *The Imam and the Pastor*, that tells the story of an interfaith reconciliation in Nigeria. Religious leaders who attended from all 18 of Iraq's provinces found the film "resonated deeply" with their concerns, and they requested copies to be distributed around Iraq. USIP is now developing a curriculum on religious reconciliation and pluralism to accompany the film.

Practice: Seek Repentance and Forgiveness

It is of little use to acknowledge responsibility for the suffering of victims, however, if nothing changes for them, their families, or the society. The next step in this practice norm is redressing the suffering of victims. Taking responsibility through concrete action to address the consequences of abuse must occur, or repentance stays on the surface and does not impact either individuals or their society.

In June of 2009, the U.S. Senate passed "Resolution 26: Apologizing for the enslavement and racial segregation of African Americans." This Senate apology passed by voice vote almost 150 years after the end of the Civil War. What should have been a momentous moment in U.S. history, signaling a profound change in the course of American race relations, was instead an example of what German theologian and Nazi resistor Dietrich Bonhoeffer called "cheap grace." Tacked onto the end of the resolution is a disclaimer that says nothing in the resolution authorizes or supports reparations for slavery. In his book *The Cost of Discipleship,* Bonhoeffer makes it crystal clear that apologies that don't cost you anything don't change anything. In the section on the difference between "cheap" and "costly" grace, Bonhoeffer explains that cheap grace is the idea that forgiveness just wipes the past away. That is what is cheap about it. All that means is "Of course you have sinned, but now everything is forgiven, so you can stay as you are and enjoy the consolations of forgiveness."[17]

This is not unlike the role of repentance and forgiveness in domestic violence—battered women can be pressured to "forgive, forgive" without real repentance and change on the part of their batterers. This pressure to forgive on the part of victims without repentance and change on the part of victimizers is sometimes given a religious interpretation. It is, however, not in line with this practice norm, as the result is often to help justify the violence, not end it. "Countless women have told me that their priest or minister had advised them, as 'good Christian women' to accept beatings by their husbands as 'Christ accepted the cross.' An overemphasis on the suffering of Jesus to the exclusion of his teaching has been used to support violence."[18] The "forgive, forgive" dynamic in domestic violence fails at the crucial step of recognizing that unequal power relations are at the root of violent relationships, whether personal, national, or international. The "spiral of violence" will not be interrupted unless the power inequalities that helped to give rise to the violence are changed.

Apologies, even apologies long overdue, can, however, be powerful in transforming relations of enmity. These are apologies that illustrate the capacity for "self-transcendence" that Alan Geyer argues so persuasively is required for this Just Peace practice to be effective. "Peacemaking, whether in personal, group, or international relations, requires a variety of capacities for self-transcendence" including a capacity for empathy, an ability to overcome pride and defensiveness, and the ability to let go of the past.[19] There are some powerful examples in human history, as Donald Shriver argues in his book, *An Ethic for Enemies: Forgiveness in Politics*. Among the most astonishing was the address to the Bundestag by German President Richard von Weizsacker on the fortieth anniversary of the end of World War II. Shriver writes, "What impressed the world about this speech was its lengthy, unflinching, excuseless enumeration of Nazi crimes and many degrees of association with those crimes by millions of Germans in the years 1933–45." In part, von Weizsacker said, "Who could remain innocent after the burning of the synagogues, the looting, the stigmatizing with the Jewish star, the withdrawal of rights, the unceasing violations of human worth? . . . As human beings, we seek reconciliation. Precisely for this reason we must understand that there can be no reconciliation without memory."[20]

Conclusion

This practice norm has a series of interconnected steps designed to engage a situation of grave injustice with openness to painful and long hidden truths, change the power inequalities that gave rise to the injustice in the first place by the search for real repentance that includes redress of past wrongs, and make an effort toward restorative justice. Forgiveness then becomes a way to break with the past and find a new path forward in a changed relationship.

All around the world, there is increasing interest in local, regional, state, and international conflicts in how this practice norm can function to change the desire for revenge that is such an engine of violent conflict. The Abrahamic traditions have rich and diverse contributions to make to this dynamic; religious leaders from all three traditions, as well as others, have played or could play a significant role in helping to lead on how people can change their relationship to the past, live in a different present, and find a new future together.

Notes

1. I have developed this argument more expansively in my paper, "Religious Conviction in a Diverse World: A Jewish Perspective on Fundamentalism and Relativism," in *Between Relativism and Fundamentalism,* ed. Peter L. Berger (Grand Rapids, MI: Eerdmans, 2010).

2. For more detail on the story, see Abdullah Yusuf Ali, *The Meaning of the Holy Qur'an* (Beltsville, MD: Amana, 2001). He offers comparative notes of the biblical and Qur'an stories.

3. Muhammad Asad in his translation and commentary on the Qur'an has detailed notes on the Qur'an command of forgiveness without acknowledging guilt.

4. Qur'an 68:4: "And thou (standest) on an exalted standard of character."

5. Qur'an 21:107: "We sent thee not, but as a Mercy for all creatures."

6. Qur'an 33:21: "Ye have indeed in the Messenger of Allah a beautiful pattern (of conduct) for any one whose hope is in Allah and the Final Day, and who engages much in the Praise of Allah."

7. For more details on the conquest of Makkah and the Prophet's forgiveness and general amnesty, see M. Tayyib Budayuni, trans., *'Allama Shibli Nu'mani, Seerat-un-Nabi* (New Delhi: Kitabbhavan Press, 2000), 146–60.

8. Safi-ur-Rahman al-Mubarakpuri, *Ar-Raheeq al-Makhtum, Maktba Dar-us-Salam* (Riyadh: Maktaba Darus-Salam Publication, 1996), 136–40, 446–48.

9. Mia 'Abid Ahmad, *Shaan-e-Muhammad* (Pakistan: Idara Adb wa Thaqafat, 1988), 66.

10. Hannah Arendt, *The Human Condition* (Chicago: University of Chicago Press), 238.

11. New Revised Standard Version.

12. Or church-based.

13. Reinhold Niebuhr, *The Irony of American History* (New York: Scribner, 1952), 42.

14. Andrew Trocmé, *The Politics of Repentance* (New York: Fellowship Publications, 1953), 74.

15. Dorothy Shea, *The South African Truth Commission: The Politics of Reconciliation* (Washington, DC: USIP Press, 2000), 6.

16. *Confronting the Truth: Truth Commissions and Societies in Transition,* DVD (Washington, DC: USIP Press, 2007).

17. Dietrich Bonhoeffer, *The Cost of Discipleship* (New York: Touchstone, 1995).

18. Susan Thistlethwaite, "Religion: Why Did Jesus Die?" *Time* (April 12, 2004): 60.

19. Alan Geyer, "Acknowledge Responsibility for Conflict and Injustice and Seek Repentance and Forgiveness," in *Just Peacemaking: Ten Practices for Abolishing War,* ed. Glen Stassen (Cleveland: Pilgrim Press, 1998), 87–94.

20. Donald Shriver, *An Ethic for Enemies: Forgiveness in Politics* (New York: Oxford University Press, 1995), 71.

CHAPTER 5

Practice Norm 5

Advance Democracy, Human Rights, and Interdependence

Definition

*T*he phenomenon of democratic peace is well attested to: no democracy with human rights fought a war against another democracy with human rights in all the twentieth century (although some funded or fomented wars by others). This does not mean democracies do no evil, but on the average they make wars less often and spend less on their militaries than dictatorships do. Several factors have been researched by political scientists to explain this striking decrease in war making. International institutions can help to strengthen democracy globally; however, the ideal of the advancement of democracy should not be understood to condone war making in order to force democracy on other regimes. And the establishment of democratic governance should never be at the expense of minority rights. Human rights organizations must be recognized for their significant place as independent and articulate reporters of abuses perpetuated by any and all governments, and for their steady pressure toward democracy with human rights. Interdependence can also be a tool of peacemaking because it gives countries a stake in one another's well-being when it is a truly mutual dependence and not a one-sided dominance of the weak by the strong.*

Introduction

The themes of human rights, democracy, and interdependence are woven through the historical and contemporary writing of Islamic, Jewish, and Christian theologians, especially those for whom the call to peacemaking is grounded in, and challenged by, their engagement with real-world political, economic, and cultural challenges. This chapter provides three complementary perspectives on human rights, democracy, and interdependence. Louay Safi and Blu Greenberg focus their contributions on traditional texts in Islam and Judaism, whereas Matthew Johnson focuses on the special story of the African American Christian churches in the freedom struggle. All three highlight texts that support the importance of human rights in traditional teaching, and all three identify contemporary cases where new perspectives are evolving in response to changing historical and cultural realities. Although the three contributions take somewhat different paths, together they suggest ways in which their three traditions support, challenge, and provide opportunities for continued progress in the areas of human rights, democracy, and interdependence.

Muslim Reflection

Louay M. Safi

The Universal Declaration of Human Rights (UDHR) adopted by the United Nations in 1948 represented an advanced stage in the struggle to recognize the equal dignity of all human beings. In Western society, the Magna Carta and the Declaration of Independence served as preludes to the Universal Declaration. Less known are the various expressions in support of equal dignity of people in the Islamic tradition. As contemporary Muslim societies struggle today to establish human rights protections, they can rely on a long tradition of advancing individual rights and freedom, including religious freedom and gender equality. Ever since the Qur'an declared religious freedom and the equal dignity of all people,[1] early Muslim scholars and leaders articulated those values into working ideas and traditions that were suitable to their own social and historical conditions.

This essay explores some of the textual pronouncements and scholarly articulations in classical sources, because they provide a firm moral and intellectual foundation for a human rights tradition rooted in Islamic values and worldview. Given space restrictions, the focus here is on religious freedom and gender equality, leaving other aspects of human rights for future discussion.

Religious Freedom and Equality

Early jurists recognized that non-Muslims who have entered into a peace covenant with Muslims are entitled to full religious freedom and equal protection of the law as far as their rights to personal safety and property are concerned. Thus Muhammad bin al-Hasan al-Shaybani (749/50–805 CE) states in unequivocal terms that when non-Muslims enter into a peace covenant with Muslims,

"Muslims should not appropriate any of their [the non-Muslims] houses and land, nor should they intrude into any of their dwellings."[2] Similarly, early Muslim jurists recognized the right of non-Muslims to self-determination, and awarded them full moral and legal autonomy in the villages and towns under their control. Therefore, al-Shaybani, the author of the most authoritative work on non-Muslim rights, insists that the Christians who have entered into a peace covenant (*dhimma*)—and hence became *dhimmis*—have all the freedom to trade in wine and pork in their towns freely, even though such practice is considered immoral and illegal among Muslims.[3] However, *dhimmis* were prohibited from doing the same in towns and villages controlled by Muslims.

There is ample evidence in the Qur'an that individuals should be able to accept or reject a particular faith on the basis of personal conviction, and that no amount of external pressure or compulsion should be permitted: "No compulsion in religion: truth stands out clear from error" (Qur'an 2:256). By emphasizing the individual's right to freely follow his or her conviction, the Qur'an reiterates a long-standing position, which it traces back to one of the earliest known prophets, Noah.[4]

Not only does the Qur'an recognize the individual's right to freedom of conviction, but it also recognizes moral freedom to act on the basis of individual conviction.[5] The principle that the larger community has no right to interfere in one's choices of faith and conviction can be seen further in the fact that the Qur'an emphasizes that the individual is accountable to the Creator alone for moral choices made in this life.[6]

Despite the Qur'anic emphasis on the freedom of conviction and moral autonomy, most classical jurists contend that a person who renounces Islam or converts to another religion commits a crime of *ridda* (apostasy) punishable by death. However, because the Qur'an is unequivocal in supporting religious freedom,[7] classical jurists who advocated the death penalty for *ridda* (renouncing Islam) relied on two *hadith* texts, and the precedent of the Muslims fighting against Arab apostates under the leadership of Abu Bakr, the first caliph. However, both *hadith* statements cannot stand as credible evidence because they contravene numerous Qur'anic sources. The *hadith* even contradicts the practices of the Prophet, who reportedly pardoned Muslims who committed *ridda*.

Gender Equality

When approaching Islamic sources to shed light on the issue of women's rights, a clear distinction emerges between the rights of women in the public sphere and their rights in the area of family law. For while Islamic sources differentiate men's and women's responsibilities within the family, all limitations on women's rights imposed by classical scholars in the public sphere were based on either faulty interpretations of Islamic texts or practical limitations associated with the social and political structures of historical society.

The Qur'an is unequivocal in assigning equal responsibilities for men and women for maintaining public order: "The believers, men and women, are protectors one of another; they enjoin the right (*ma'ruf*) and forbid the intolerable (*munkar*); they observe regular prayers, practice regular charity, and obey God and His Messenger" (Qur'an 9:71). Since men and women are entrusted with the same public responsibility to enjoin the right and forbid the intolerable, one should expect that they would enjoy equal political rights. Yet it is obvious that classical jurists deny women political equality with men. The question therefore arises as to what is the basis of the classical position? Jurists who deny women the right to public office base their arguments on one Qur'anic and one prophetic statement. The Qur'anic statement reads, "Men are the protectors (*qawwamun*) of women, because God has given the one more (strength) than the other, and because men support women from their means" (Qur'an 4:34). The word *qawwamun*, which connotes "support" and "protection," has come to signify authority as well.

The fact that *qawwamun* also signifies authority is not difficult to see, as the remainder of the above Qur'anic statement empowers men with the right to discipline women guilty of mischief. But can the above verse be used to deny women access to public office? The answer is an emphatic no. For the authority implied by *qawwamun* and the obedience it entails is relevant—even under classical interpretation—within the confines of the family. The Qur'an does not intend to give authority to every single man over every single woman. Nor do those who extend the implication of this verse to the public sphere expect that any single woman in society should obey any single man, known to her or not. If this is the case, no one can invoke the notion of *qawwamun* to deny women access to public office.

The other textual evidence used by classical jurists, and by some contemporary traditionalist jurists, is in the form of a *hadith* text that states, "They shall never succeed those who entrust their affairs to a woman."[8] Reportedly the statement is a comment made by the Prophet upon hearing the news of the accession of Buran, the daughter of King Anusherawan, to the Persian throne after the passing away of her father. There are several reasons to show that this *hadith* does not stand up to close scrutiny and cannot undermine the principle of moral and political equality between the sexes, which is firmly established in the Qur'anic texts. First, the *hadith* statement is not given in the form of a directive, but an opinion that has to be understood in its historical and cultural context. That is, the *hadith* has to be interpreted in the context of a historical society where women were not active participants in political life, and in the context of a political culture that places the hereditary rule over the principle of merit in deciding political succession. Second, the *hadith* is a single statement that has no support in the most authoritative Islamic source—the Qur'an. Third, the *hadith* stands in a direct contradiction with the principle of moral and political equality of the sexes, a principle established by numerous Qur'anic verses. Finally, the *hadith*, being a singular narration (*khabar ahad*), is of a lesser degree of certainty than the Qur'anic narration (*khabar mutawatar*) and hence cannot overrule principles established in the Qur'an.

Islamic sources support the right of women to have full access to public office and to enjoy complete equality with men in public life. The discussion of the notion of *qawwamun,* which provides men with a degree of authority over women, must be confined to the realm of family life. It is in the family, and in the family alone, that all of the practices cited by the critics of *shari'ah* as instances of gender inequality can be found, namely polygamy, unequal inheritance, and interreligious marriage.[9] It is important to recognize the complexity of the issues involved in the debate on gender equality and gender roles, and the need for undertaking further research to examine the sociohistorical meaning of biological differences between the sexes and the sociopolitical significance of psychological differences—if any—between genders. However, the debate is neither relevant nor helpful for the purpose of elaborating human rights. The findings of all empirical studies on the issue of sexual differences have been disputed on ideological grounds and have been interpreted in support of competing normative positions. There is nothing to suggest that human beings would ever subordinate their moral beliefs to empirical knowledge—at least not in a historically relevant timeframe.

This brief examination of the Qur'anic discourse reveals the significance it places on the equal dignity of human beings. While the Qur'an urges people to adopt high moral standards, it makes it quite clear that people are ultimately accountable to their creator for their moral failings. Those who have been more fortunate to lead a moral life should strive, with tolerance and sympathy, to persuade others to adopt their vision of a good life, but they should never go to the extent of imposing their morality on others. This attitude allowed early Muslims to embrace diverse cultural groups and to cooperate and peacefully coexist with a plurality of religious communities.

The tolerant attitude and pluralistic outlook were later diluted, giving rise to a more intrusive approach in which the lines separating the moral from the legal became blurred. The traditionalist stance was further compounded by undermining the principle of moral equality between men and women advanced in the Qur'anic texts. This was done by giving more weight to particular pronouncements, while ignoring universal principles and general purposes. Gradually, therefore, the moral autonomy of individuals and groups was severely compromised. Interestingly, though, in their zeal to assert Islamic morality through legal enforcement, the traditional jurists unwittingly undermined the moral fabric of society. This is because moral character does not develop under conditions of rigid restrictions on free speech and action. By definition, a moral choice presupposes that the individual has also the choice of acting immorally or in accordance with standards that do not rise to the level of moral action. Take this choice away and morality cannot be distinguished from hypocrisy and duplicity.

There is a dire need today for Muslims to undertake a legal reform so as to restore the principle of moral autonomy to both individuals and cultural groups. By so doing, Muslims will have a greater opportunity to rid their communities of oppression, corruption, and hypocrisy. They will also have the chance to join hands with an increasing number of individuals and groups belonging to the various religious communities of the world to fight global injustice and oppression. The Universal Declaration of Human Rights should be viewed as a common thread that can bind the efforts of people belonging to diverse moral communities the world over.

Jewish Reflection

Blu Greenberg

Judaism has a long history of developing human rights, beginning with its foundation document, the Torah.[10] A work of history and theology, the Torah tells several major stories: God's creation of the universe, a family embracing monotheism, a people enslaved and then redeemed, a newly freed community entering into a covenant with God, and finally a nation making its way to the Promised Land. While all of these narratives are paradigmatic for universal human rights, two particularly stand out: redemption from slavery and a life of independence, security, and peace on one's own land. The theological message of these narratives is clear: what God did for the Jewish people, God will do for all of humanity.

But more than narrative, the Torah is a book of how to live in a covenantal relationship not only with God, but with other human beings, and not only along those early journeys, but for all time. Thus the Torah is filled with ritual and ethical law. These two discrete categories of law are wholly interdependent, which is why the prophets rail against those who perform ritual but neglect ethics. "Of what use to me are your many sacrifices? says the Lord . . . Purify your selves . . . Put away your unjust actions" (Isa. 1:11–16).

The ethical laws of the Torah, as well as the narratives from which ethical behavior is extrapolated, constitute the hub and heart of human rights in

Judaism. As Jews moved through several millennia of history, a remarkable rabbinic process of both preserving and renewing Torah law greatly expanded these rights. Many of contemporary society's basic rights can trace their roots back to Torah and Jewish tradition.[11]

Yet the term "human rights" did not enter the Jewish vocabulary until the mid twentieth century.[12] This is largely because most statements of Jewish ethical law throughout the ages were framed as duties rather than as entitlements characteristic of contemporary documents. For example, the standard bearer of human rights today, the United Nations Declaration of Human Rights, states, "Everyone has the right to life, liberty and security of person" (Article 3), whereas the Torah states, "Thou shall not kill . . . kidnap . . . oppress a slave."[13],[14] In fact, this difference in formulation relates to a much larger issue—the element of divinity. Absent in secular documents, the notion of a Divine Commander is ever present in Jewish ones.[15] Ethical laws in the Torah often carry a tagline: "because I, the Lord, have commanded you"; "because I, the Lord your God, redeemed you from bondage in the land of Egypt"; "because I remember the love and faithfulness of your ancestors." In violating the human rights of others, one violates God's law.

Divine accountability adds heft to prescriptions for behavior.[16] The Talmud rules that if one violates the rights of her neighbor, she must first ask for and receive forgiveness from the neighbor and only then will the healing forgiveness of Yom Kippur be granted by God.[17] These teachings—that relationships between human beings exist simultaneously in partnership with God and must meet God's standards—do have powerful implications for human rights. When righteous Gentiles were asked why they risked their lives and their children's in order to save Jews in the Holocaust, they answered that it was an obligation of their faith to respect the right to life of others.[18]

The Dignity of All Humans

The philosophical core of human rights in Judaism is found in the biblical account of the creation of humanity: "And God created *adam* in His image, in the image of God He created him, male and female He created them" (Gen. 1:27). But what does a human image of God mean? With what inalienable rights does an individual enter life on Earth? In a Talmudic passage describing the court's cautionary words to witnesses who are about to testify in a capital case, three innate human dignities are noted:

> You must know that . . . [for these reasons] the human being, *adam*, was created as a single being: to teach you that anyone who destroys a single life Scriptures considers him as if he destroyed a whole world, and anyone who preserves a single life, Scriptures considers him as though he has preserved a whole world; and a

single being was created . . . for the sake of peace so that one should not say to his fellow, 'My ancestor was greater than yours [equality]'; and to proclaim the greatness of God . . . who stamped every human being from the same mold [the first single being] yet not one of them is like any another.

We learn from this that every human being should see himself or herself as created in the image of God, endowed with infinite value, equality, and uniqueness and should treat every other human image of God as similarly endowed.[19,20]

These three dignities are a noble vision of life yet hardly a description of reality, neither at the moment of creation nor now, untold civilizations later. In a world of slavery, war, uneven wealth, gender inequity, and racial discrimination, the idea that every human is unique, equal, and of infinite value seems like fantasy. Judaism deals with the theological conflict betweeen reality and the ideal by keeping alive the messianic dream even as it delivers a stream of realistic guidelines to help steer the course. Visions of "ploughshares into pruning hooks" and "the lion shall lie down with the lamb" coexist with myriad laws that acknowledge human frailties and protect the rights of others. If a human being is of infinite value, then his life and limb must be carefully protected. If one person is equal to every other, her rights must be assured. If each man, woman, and child is unique, their individual dignities must be honored. Below are several examples that fit each category.

Protection of Life and Limb

"You shall not stand idly by the blood of your neighbor" (Lev. 19:16). Associating the shedding of blood with bystanding underscores the gravity of the crime. Bystanding is a major issue in human rights. How much human misery could have been avoided if not for the complicity of the bystander who sees evil or ill fortune but chooses not to act?[21] "You shall rise before the aged and show deference to the old man" (Lev. 19:32). Respect for the elderly counters the tendency to measure people in terms of productivity and utilitarian worth, abandoning them when they no longer serve these purposes. "When you build a new house, you shall make a parapet for your roof so that . . . no one falls from it" (Deut. 22:8). One is as liable for prevention of injury as for remedy after the fact. "And you shall construct cities of refuge throughout the land [to protect the accidental manslayer until he stands judgment]" (Num. 35:12; Deut. 19:2ff). The presence of such cities prevented the land from descending into the lawlessness of blood avengers, sadly a characteristic of some societies even today.

Equality

Rule of law ensures equality. The Torah's range on this subject is wide, from general admonitions of "Justice, justice shall you pursue"[22] to more specific directives such as "You shall not be swayed by the crowd nor show deference to the poor in administering the law" (Exod. 23:2–3).[23] Every aspect of law is included: the establishment of a court system, appointment of judges, the prohibition against false testimony and bribery, inheritance, debt repayment, business ethics, honest weights and measures, protection of property, the right to work and to land ownership that assures a source of income, and, of course, the prohibitions against bodily injury and capital crimes—all these come under the Torah's sacred canopy. Even the king is not above the law. He must copy the words of the Torah and adhere to it.

The laws of Sabbatical and Jubilee years (Deut. 15:1ff) served to rebalance wealth, thereby protecting the poor. In the Sabbatical year, debts were canceled; in the Jubilee, property reverted to its original tribal heirs. To ensure that the spirit of laws redistributing wealth not be violated, the Torah warned against a secretive, self-serving stinginess in the face of a poor person: "Beware lest you harbor the base thought that the Jubilee year of remission is coming . . . so I'll not lend" (Deut. 15:9).

The right to education for self-sufficiency finds its core in the Torah. "And you shall teach these words [details of the covenant] to your children" (Deut. 11:19). The rabbis interpret this verse as mandating universal education, also that a father must teach his son a craft, find him a wife, teach him to swim. "He who does not teach his son a craft, is teaching him to steal" (Babylonian Talmud *Kiddushin* 29b).[24]

"Do not afflict the orphan and widow" (Exod. 22:21). This theme runs throughout sacred Jewish literature. Orphans and widows symbolize the most vulnerable elements of society. They need deferential care. Derelictions of duty, such as neglect of widows and orphans or pretending that you don't see your neighbor's ox gone astray (Deut. 22:1–3) may escape scrutiny by others, but the Torah cautions against surreptitious violations of equality as much as against obvious crimes and misdemeanors. And of course there is the golden rule of human rights equality: "Love your neighbor as yourself; I am the Lord" (Lev. 19:18).[25]

Uniqueness and Dignity

"You shall not go up and down as a talebearer among your people" (Lev. 19:16). Slander is a serious violation for it robs a person of dignity. The Torah brings multiple injunctions against evil speech: "You shall not repeat a false or slanderous report" (Exod. 23:1); "You shall judge your neighbor in righteousness [i.e., give the benefit of doubt]" (Lev. 19:15); "You shall not oppress a convert with insulting words" (Exod. 22:20); "You shall not curse your judges or political leaders" (Exod. 22:27). To all this was added the admonition in the Psalms, "Guard your tongue from speaking evil and your lips from speaking guile" (Ps. 34:13).[26]

"When you reap the harvest of your land, you shall not reap all the way to the edges of your field, nor gather the gleanings of your harvest. You shall not pick your vineyard bare, nor gather the fallen fruit of your vineyard; you shall leave them for the poor and the stranger" (Lev. 19:9ff). Not only must the haves provide for the have-nots by right, they must also provide anonymity—to preserve pride and dignity of the gatherers.

"You shall not abuse a needy and destitute laborer, whether fellow-countryman or stranger in any of the communities of your land. You must pay him his wages on the same day, before sunset, for he is needy and urgently depends on it" (Deut. 24:14–15). The law of the day laborer—the mark of a just society—eases the laborer's anxiety. How many stories have been told of cruel employers who torment the day laborer by withholding, deducting, or reducing wages for some flimsy reason?[27]

"If you take your neighbor's garment as [debt] pledge, you must return it to him each evening before the sun sets; it is his only clothing, the sole covering for his flesh. In what else shall he sleep?" (Exod. 22:25–26).[28] The right to a warm night's sleep under a blanket is one of the great measures of a free person.

Respecting the dignity of human beings can also be learned from treatment of animals. "You shall not plough by harnessing ox and donkey together [for they pull at different speeds]" (Deut. 22:10). "Do not muzzle an animal working in produce it enjoys eating" (Deut. 25:4). No act is too trivial. "If, along the road, you chance upon a bird's nest . . . with the mother sitting on her young, shoo away the mother before taking her young." (Deut. 22:6–7). So important was kindness to animals that the promised reward for complying with this commandment was long life.

Finally, in addition to laws, the interlocking themes of peace, freedom, and self-determination that sustain humanity are manifest throughout the Bible.[29] The entire Pentateuch, the first five books of the Bible, can be read as a treatise entitling a nation to peace and freedom, directing the people to their homeland. Each of the annual pilgrim holidays, Tabernacles, Passover, and Pentecost, is connected to Exodus and liberation. The idea of the Sabbath, Judaism's major contribution to the world, is a paradigm for peace. The Sabbath testifies both to Creation and Exodus, visions of human being as image of God and of liberation. The Sabbath experience implements those noble visions. Laws of cessation of work, imitating God's rest on the seventh day, enable human beings to refresh themselves, body and spirit. The Sabbath is a day of being, not doing, a day for reevaluating one's priorities of family, community, and faith. Every person, from every stratum of society, is entitled to a day of rest, of peace, of feeling free, of experiencing present dignity and future hope.

Beyond Torah

The Jewish ethical tradition did not stop with the Bible. Throughout the centuries until today, rabbis of every generation interpreted and expanded human rights laws.[30,31] Some of the original rights in Judaism, having entered the system so early, were progressive for biblical times but required correction in history. Such is the case with slavery. Paradoxically, although the biblical Exodus is the paradigm for all human liberation movements, slavery itself was never outlawed in the Torah. But the process began there, first by setting limits on slavery. The Jewish slave must be properly fed and clothed and given a Sabbath day of rest like his master. If a slave is abused, he goes free. A Jewish slave is set free after six years, with his wife with whom he entered. By Talmudic times, the limits on slavery were so tight that the Talmud opines, "When a man acquires a slave, he acquires a master."[32] Finally, recognizing that even the most benign form of slavery was a violation of human dignity, enslavement of one human being by another was de facto forbidden in the Jewish tradition.[33]

The Evolution of Human Rights: Challenges and Changes

With all this, does Judaism have a perfect record of human rights? Was the image-of-God concept operative in every aspect of law? One would be hard pressed to say that freedom of religion was a fundamental biblical right. We read of commandments to stone the blasphemer (Lev. 24:16), destroy all places of idolatry in the land (Deut. 21:18–22; 18:10), burn apostate cities and kill all their contaminating inhabitants including women and children (Deut. 13:15–17). These are difficult readings for lovers of Torah. However, in postbiblical Judaism, the rabbis eliminated all forms of death penalty for idol worshipers, apostates, and sinners.[34] In any event, history would have challenged acts of religious coercion. Such laws became irrelevant to a people exiled from their homeland and powerless inside a larger host culture. When the Jewish people finally regained independence on their own land, they did so in a climate of religious pluralism and coexistence that had developed during the two-thousand-year-long Diaspora.

One area of human rights that did not adequately develop until recent times is gender equality, by now a feature of most Western societies. In biblical times, women were under the protection of a benevolent patriarchy, but this confined them. Full rights to education, ritual celebration of life-cycle events, and leadership roles were lacking throughout much of Jewish history. Under the impetus of twentieth-century feminism that has largely changed. But some pockets of inequity remain; one example is traditional Jewish divorce law where the husband continues to have leverage over a wife who initiates divorce.[35]

A second area where Jewish tradition lags behind Western culture is in attitudes toward homosexuality. Biblical law is harsh (Lev. 20:13). Rabbinic law eliminated punishment but retained strong negative attitudes. During the past few decades, Jewish liberal denominations have moved away from negativity, but the Orthodox have not. While no one advocates biblical stoning, one still hears language of "abomination" in ultra-Orthodox circles and "sickness" in modern ones. This sits in stark contrast to the current cultural coinage of the gay revolution in which homosexuality is presented as an equal option to heterosexuality.[36]

A third issue that Jewish tradition must grapple with—as indeed must all religions and nationalities—is the matter of hierarchy of privilege in human rights. The great disparities in our global world have more to do with this than with lack of resources. Foreign workers, way down the social scale, suffer the least protection of rights everywhere. In the Bible, a dialectical tension seems to exist between the recognition of an in-group and the stress on the need for universal concern.[37] "Love your neighbor as yourself" exists alongside "Love the stranger in your midst" (Deut. 10:19). The non-Jewish slave is treated differently but may not be mistreated (Deut. 24:14–15). One may not wrong one's brother or a stranger in buying and selling (Lev. 25:14, Exod. 22:20). "The *ger*, the outsider who resides with you—you shall love him as yourself, for you were strangers in the land of Egypt: I the Lord am your God" (Lev. 19:33–34). In many ways, family solidarity and preferential treatment of one's own are quite normal, a real-time response to a world of the universal and the particular.[38] Still, at times in-group behavior can spill over into bias and discrimination, and a nation must be ever vigilant.[39]

Democracy

What about democracy, the second high correlate of Just Peacemaking? Although Jewish tradition is rich with writing about tolerance, equality, and human rights, the term "democracy" is not found in traditional Jewish sources since, until recently, the Jewish nation had no opportunity or experience in democracy building. The last time Jews controlled a land of their own, a democracy model was in the early stages of formation.[40] In the twentieth century, we have seen the widespread push for human rights lead to a global and peaceful advance for human rights in Latin America, Europe, Asia, and Africa. So, too, the affirmation of human rights as God's gift and demand in the Torah has led Israel to establish a democracy at its moment of independence. Democratic laws in current-day Israel draw on both secular and religious traditions, and sometimes these come into conflict. Like all democracies, there are important struggles within Israel—and in some ways among the Jewish people—over the implications of democracy and the space between its ideals and its practices. Many of the accoutrements of democracy had long been in place: an emphasis on peace between nations, a commitment to rule of law, and the vast compendium of human rights, honed throughout the centuries. I believe that it was the latter, the Jewish rights tradition, that bridged an ancient Diaspora community to its fullest place alongside the true democracies of modern times. Israel's ongoing challenge has been to find a way to support democracy for the people of Palestine. This is the elephant in the room. Much should be said on this challenge and problem, but here, in this small space, is not the place.

With all its shortcomings, the story of human rights in Judaism is a remarkable one, enriching all of society and culture for several millennia. In Torah and the rabbinic literature that follows are found many of the roots of current principles and practices of human rights. The roots of democratic values (tolerance, equality, human dignity, and the rule of law) are also present— although in historical forms and texts that need to be understood and applied in current contexts. The level of sensitivity that Jewish tradition has taught is nothing short of extraordinary. Send the mother bird away so that she will not suffer anxiety when her eggs are taken; return the debtor's blanket or coat security deposit each night lest the poor fellow become chilled. These laws help shape and connect our current commitment to human rights, democracy, and interdependence.

Christian Reflection

Matthew V. Johnson Sr.

There is a sense in which African Americans are ground zero for the national and international struggle for full democracy in the United States. There is an unspoken understanding in the African American community that if all people's rights are not protected, we will likely be among the first disenfranchised. The only way to make a country—or a world for that matter—safe for anybody is to make it safe for everybody. The only way to ensure the human rights of anyone is to ensure them for everyone. African Americans have traditionally understood this and reflected it in the spirituality, ethics, and practice of their own struggle: from the women's struggle to the innovative immigration legislation that remains one of the least appreciated yet most far-reaching pieces of legislation to emerge from the civil rights movement, which was in fact a misnamed human rights movement. Martin Luther King Jr. said, "We have moved from the era of civil rights to the era of human rights, an era where we are called upon to raise certain basic questions about the whole society."[41]

This essay does not attempt to catalog or explore the full range or history of Christian writing related to democracy, human rights, and interdependence. Rather, it follows a few streams within Protestant Christian churches and traditions over the course of the last three centuries. It provides examples of how Christian teaching and text have supported these historic struggles and in fact have shaped "an ethic of struggle" that offers examples and promise for the broader effort of Just Peacemaking.

All Americans have benefited from the efforts to secure human dignity, rights, and civil enfranchisement that have been incubated for more than a century in the African American Church. While the struggle was certainly not confined to or exhausted by the efforts of the Christian Church in the African American community, it is impossible to imagine either the struggle or the progress made without it. Author and activist Cornel West rightly pays tribute to the free-church Puritan contribution to forming democracy and to Socratic themes in philosophy that question authority, as well as to the contribution of African American struggle and its realism, the tragicomic hope of the blues, jazz, and the black freedom struggle.[42]

However, as in any spiritual tradition grounded in scripture, experiences like challenges to authority, religious or secular, or any action of grave consequence call for a justification in and through the scriptures that provide the foundation for faith and practice. This is of the utmost importance in the Christian tradition because there are New Testament scriptures that seem to call for unquestioning obedience to established authority, a particularly painful position for African Americans suffering under slavery and the oppression of Jim Crow laws and attitudes. The dismal condition of both of these historic institutions seemed to beg for revolt. Moreover the implication in some circumstances would suggest that compliance took place because the state reflected the will of God. Scripture would be invoked to support the position of those who resisted any alteration in the status quo. Paul, for instance, writes, "Let every soul be subject unto the higher powers. For there is no power but of God: the powers that be are ordained of God. Whosoever therefore resists the power, resists the ordinance of God: and they that resist shall receive to themselves damnation" (Rom. 13:1–2).[43] But the climax of this passage, in verses 6-7, shows that Paul's focus here is on urging Christians to pay their taxes—"taxes to whom taxes are due, revenue to whom revenue is due." He was urging them not to participate in an impending tax revolt against the Roman government. A tax revolt of this sort had resulted in the exclusion of Jews and Christian Jews from Rome only a few years prior to Paul's writing the Epistle to the Romans.[44]

In what would be called an exercise in "canonical criticism" in the classic critical tradition of biblical studies, African Americans and others opposing oppressive authority and institutionalized injustice referred to other texts that superseded those calling for strict obedience and conformity. Often these challenges were embedded in paradigmatic narratives featuring significant models of the faith that lent them their peculiar rhetorical force and spiritual authority over the otherwise captive will of the faithful. When the Apostle Peter was faced with the order to refrain from teaching or preaching in the name of Jesus under pain of penalty and punishment, he boldly proclaimed, "We ought to obey God rather than men" (Acts 5:29). Clearly, this text established a precedent for revolt when the exercise of secular or religious authority conflicts with or contradicts the will of God as it is understood. In addition, this precedent marked the path within the Christian tradition toward the sacred exercise of the individual conscience in matters of right and wrong—a hallmark of the democratic tradition.

Democracy and the Protestant Tradition

Democracy in the modern world originated historically during the Puritan period of the sixteenth and seventeenth centuries in England. Puritans believed churches should not be governed by a hierarchy allied with a king; Christ, not a hierarchy, is Lord, and congregations gathered together should seek Christ's will. Their experience of democracy in the congregation and their strong sense of obligation under God to shape church life in accord with God's will were transferred also to the state. Their strong sense of obligation under God to shape life in accord with God's will applied to all of life, including the state. There is but one God, and God is sovereign over all of life. The state is not like an organic family to be ruled over by a single ruler, but like a ship with a teleological purpose: the ship of state has the purpose of sailing toward peace and justice, which the Bible teaches is God's will. "It is the ruler's duty . . . to see that it reaches its appointed destination." In this the Calvinists were insisting on a theme that Thomas Aquinas (1225–74) had articulated before them. They added a strong sense of obligation for every person to participate in the struggle for justice and right order.[45]

In this, the Puritans were recovering greater attention to the Hebrew prophets and the Hebrew scriptures. The prophets regularly challenged kings, insisting that God's will for justice for the powerless, the widows, orphans, the poor, and alien immigrants was above the king, not vice versa. Thus Cornel West writes of the Jewish prophetic commitment to justice for all peoples "formulated in the Hebrew scriptures and echoed in the foundational teachings of Christianity and Islam." The prophets prophesied not only to Israel, but to the other nations also. "The gospel love taught by Jesus and the message of mercy of Muhammad both build on the Jewish invention of the prophetic love of justice."[46]

The African American Church and the Ethic of Struggle

This essay focuses on African American Christian tradition in part because U.S. democracy excluded African Americans and other minorities. The struggle of African Americans for human rights is crucial for fulfilling the democratic vision rather than distorting it. It has been too often overlooked as crucial for redeeming the democracy project. The appearance of democracy as an institution in the modern world was in most, if not all, cases accompanied by intense and sometimes bitter struggle against reactionary forces. Even as the flagship democracies of the West came into existence, they were accompanied by varying degrees of compliance with espoused principles, values, and public proclamations. The Western "democracies" have been consistently guilty of tragically compromising their own claims with respect to their own "citizens," as well as their willingness to aid and support antidemocratic and repressive regimes around the world when it served their imperial and practical economic interests.

The commitment to democratic values and ideals has ranged from very warm when in the interests of the ruling party, class, or race, to ice cold when it comes to subjects, servants, and slaves. Consequently many of those who have been subject to the utter hypocrisy of existing Western democracies have developed a method of interpretation or hermeneutic of suspicion and a healthy skepticism toward assumptions that "democracies" imply a cure or end to human oppression, the institutionalization of justice, the absence of repressive violence, or the subjection of political values to the economic interests of the ruling class or race, both within a given state and in external relations with other sovereign states. Yet this hermeneutics of suspicion and healthy skepticism does not undermine belief in democracy, but rather makes all the more urgent its true realization from the perspective of historically oppressed peoples.

The African American Christian faith is characterized by an ethic of struggle. The civil rights movement is often referred to in the church as "the struggle." Yet the use of the term "struggle" transcends the civil rights movement to include all efforts at establishing complete legal, institutional, cultural, and social recognition of African American humanity. In his 1993 matchless masterpiece, *There Is a River: The Black Struggle for Freedom in America*, Vincent Harding articulates this ethic of struggle and its long history in the African American community from the Middle Passage through the 1960s in the context of its unmistakable spiritual undertones and overtones. The phrase "the ethics of struggle" refers to the historical efforts to resist oppression from the point of contact with oppressive forces up to the present moment. "The struggle" has profound spiritual resonance, and participation in it is considered by those committed to resist oppression not only inevitable, but an essential component of spiritual life. The notion of the struggle sanctifies individual and collective striving for full humanity and sanctifies the end of full humanity for all people, rendering it an aspect of God's will.

There is a profound and pervasive scriptural resonance with the ethic of struggle in the African American biblical hermeneutic. There is a deep sense in which the Christian struggle to self-actualize or live into one's potential is an ongoing, in fact lifelong process. So while for some salvation, grace, or sanctification may be experienced as a static state imposed externally from the divine transcendence, "the struggle" for the salvific *summum bonum* (greatest good) is experienced as appropriate to the life of piety. This is how certain texts are read. For instance, "Brethren, I count not myself to have apprehended: but this one thing I do, forgetting those things which are behind, and reaching forth unto those things which are before, I press toward the mark for the prize of the high calling of God in Christ Jesus" (Phil. 3:13–14). Hence the Apostle Paul's confession is seen as the model for all would-be Christians. So struggle is not only expected, but an integral part of the Christian ethic. This sense of the inherent dimension of struggle, the exertion of effort under duress, as an expression of authentic Christian practice is communicated in other places as well with the use of the race or contest metaphor. "And if a man also strives for masteries, yet is he not crowned, except he strive lawfully" (2 Tim. 2:5). Or again, "Wherefore seeing we also are compassed about with so great a cloud of witnesses, let us lay aside every weight and sin which doth so easily beset us, and let us run with patience the race that is set before us, looking to Jesus the author and finisher of our faith; who for the joy that was set before him endured the cross, despising the shame, and is set down at the right hand of the throne of God" (Heb. 12:1–2).

In the last passage quoted above one can easily see how this sense of struggle is inclusive of the larger community, even that which transcends the living to incorporate those who have since died with the ends of the struggle yet unrealized. Texts such as these fit well into the African American worldview, which bore the inflection of African heritage, where the community is always inclusive and aware of the contributions of the ancestors. The flight from Egypt to freedom would be incomplete, and perhaps even hollow, did we not bear along Joseph's bones.

The sanctification of the struggle is also related to another dimension of the African American Christian tradition. This dimension is connected to the hermeneutics of suspicion. Since African Americans have known the fragility of human rights through the failings and reversals they have experienced throughout their history, there is a sense of vigilance. In order for democracy to be advanced, given that there are always forces at work that motivate some to disenfranchise others through a variety of means, given that power tends to corrupt and all governments remain flawed and subject to exploitation by individuals and groups in power, vigilance becomes a necessary and key component for the advance and preservation of democracy and human rights.[47]

The African American Christian tradition has developed a strong prophetic component. In order to maintain and advance democracies, governments must be called to account in light of their initial commitments and fundamental ideals.[48] The African American Church has historically called America to account for the distance between promise and fulfillment, its ideals and its reality. For many, it is difficult to read the glowing language of the United Nations Declaration on Human Rights of the late 1940s in the immediate aftermath of World War II, sponsored by the United States, knowing the depth of the toxic hypocrisy of a violently racist country where it was practically legal to kill African Americans, bomb their houses of worship with impunity, deny them the right to vote, and dare them to exercise fundamental citizenship rights. African Americans are acutely aware that the language of democracy is far from the political reality of democracy, and aware of the necessity of being vigilant in maintaining the health of democratic systems.

This tradition goes back to the very historical foundations of modern Western democracies. The African American contribution to democracy through the ethic of struggle manifests itself through the pursuit of freedom from the American and French Revolutions and is extremely complex and multilayered. They pursued freedom through a variety of strategies. Those held in bondage did not fail to notice the patriots' lofty rhetoric and the contradiction with their continued plight. In 1773 a group of slaves in Boston sent a petition to the Massachusetts legislature, which in effect congratulated it for embarking on the historic path of freedom, agreed with the colonists' right to resist the slavery of being taxed without representation, and begged that when—God willing—the hostilities were decided in the colonists' favor, they would consider the plight of those of darker hue living in the colonies who remained in that condition.

Perhaps skepticism may be too strong a word, but it captures the depth at which the consistent failings of the American democratic project to provide consistent and equal access to all of its citizens to the same rights, duties, and privileges strike at the heart of faith in its virtues and thus its national and international claims of commitment. Yet even for a people so deeply disappointed through the years, African Americans have nevertheless maintained a commitment to the ideals and project of democracy for all people. Fully aware of the faults and failings of extant institutional incarnations, they press on. This pressing on against odds is spiritually significant and reflects the depth of the African American Christian spirituality that grounds it. It is the spirituality that does not require perfection in a historical manifestation to preserve commitment to an ideal, particularly an ideal grounded in the value that each individual holds in the sight of God as he or she understands God. This is key. Frederick

Douglass (1818–95) reminded us that without struggle, democracy cannot be realized in the face of the tendency of the privileged to preserve their privileges. Without this tenacious and persistent spirituality that sustains the ideal in the face of hypocrisy and disappointment, the struggle itself would have long ago succumbed to the monumental disillusionment that lurks in the shadows of every historical movement for peace, freedom, and justice.

The Struggle and Christian Scripture

The historical context of the African American struggle for full democracy and the values it entails, such as freedom, equality, equal protection under the law, bodily integrity, and a measure of economic security and political self-determination, provided for a unique hermeneutical lens through which the Christian scriptures were approached. Struggle was an essential component. This was not simply organized political struggle, but the extreme duress of daily experiences fraught with physical danger and mental anguish. The American caste system placed African Americans not only outside the political process, but through a cultural classification system fraught with debilitating implications sought to deprive their humanity of fundamental worth and dignity. Hence the struggle to realize democracy and bring about a peaceful social order through its realization had a meaning that moved beyond merely gaining access to political power and reached a depth that was essentially spiritual and profoundly religious.

The deep faith of the African American Christian Church provided the matrices by which the meaning and contours of the struggle were determined. Scripture, daily life, and the struggle for human dignity naturally bled into each other to the point where discussion of one always already implied the other. Hence Jesus's association with the disinherited became a key theme in understanding the faith, as well as a sense of assurance under difficult, challenging, and trying circumstances.[49] Texts such as Jesus's announcement of his ministry took on an urgent and immediate meaning in the context of struggle. "The Spirit of the Lord is upon me, because he hath anointed me to preach the gospel to the poor; he hath sent me to bind up the broken hearted, to preach deliverance to the captives, and recovering of sight to the blind, to set at liberty them that are bruised" (Luke 4:18). The scripture came alive with profound spiritual and emotional resonance with profound existential and historical consequences.

The fact that full human dignity and peace implied in the promise of democracy was not a present reality led to two other significant developments in this particular hermeneutic. The first was an emphasis on prophetic scriptures. These scriptures entailed an ongoing indictment of prevailing realities and condemnation of injustice. Amos's call to "let justice roll down like water and righteousness like a mighty stream" (Amos 5:24) captured both the longing for the future realization of human dignity and the indictment of prevailing realities. It affirmed the presence of God on the side of the oppressed, giving African Americans a sense of transcendent purpose and meaning in their struggle. It affirmed a dignity grounded in divine recognition that assured the legitimacy of their claims. Second, this longing animated the eschatological dimensions of scripture—those aspects looking to the end of time—giving them concrete relevance to immediate historical circumstances. "And he shall judge among the nations, and shall rebuke many people: they shall beat their swords into plowshares, and their spears into pruning hooks: nation shall not lift up sword against nation, neither shall they learn war any more" (Isa. 2:4). These scriptures in turn acted on the faith expressions of African Americans, giving universal significance and relevance to their particular struggle, so that it was more often than not expressed in terms inclusive of all people. This vision was eloquently summarized and attested to in the now iconic rhetoric of Rev. Martin Luther King Jr.'s "I Have a Dream" speech.

Over the centuries, Christian scripture has provided a foundation for the Protestant Christian churches to envision and enact practices that support democracy, human rights, and interdependence—across lines of race and class, geography and gender, age and status. Evolving directly from the Hebrew prophetic traditions, the teaching of Jesus strengthened a Christian commitment to Just Peacemaking. Historically and imperfectly, the Christian churches have built on these foundations with their teaching, their social engagement, and, in many cases, even the structure of their church communities. This is especially true of African American Christian churches—whose struggle has both modeled and drawn on other international efforts to promote human rights, democracy, and interdependence.

"The struggle" transcends individuals, groups, and even issues. It has been a part of the African American Christian tradition to see the struggle as inherently connected to all struggles around the world. In other words, inherent in the African American tradition is the conviction that the struggle for justice is interrelated all over the world. The commitment to justice is a Christian commitment, and it does not begin and end for African Americans with just African Americans. This notion is best encapsulated in the quote from Martin Luther King Jr. that "a threat to justice anywhere is a threat to justice everywhere." Whether it is the struggle of Palestinians for a homeland, or Israelites for security in the aftermath of monumental persecution, or the victims of ethnic cleansing the world over and especially in Africa, African Americans have not only proven sympathetic, but have affirmed the ethical responsibility of Christians to be in the forefront of righting those wrongs, correcting identifiable injustices, and searching for solutions.

Conclusion

Religious and cultural differences are often cited as reasons that "democracy" and "human rights" cannot be considered as universal norms. The advantage of a Just Peace practice norms approach to these interrelated concepts is that they are not treated as abstract universals. As is clear from the three different religious reflections on this norm, religious teachings are a resource for different, sometimes overlapping, approaches to how to practice participatory political systems and secure actual equality. Inequalities, particularly of race and gender, occur even within systems that declare themselves to be democracies. A practice norms approach does not hold up democracy as a "cure-all" for equality, but stresses the need to continue to deal with these in every context in specific ways.

Notes

1. "O humans! We have created you from a single pair of male and female and made you into nations and tribes that you may know one another. The best of you in the eye of God is the most righteous of you." (Qur'an 49:13).
2. Muhammad bin Ahmad al-Sarakhsi, *Sharh Kitab al-Siyar al-Kabir* (Pakistan: Nasrullah Mansur, 1405 A.H.), vol. 4, 1530.
3. Ibid.
4. "He [Noah] said: O my people! See if I have a clear sign from my Lord, and that he has sent mercy unto me, but that the mercy has been obscured from your sight? Shall we compel you to accept it when you are averse to it!" (Qur'an 11:28). "The message of freedom of belief and conviction, and the call to religious tolerance is reiterated time and again through various Prophets: And if there is a party among you that believes in the message with which I have been sent, and a party which does not believe, hold yourselves in patience until Allah does decide between us: for He is the best to decide. The leaders, the arrogant party among his people, said: O Shu'ayb! We shall certainly drive you out of our city, and those who believe with you, or else you shall have to return to our ways and religion. He said: 'What! Even though we do not wish to do so'" (Qur'an 7:86–87).
5. "Say: O my people! Do whatever you may: I will do (my part). But soon will you know on whom an anguish of ignoring shall be visited, and on whom descends an anguish that abide" (Qur'an 39:39–40). "Say: Everyone acts according to his own disposition: But your Lord knows best who it is that is best guided on the way" (Qur'an 17:84).
6. "O you who believe! Guard your own souls: If you follow (right) guidance, no hurt can come to you from those who stray. The goal of you all is God: It is He that will show you the truth of all that you do" (Qur'an 5:105). "So if they dispute with you, say: I have submitted my whole self to God and so have those who follow me. And say to the People of the Book and to those who are unlearned: Do you (also) submit yourselves? If they do, they are in right guidance. But if they turn back, your duty is to convey the Message; And in God's sight are (all) His servants" (Qur'an 3:20).

7. In fact, one cannot find in the Qur'an any support for the *ridda* penalty. The Qur'an makes two references to *ridda*: "Nor will they cease fighting you until they turn you back from your faith if they can. And if any of you turn back (commit *ridda*) from their faith and die in unbelief, their works will bear no fruit in this life; and in the hereafter they will be companions of the fire and will abide therein" (Qur'an 2:217). "O you who believe! If any from among you turn back (commits *ridda*) from his faith, soon will God produce a people whom He will love as they will love Him—humble with the believers, mighty against the disbelievers, thriving in the way of God, and never afraid of the reproaches of detractors. That is the grace of God, he bestows on whom He please; and God encompasses all and he knows all things" (Qur'an 5:54). In both cases the Qur'an does not specify any physical punishment here and now, let alone a death penalty. The Qur'an rather warns those who renounce their faith of disgrace and ill fate. To the contrary, the Qur'an provides a direct evidence, albeit open to interpretation, that *ridda* is not punishable by death: "Those who believe then disbelieve, then believe again, then disbelieve and then increase in their disbelief—God will never forgive them nor guide them to the path" (Qur'an 4:137).

8. Reported by al-Bukhari, al-Tirmidhi, and al-Tabarani.

9. Empowering women through public work, education, and legal reform addresses cases of injustice stemming from polygamy, while separating moral from legal obligations addresses interreligious marriage. Unequal inheritance, on the other hand, is connected with exempting women from any obligation to spend on the household, even when they enjoy high income, and hence must be dealt with in any legal reform by considering both rights and obligations within the family.

10. The Torah has several connotations. Here I refer to its classic meaning, the Pentateuch, or Five Books of Moses. Torah also has come to mean the entire canonical text including all of prophetic literature and the five scrolls, Song of Songs, Esther, Ecclesiastes, Ruth, and Lamentations. Torah has also come to mean the study of Torah, including the great enterprise of Talmudic study.

11. See Haim H. Cohn, *Human Rights in Jewish Law* (Hoboken, NJ: KTAV, 1984). Cohn, a justice of the Supreme Court in Israel, compares the rights in UNDHR to Jewish law.

12. The *Encyclopedia Judaica*, the definitive 22-volume reference work about Judaism originally published in 1961, now in its second edition (2007), and covering every imaginable topic has no entry for Human Rights, equivalent to the omission of a topic entitled "Judaism." But it does cover every significant right under individual headings.

13. Exodus 20; Deuteronomy 5; Leviticus 25.

14. See Article 29.2 of the UNDHR, "securing due recognition and respect for the rights and freedoms of others."

15. While the language of human rights in the UNDHR is decidedly secular, the underlying premise of the document—which appears in prominence in the Preamble—is that human beings are created with innate dignity and certain inalienable rights. How did the U.N. drafters arrive at this core of human dignity? It would be interesting to explore the history of the Preamble.

16. In contrast to negative injunctions—the violations of which are often prosecutable in courts of law and thus command compliance—positive precepts such as the

commandment to take care of widows and orphans or tithe oneself for the poor can easily fall by the wayside. Thus the need for gravitas of God's law.

17. Babylonian Talmud *Yoma* 85b.

18. What is remarkable about these postwar testimonies is how modest these rescuers are, a lesson in true religious humility. See the annual publications of the Jewish Foundation for the Righteous, http://www.jfr.org/site/PageServer.

19. I am indebted to my husband, Irving Greenberg, for teaching this core definition of inalienable human rights in Judaism. See "Covenantal Pluralism," in *For the Sake of Heaven and Earth: The New Encounter between Judaism and Christianity* (Philadelphia: Jewish Publication Society, 2004), 187.

20. Moreover, these rights serve as the foundation of democracy, where all are treated as equals, their individuality is respected, and their lives are protected.

21. There is no equivalent to the law of the bystander in the UNDHR or other human rights documents.

22. The rabbis of the Talmud interpret repetition of the noun to mean pursue justice by just means.

23. Nor, or course, favor the rich (Lev. 19:15).

24. Babylonian Talmud *Kiddushin* 29a.

25. Interestingly, this sweeping biblical human rights commandment was deemed by the rabbis to be too diffuse, so they formulated a more practical thou-shall-not from it. The great teacher Hillel taught, "What is hateful to you, do not do unto another."

26. Also, "You shall not wrong one another" (Lev. 25:17), which the rabbis explain refers to bad speech. Also, "One who slanders his wife, falsely accusing her of adultery, may never divorce her" (Deut. 22:19).

27. Sad to say, even the most sophisticated of contemporary societies, such as our own, harbor employers who do not heed this law.

28. This law speaks of a very needy man with meager possessions. A fuller and even more compassionate version of this law is in Deuteronomy 24:10–13. There a creditor is also admonished not to enter the house of a debtor to take back his pledge.

29. These exist in dialectical tension with conquest and settlement of a promised land.

30. Their teachings are preserved in the Talmud, codes of law, Responsa (questions sent to great rabbis for legal decisions), and commentaries on Torah and Talmud. Approximate dates: Revelation of Torah: twelfth century BCE; writing and compilation of the Talmud: first to seventh centuries CE; commentaries: spanning the last 15 centuries; major codes of law: twelfth to sixteenth centuries; Responsa literature: tenth to twenty-first centuries. The process of a written legal tradition never stopped.

31. Whole tractates of the Talmud and whole treatises were devoted to a particular human right that originated with a verse or two in the Torah. For example, in Exodus and Deuteronomy, perhaps a dozen laws dealing with property rights appear. But the rabbis of the Talmud, spanning several centuries, interpreted these few verses: their deliberations were gathered into three of the 63 large tractates of the Talmud. These three "gates" of *Bava Kamma*, *Bava Metzi'a*, and *Bava Batra* number into hundreds of pages, greatly expanding protection of one's property.

32. Babylonian Talmud *Kiddushin* 22a.

33. Centuries ago, the rabbis determined that as long as the Jubilee year was not operative, there could be no slavery (Babylonian Talmud *Arakhin* 29a). There has been no Jubilee for 2,400 years.

34. The Mishnah, redacted c. 220 CE, establishes practically insurmountable obstacles to enforcing the death penalty. See Babylonian Talmud *Sanhedrin* 40a.

35. I believe that when activist Jewish women today will bridge the matter to the human rights enterprise, such as the Committee on the Elimination of Discrimination against Women, it will generate rabbinic will for resolution. With sufficient rabbinic will to reinterpret the law, a halachic way will be found.

36. Many orthodox Jews, myself included, understand increasingly that one's sexuality is less a matter of choice than of biological determination. The dilemma arises for us: if these, too, are God's creatures, formed in the image of God, why did or does God's law reject them?

37. Distinctions between sojourner and citizen, stranger and countryman, convert and brother appear in many Torah contexts, though not all of them negative.

38. The Talmud describes this natural inclination: "The poor of your city and the poor of another city, the poor of your city come first." Family should take precedence. Those societies that tried to override family fidelities destroyed themselves and many other lives in the process.

39. An example of this is the law concerning the saving of a non-Jew drowning on the Sabbath. Throughout the ages, Jewish law and theology communicated the idea that human life is sacrosanct, and its protection takes precedence over every other commandment. No matter how holy the Sabbath is, one must violate it by jumping into the river to save a drowning countryman. But the law continues: if a stranger is drowning—an idol worshipper as non-Jews were considered to be—one may not violate the holy Sabbath to save his or her life. Thankfully, this law was observed in the breach, as later rabbinic authorities ruled against it on the basis of *darkhei shalom*: for the sake of peaceful relations with one's neighbors, one must save the life of the stranger on the Sabbath. But the fact that the law was challenged on pragmatic grounds rather than on the more noble grounds of human rights of the stranger can lead to a devaluation of the other in the minds of Jewish fundamentalists even today.

40. In the year 70 CE, the Jews were exiled from their homeland by the Romans, and the Jewish commonwealth in Palestine and the Middle East was destroyed.

41. David J. Garrow, *Bearing the Cross: Martin Luther King, Jr., and the Southern Christian Leadership Conference* (New York: Vintage: 1988), 563.

42. Cornel West, *Democracy Matters* (New York: Penguin, 2004), 16–18.

43. King James Version.

44. Glen Stassen, and David Gushee, Kingdom Ethics: Following Jesus in Contemporary Context (Downers Grove, IL: InterVarsity, 2003), 206-7.

45. Michael Walzer, *Revolution of the Saints: A Study in the Origins of Radical Politics* (New York: Atheneum, 1974), 177.

46. West, *Democracy*, 16–18.

47. Reinhold Niebuhr, *The Children of Light and the Children of Darkness: A Vindication of Democracy and a Critique of Its Traditional Defense* (New York: Scribner, 1945).

48. Cornel West, *Prophesy Deliverance* (Philadelphia: Westminster, 1982), especially ch. 1.

49. See Howard Thurman, *Jesus and the Disinherited* (Boston: Beacon Press, 1996).

CHAPTER 6

Practice Norm 6

Foster Just and Sustainable Economic Development

Definition

*J*ust and sustainable development can be understood as processes of change in *people's relationships to their environment that result in a positive improvement in their standard of living or quality of life. Just and sustainable development is not only about material prosperity, but also involves the cultivation and growth of the individual person. Just Peace cannot truly be said to exist without a resultant state of human flourishing. Local culture and ancient ways must be balanced against the aims of development and can be vital sources of human growth and satisfaction in the development process. Sustainable development also requires defense of the human rights and economic and property rights of the poor—those least able to resist the oppression of economically powerful persons and institutions— and is therefore inseparable from legal and political development.*

Introduction

The world has made some progress on reducing poverty. Two hundred million people have been brought above the poverty line of $2.50 per day since 1999. However, these gains are rapidly disappearing because of recent crises. The food crisis has already pushed between 73 and 105 million people back into poverty. The World Bank estimates that if the current financial crisis persists, as many as 53 million additional people will fall below the poverty line. There are crucial gender-specific impacts of the crisis, "such as the expected drop in women's income and girls' school enrolment and the rise in mortality rates among infant girls." An estimated 200,000 to 400,000 *more* infants will die each year, the majority of whom will be girls. Furthermore, these negative impacts will not only increase poverty, they will jeopardize future development.[1]

Christian, Jewish, and Islamic teachings are clear that taking care of the poor is a profound religious responsibility, as well as a way to peace. The Babylonian Talmud keeps these two themes together: "The world will not be at peace before God until people are generous and provide food for the poor" (Babylonian Talmud *Eruvin* 86a).

An example of this practice norm of just and sustainable economic development is found in Egypt being applied today and can be seen in the work of Misr el-Kheir (MEK), a development nongovernmental organization under the direction of Shaykh Gomaʿa. MEK has enjoyed astounding success in just a few years, bringing Egyptian Muslims and Christians together to fight poverty, illness, and illiteracy in Egypt based on a holistic approach to development informed by religious values. A sample of MEK projects, all of which are offered to both Muslims and Christians, includes helping establish small-scale livestock, fishing, kiosk, sewing, field vehicle, and other projects to raise the incomes of the poor; rebuilding demolished houses in Aswan and home improvement projects in other states; seasonal nutrition programs; feeding the elderly year round; rescuing the poor and illiterate from debt and predatory lending practices that have landed thousands in jail; expanding medical centers that help the blind recover their sight through simple operations; training people in upper Egypt for primary medical treatment in villages where no medical services are available; funding stem-cell research to treat diabetes, an enormous problem in Egypt; constructing schools and training social workers to assist in them; and providing specialized training to help children with special needs.

Christian Reflection

Pamela K. Brubaker

The literature on poverty and terrorism shows that "there is a correlation between conditions of extreme poverty, injustice, hopelessness, marginalization, and political oppression and the likelihood that people may use violence, including terrorism, to protest their fate."[2] These conditions are also expressions of structural violence, which cause unnecessary suffering and death. Thus they are a matter of concern for Just Peacemaking, addressed in part by this practice.

The Great Command: Love of God and Neighbor

Scripture calls us to address these injustices as a crucial aspect of our Christian faith and life. When Jesus was asked what was the greatest of the commandments, he responded, "You shall love the Lord your God with all your heart, and with all your soul, and with all your mind, and with all your strength . . . You shall love your neighbor as yourself. There is no other commandment greater than these" (Mark 12:30–31).[3]

In Luke's Gospel, the lawyer who asked the question follows up by asking, "And who is my neighbor?" Jesus tells the story of the Samaritan who cared for the man beaten and robbed on the road from Jerusalem to Jericho, after religious leaders had passed him by. Jesus then asks who was a neighbor to this man, and the lawyer answers, "The one who showed him mercy." Jesus responds, "Go and do likewise" (Luke 10:25–37).

Some contend that Christians are called not just to mercy, but also to justice. Martin Luther King Jr. offered such an interpretation in a sermon: "On the one hand we are called to play the good Samaritan on life's roadside; but that will only be an initial act. One day we must come to see that the whole Jericho road must be transformed so that men and women will not be constantly beaten and robbed as they make their way on life's highway. True compassion is more than flinging a coin to a beggar; it is not haphazard and superficial. It comes to see that an edifice which produces beggars needs restructuring."[4]

The prophetic tradition of the First Testament supports this understanding. Micah 6:8 offers a succinct summary: "What does the Lord require of you? To do justice, to love kindness and to walk humbly with your God."

The Sabbath and Jubilee traditions of the Hebrew Bible, which Jesus draws on in the Lord's Prayer (Matthew 6:9–14) and the announcement and vision of his ministry in Luke 4 "to bring good news to the poor . . . proclaim release to the captives . . . to let the oppressed go free," prescribes specific practices for correcting injustices.[5] When Jesus instructs us to pray "give us this day our daily bread," he is evoking the tradition of the wilderness feedings in Exodus 16, where each family is given enough manna for their daily needs and which establishes a Sabbath on the seventh day for rest. The next line of the prayer, "forgive us our debts as we forgive our debtors," evokes other elements of these traditions. In the Sabbath year instructions, not only was the land to lie fallow every seventh year, it was also to include debt release (Exod. 23:10–12; Deut. 15:1–81) to maintain social justice—"there will be no one in need among you."

The Jubilee tradition (Lev. 25:1–55; 27:16–24; Isaiah 61; Luke 4:18–19, "the acceptable year of the Lord's favor") adds a new feature to the Sabbath year. During the fiftieth year (after seven cycles of Sabbath years), the land is to be returned to the families who lost it because of poverty and debt. The World Council of Churches declares that the "Jubilee fully restores the access by the poor to the resources of production and well-being. It goes far beyond distributive justice to restitution of people's capacity and means to provide for life."[6] In other words, it promotes just, sustainable development.

Feeding the Hungry, Reducing Poverty, "Passing on the Gift"

Christian churches have attempted to foster just and sustainable economic development through a variety of approaches. These include charitable giving or aid; education and health care provision, which are conditions for economic development and central to human development; economic development projects; reform of unjust economic policies; and support for alternatives to neoliberal corporate-led development.

Christian churches excel at providing short-term disaster relief and aid within the United States and globally through organizations such as Church World Service, World Vision, Bread for the World, and Caritas Internationalis. At the same time, it can be difficult for churches to analyze and address root causes of poverty, but this is a necessary task in order to foster just and sustainable economic development. Organizations are committed to longer-term solutions to poverty, such as microloans and development projects.[7] Many Christian denominations and ecumenical organizations support the United Nations (U.N.) Millennium Development Campaign to reduce hunger and poverty. For instance, the Micah Challenge is a global coalition of Christians, affiliated with the World Alliance of Evangelicals. They are grounded in Micah 6:8 and intend to hold governments "to account for their promise to halve extreme poverty by 2015" and "encourage Christians worldwide to deepen their commitment to the poor and to speak out to leaders to act with justice."[8]

Heifer Project International (an ecumenical organization, with interfaith partners) is an innovative example of a hunger alleviation program that helps people obtain "a sustainable source of food and income" by providing animals to them. Its founder, Dan West, served as a relief worker in Spain following the Spanish Civil War. While distributing milk to hungry children, he realized that they needed "not a cup, but a cow." From its beginnings as a national project in 1942, the project included two crucial practices: (1) local communities decide who among them receive the first cows and other kinds of animals, and (2) these families then "pass on the gift" by giving their firstborn animals to other families chosen by the community. The animals provide needed food and income that contributes to school fees, health-care costs, and small-scale development projects. Heifer provides training in organizational development and care for the animals and environment, to promote sustainable agricultural practices. The effectiveness of this approach has been documented by independent assessments of projects in the United States and other countries. Over eight million people in 128 countries have benefited. Although this is not an insignificant number, it does not begin to meet the needs of the billion or more rural people who live in absolute poverty. However, it offers a model of people-centered development and a "gift economy" as a supplement or alternative to corporate-led, profit-oriented capitalism.[9]

Correcting Injustices, Rethinking Capitalism, Supporting Alternatives

This practice of fostering just and sustainable economic development must also work to correct economic injustices. Jubilee campaigns for cancellation of the external debt of poor countries are one example of this approach, grounded in the Sabbath and Julibee traditions discussed earlier. The Lutheran World Federation (LWF) has made illegitimate debt a focus of its work. They note "the debt burden has increased and is today a major barrier against eradication of poverty and fulfillment of basic human rights for all." They charge that the international financial institutions "and the dominant nations in the world have to accept their responsibility for the bad policies, decisions and practices, which led to the current debt crisis." Since 2004, the LWF's Latin American member churches have conducted an advocacy program focusing on the illegitimacy of the region's foreign debt.[10] They affirmed the Norwegian government's decision to unilaterally and unconditionally cancel about $81 million of illegitimate foreign debt owed to them by Egypt, Ecuador, Jamaica, Peru, and Sierra Leone. Norway did not link cancellation to its development aid, a positive contrast to cases where "supposed debt relief has gravely distorted the amounts actually granted to the poorer countries for their development."[11]

Some Christians contend that the present capitalist system itself is unjust. In his chapter "Rethinking Human Rights," in *Peace-Building by, between, and beyond Muslims and Evangelical Christians,* David L. Johnston challenges evangelicals "to marry civil and political rights to social, cultural, and economic rights." He points out that this "challenges the prevailing neoliberal capitalist paradigm to the core." Citing Jesus's admonition that "you cannot serve both Mammon and God (Matt. 6:24; Luke 16:13), Johnston denounces the central role played by the market as "inhuman and oppressive for the weakest elements of society, as well as idolatrous." This realization "should press Christians to rethink the present capitalist system, including the role of powerful multinational corporations . . . as well as their role in virtually dictating U.S. politics."[12] The World Alliance of Reformed Churches charged that "the root causes of massive threats to life are above all the product of an unjust economic system defended and protected by political and military might. *Economic systems are a matter of life or death.*"[13]

The World Council of Churches (WCC) has been analyzing neoliberal economic globalization through its "Alternative Globalization Addressing People and Earth" or AGAPE process. "The call to love and action" at the WCC 2006 Assembly in Brazil described its impact:

This process has examined the project of economic globalization that is led by the ideology of unfettered market forces and serves the dominant political and economic interests. The international financial institutions and the World Trade Organization among other such institutions promote economic globalization. The participants in the AGAPE process shared their concerns about the growing inequality, the concentration of wealth and power in the hands of a few and the destruction of the earth—all aggravating the scandal of poverty in the South and increasingly in the North. In recent years the escalating role of political and military power have strongly surfaced. People all over the world experience the impact of imperial forms of power on their communities.[14]

The AGAPE Background Document identifies several alternatives to the dominant economic system. These include the sustainable livelihoods of many indigenous communities, the Christian economy of communion in the Focolare movement, and Islamic banking.[15]

The WCC and its member churches advocate for more just and sustainable policies at the World Bank, the International Monetary Fund, the World Trade Organization, and the Group of Twenty (G-20) Finance Ministers and Central Bank Governors. They work with the U.N. General Assembly and U.N. agencies, as well as with social movements like the World Social Forum, to correct economic injustices and to develop alternatives to neoliberal corporate capitalism. The WCC Central Committee has adopted statements on "Just Trade" (2006), "Eco-justice and Ecological Debt" (2009), and "Just Finance and an Economy of Life" (2009). The global financial crisis is both moral and systemic: it "points to the immorality of a system that glorifies money and has a dehumanizing effect by encouraging acquisitive individualism."[16] The current economic system is neither just nor ecologically sustainable. Feminist theologians charge that economic systems and policies must place paramount value on caring and provisioning for human life if they are to be just and sustainable.[17] Economic paradigms must be reordered "from consumerist, exploitive models to models that are respectful of localized economies, indigenous cultures and spiritualities, the earth's reproductive limits, as well as the right of other life forms to blossom."[18]

Although Christians (and others) may rightly disagree about the effectiveness and value of capitalism as an economic system, we must look critically and constructively at our policies and practices so that they become more just and sustainable, and help end structural violence and promote Just Peace. The biblical imperative clearly is the recognition that "it is God's will on Earth that all people, regardless of class, gender, religion, race, ethnicity or caste enjoy the fullness of life in harmony with each other and nature."[19]

Muslim Reflection

Waleed El-Ansary

> Indeed God does not alter (*yughayyiru*) the state of a people unless they have altered (*yughayyiru*) the state of their souls (Qur'an 13:11).

The above Qur'anic verse suggests that the key to just and sustainable development from an Islamic perspective must begin with change within ourselves, indicating the *human* focus of development. This change (*taghir*) is clearly different from any materialistic conception of development, which may be neither just nor sustainable. The Islamic perspective is thus in full agreement with the first principle of this Just Peacemaking practice that, as stated earlier in this chapter, "Just and sustainable development is not only about material prosperity, but also involves the cultivation and growth of community organization and the individual person."

Islam, as other religions, sees the end of the human state in the perfection of our spiritual possibilities, defining a human as a creature born for transcendence, or going beyond oneself. Development must therefore address our physical, intellectual, and spiritual needs, balancing all three in such a way that no single dimension is emphasized at the expense of others. As Shaykh Ali Goma'a (b. 1952), the grand mufti of Egypt, points out, this balance of all three dimensions of our being is exactly what the Prophet aimed to achieve when he founded the mosque in Medina as the first public institution. The mosque was used for providing refuge for the poor, hosting delegations, performing ritual acts of worship, delivering religious lectures, organizing military assignments, awarding those who had proven their courage and valor in battle, strategic planning, and religious preaching.[20]

The Qur'an also explicitly addresses a hierarchy of needs, stating, for example, "It is He who produces trellised and untrellised gardens, date palms, crops of diverse flavors, the olive, the pomegranate, alike yet so different. Eat of the fruit thereof when it ripens, and pay the due thereof on the day of its harvest, and do not be prodigal. Truly, God does not love the prodigal" (Qur'an 6:141).

Traditional commentary notes how this verse addresses all three dimensions of our being: "First, it calls on us to ponder the wonder and wisdom of God's multi-colored creation, which brings the greatest joy to our mind. Secondly, it encourages us to eat, which is a pleasure for our physical body. Thirdly, it calls us to purify our soul through giving our wealth away in charity, which helps foster inner peace and happiness. Finally, the verse prohibits us from being prodigal, so that we will learn to live a balanced life."[21]

Accordingly, Islamic doctrine is in full agreement with the second principle of just and sustainable development that "peace cannot truly be said to exist without a resultant state of human flourishing." The Qur'an states, "[Prophet], when your Lord said to the angels, 'I am appointing *on earth a vice-regent (khalifah)*,' they said, 'What, will You appoint therein one who will *spread corruption and shed blood*' (Qur'an 2:30, emphasis added)?

According to traditional commentators, the angels knew that Adam was endowed with free will and that he therefore had the ability to go against the divine command, unlike the world of nature. "The angels saw the jumble of emotions and desires which were to constitute the human being, and concluded that humans would unavoidably be driven to foment chaos and violent conflict in their insatiable quest for domination and control."[22] Because we are made for the Infinite, the search for the Infinite in the finite necessarily leads to violence against humanity and nature. The Qur'an asks, "If you turn away, could it be that you will go on to spread corruption in the land and sever your ties of kinship" (Qur'an 47:22)? That is, if one turns away from the way of God, one's evil deeds lead to both corruption of the earth and dissolution of ties between human beings. Focusing only on material needs and wants at the expense of a hierarchy of needs leads to lopsided development that fails to provide people with psychological and spiritual fulfillment on one hand, and fails to keep nature clean and self-replenishing on the other. Accordingly, the environmental crisis is not simply the result of bad engineering or social organization, but a spiritual crisis.

Islam therefore envisions the process of development as having two components: *theoria*, in the Latin sense of this term meaning vision and not theory as ordinarily understood in English, and *praxis*, the practical steps taken to realize this *theoria* on the level of and through action. The Qur'an accordingly emphasizes the need for faith (*iman*) in conjunction with good works (*'amal saliha*).[23]

The Islamic perspective is thus consistent with the third principle of this practice that "local culture and ancient ways must be balanced against the aims of development and can be vital sources of human growth and satisfaction in the development process." In Islam, all human activity must be carried out in accordance with God's will as embodied in the divine law (*shari'ah*), according to which *some* members of the community must practice *each* profession to fulfill the needs of society. The same applies to other collective duties (*fard kifa'i*) such as building orphanages and hospitals. If no members in the community fulfill such needs, each member of the community is held spiritually accountable. The division of labor is accordingly a spiritual *duty*, not only a right. This is distinct from individual duties (*fard 'ayni*) such as prayer, for which others cannot fulfill our own obligations.

Moreover, the division of labor must leave ample room for human creativity, enabling us to use and thereby perfect our gifts like good stewards. Even Adam

Smith (1723–90) observed that a very high division of labor employing few of human faculties can have serious individual and social costs: "The understandings of the greater part of men are necessarily formed by their ordinary employments. The man whose life is spent in performing a few simple operations . . . has no occasion to exert his understanding . . . He naturally loses, therefore, the habit of such exertion and generally becomes as stupid and ignorant as it is possible for a human creature to become."[24]

Such an excessive division of labor creates an unsustainable trade-off between the spiritual and material objectives of work. Consequently, the norms and principles of Islamic art, which are also derived from the Islamic revelation, govern the making of things in an authentic Islamic approach to development.[25] The production process is thus conceived and elevated to the level of a spiritual discipline in which what one makes is an instrument of livelihood and devotion. Accordingly, "The artist is not a special kind of man, but every man is a special kind of artist."[26]

Islamic values also require the final principle of this practice: "the defense of the human rights and economic and property rights of the poor—those least able to resist the oppression of economically powerful persons and institutions—and is therefore inseparable from legal and political development."[27] The Prophet of Islam stated, "Access to three things should never be cut off: water, pasturage, and fire."[28] He also stated, "Access to water should not be cut off to prevent the cultivation of extra pasturage."[29] The point is that certain resources are public goods, which everyone has the right to access according to need, "leaving the rest to be used by others or otherwise leaving these resources to proceed along their natural cycle."[30]

Of course, the same principle applies to many other natural resources, but the Prophet highlighted these particular goods given their primary importance.[31] Private monopolies over fundamental resources constitute a form of injustice according to this perspective, and legal scholars infer from these Prophetic sayings that "Muslim rulers have the right to enact laws to prevent the monopolization of resources necessary for the well-being of the populace and the environment."[32]

Water provides a particularly important example, since every living being needs it to survive. In fact, the Prophet threatened those who control water resources from preventing wayfarers from quenching their thirst: "There are three people whom God will not look at on the Day of Judgment, nor purify, and they will face an agonizing torment. One of them is someone who owned a source of water on a causeway, but did not allow wayfarers to drink from it."[33]

Although Islam recognizes the need for public property, it also recognizes an important role for private property so long as it does not encroach upon the public right of access to the essentials of life. Qur'an 11:61 states, "It is He who brought you into being from the earth and had you inhabit it (*isti'marakum fiha*)." According to traditional commentary, God commands humanity in this verse to develop the earth to establish a just and virtuous society.[34] This requires institutions of both private and public property so that we avoid wasting our God-given talents and resources, either by underutilizing them and thereby failing to fulfill real needs, or by exploiting them in the service of greed rather than humankind.

Islam has enjoined the duty of preserving the environment both on individuals, in their capacity as the original owners or inheritors of that property, and on the state, which is responsible for protecting individual property and for prosecuting those who would squander their resources to the detriment of themselves and society as a whole.[35]

From the Islamic point of view, private property provides incentives for people to work hard and diligently, and the Prophet himself made the following declaration utilizing private property to promote proper cultivation and development: "Whoever revives a plot of dead land is entitled to it. As for the previous neglectful owner, he has no right over it."[36] In this Prophetic tradition, "dead plot of land" refers to land that has not been cultivated or developed and has therefore not been "brought to life" from its untended state, which is likened to death. (Of course, this tradition must be understood in context, and does not provide a justification for exploiting environmentally sensitive and crucial regions such as the Brazilian rain forests, especially since the Prophet also set aside natural reserves called *hima*.[37]) This Prophetic tradition therefore demonstrates respect for those who work hard on one hand, while providing incentives for work on the other.

At the same time, Islamic law obligates Muslim rulers to prevent any small elite from controlling goods and resources and thereby denying the general populace access to them. The caliph 'Umar al-Khattab (c. 590–644) provided a powerful precedent for this during his reign when he confronted a group of people who had "set aside a plot of land for themselves, but then left it alone for a long time without developing it, while at the same time preventing others from doing so."[38] They rationalized this by manipulating the apparent meaning of the aforementioned Prophetic tradition regarding the revival of "dead land." But this only squandered the benefits of the land for themselves and the rest of the community. In response, "'Umar one day climbed the pulpit and declared that, 'Although those who revive a dead plot of land are entitled to it, this does not include those who set aside a plot of land and leave it alone for three years.'"[39]

Similarly, 'Umar confronted Bilal ibn al-Harith (d. c. 682), to whom the Prophet had allotted a large plot of land in 'Aqia, that Bilal left undeveloped for quite some time. 'Umar inquired, "Given that you asked the Messenger of God—who never said, 'No,' to anyone—to allot you this expansive plot of land, you should divide it up for others. You don't have the resources to develop all of it, do you?" "No, I don't actually," Bilal replied. "In that case," 'Umar continued, "determine how much you can develop yourself and hand the rest over to us so that we can divide it among the Muslim community." "By God, I won't do that!" Bilal retorted. "The Messenger of God set this land aside for *me*!" "By God, you *will* in fact do it!" 'Umar exclaimed, after which he proceeded to appropriate the land that Bilal was unable to cultivate or develop, dividing it up among the Muslim community.[40]

In short, Islam prohibits the unproductive hoarding of wealth. And other precedents from the Islamic legal tradition such as the collection of the alms tax (*zakat*) on wealth that has neither been invested nor actively used for more than a year reaffirm that 'Umar properly understood the Prophet's intent and the spirit of this tradition.[41] It is also important to note that Islamic law forbids any single generation or religious community from consuming all the available resources at the expense of other generations and communities. Shaykh Ali Goma'a provides several examples of this principle in the history of Islamic civilization, outlining how people of various ethnicities and religions shared resources, and how all those who worked hard could grow wealthy, regardless of religious affiliation.[42] He concludes with the following example to illustrate this point:

> From early on, the caliph 'Umar appreciated that future generations of both Muslims and non-Muslims were entitled to the benefits of the land. Thus, when Muslims conquered the rural part of Iraq, and were about to divide it up as spoils of war, 'Umar refused, arguing that the rights of future generations had to be safeguarded. If a land as expansive as this were to become the personal property of a handful of people, what would remain for subsequent generations? How would they be able to benefit from what the land has to offer? How could they escape being property-less wage workers? If they became unable to work, how would the state feasibly support them?[43]

Finally, it is fitting to close by noting how these principles of just and sustainable development are actually being applied in Egypt today, as was noted in the introduction to this chapter. In just a few years, Egyptian Muslims and Christians have, together, engaged issues of poverty, disease, and illiteracy in Egypt, motivated by their religious values. This is exactly what "fostering just and sustainable economic development" looks like from an interfaith Just Peacemaking perspective.

Jewish Reflection

Nancy Fuchs-Kreimer

"The world will not be at peace before God until people are generous and provide food for the poor" (Babylonian Talmud *Eruvin* 86a).

Every morning traditional Jews, and some not so traditional ones, recite a series of morning blessings compiled in the daily prayer book. In these prayers, Jews bless God who "gives the rooster discernment to tell day from night." Some mornings I reflect upon how odd this blessing is. Only a few times in my life have I been awakened by the sound of a rooster in my yard. Most mornings, I wake up to the chiming of my Zen alarm clock, the parts manufactured by workers somewhere in the Southern Hemisphere whom I will never meet.

This essay will relate Jewish tradition to just economic development through examining one practice, *tzedakah*, the mandated giving of a specified portion of one's income to the needy. I choose to focus on *tzedakah* not only because of its centrality in the tradition ("*Tzedakah* is equal to all the other commandments combined" [Babylonian Talmud *Bava Bathra* 9b]), but also because tracking the practice through Jewish history reveals both the challenge and the blessing of applying Jewish teachings to the concern for world peace. I plan to be transparent regarding the challenge, at the same time sharing a few of the blessings-themes peculiar to Jewish tradition that bring added nuance and depth to a discussion of social justice. We can apply these themes, rich in their grounding in a particular tradition, to universal concerns and do so with integrity, but only by flagging the complexity. The conclusion will indicate some ways in which the practice of *tzedakah* is, in some cases, evolving today into a genuinely Jewish world Just Peacemaking practice.

Tzedakah: *A Complex Tradition*

The biblical mandate for social justice, with its strong universal dimension, stands at the start of our story, and, as Pamela Brubaker's writing in this volume attests, at the unambiguous core of Christian teaching in this area as well. For most of Jewish history, however, in the context of Jewish and non-Jewish separation or even emnity, *tzedakah* involved Jewish responsibility for other Jews.

The book of Ruth contains the treasured image of the immigrant widow gleaning from the fields of Boaz, as was her right according to the Torah.[44] It is the only time in the Bible that we actually see someone practicing this law. The practices known as *pe'ah* (corners of the field), *leket* (fallen produce), and *shikh'cha* (forgotten sheaves) served as the basis for later rabbinic laws regarding *tzedakah*, required monetary contributions to the poor. The idea was the same: some of what you grow—or later, earn—is not your own. It belongs to God and you are obligated to share it.

English translations of *tzedakah* as "charity" fail to fully capture the meaning. The Hebrew root, *tz-d-k*, means justice. The biblical laws pertained to an agricultural society. The needy were individuals who had fallen into poverty through the death of a husband or father, or because they were newly arrived in the land and, as the text goes out of its way to stress, "a stranger."

When Jews established their own semiautonomous communities outside the land of Israel, *tzedakah* became a principal rule. The twelfth-century scholar Maimonides (1135–1204) remarked, "Never have I seen or heard of a Jewish community that did not have a charity fund."[45] If a community had to choose between building a shelter for the poor and a synagogue, they were required to first build a shelter for the poor.

Diaspora Jewish law was not primarily concerned with hosting the stranger in its midst. Maimonides confirms this Talmudic norm. "In the case of a Jew and a non-Jew, the Jew takes precedence . . . a poor person of your own city and a poor person of another city, the poor of your city takes precedence" (Babylonian Talmud *Bava Metzi'a* 71a). This makes sense. The rule was formulated in the context of hostile relations between Jews and non-Jews. If Jews did not take care of their own, who would?

In America, from the day the first Jews landed in New York Harbor in 1665, they established their own mechanisms to collect funds and deliver services to maintain their community members. It was the condition of their being admitted. Jews have built a network of institutions from hospitals to free loan societies and have been a model in their ability to elicit funds and support their community. At the same time, many Jews in America, finding increasing welcome in the general culture, abandoned traditional religious life but sustained a commitment to justice, now applied to the least well off of any background.

Most dramatically in the twentieth century, *tzedakah* as a recognized term was split down the middle, serving as a legacy for two very different groups of Jews. On the one hand are those whose primary expression of Jewish identity is their commitment to universal social justice; on the other, religiously observant Jews, closer to the traditional texts and practices, who focus on building networks of support primarily for their own community. Today, in applying the tradition of *tzedakah* to the practice of "just and sustainable economic development," we are speaking of a practice that needs to be applied to people in the direst of economic circumstances, for the most part in the developing world, for the most part not Jewish.

Themes

Several powerful themes emerge from a study of *tzedakah* that characterize a distinctive, if not unique, Jewish approach to this peacemaking practice.

1. The redistribution of material wealth is a *requirement*. It is neither a choice nor an act of kindness to share one's bounty with those in need. Proverbs 14:31 states, "Anyone who withholds what is due to the poor blasphemes against the Maker of all." Loving-kindness is also a Jewish virtue and an entire tradition (*Gemilut Hesed*) speaks to the generous deeds one does for the poor and rich alike, with one's money and with one's body, for the living and the dead (Mishnah *Sukkah* 49b). But *tzedakah* is something specific: for living people, for poor people, performed with money. And not optional.

2. The verse in Proverbs goes on to say, "He who gives to the poor, honors God." Not only is giving based on laws that ground it in God's command, it is linked to our spiritual lives in *specific, practical ways*. *Tzedakah* is connected to prayer and repentance in the liturgy of the Days of Awe. It is woven into specific laws regarding holidays such as Passover and Purim. People give *tzedakah* in connection with offering prayers of healing, in celebration of joyous events, in memory of the dead, at the start of the Sabbath. A traveler given *tzedakah* to deliver at his destination will be protected from harm on the journey (Babylonian Talmud *Pesachim* 8a), a practice that is continued today by even some secular Jews.

   The Hasidic rabbi and legal authority Mordechai haKohen (1835–1911) reported that his grandfather not only gave a tenth of his profits to the poor, when he was part of an unsuccessful business venture he tithed his savings, donating to *tzedakah* a tenth of his losses, reasoning that the tradition teaches we should bless bad tidings as well as good.

   When the great nineteenth-century Talmudist Rabbi Hayim of Brisk (1853–1918) was asked what the chief job of a rabbi was, he replied, "To redress the grievances of those who are abandoned and alone, to protect the dignity of the poor."[46] Rabbi Israel Salanter (1810–83), the founder of the Mussar movement in Eastern Europe, is quoted by the philosopher Emmanuel Levinas (1906–95) as saying, "The material needs of my neighbor are my spiritual needs." Levinas continues, "Everything begins with the right of the other person, and with my infinite obligation toward them."[47]

3. Human relationships are primary. *Tzedakah*, along with acts of *gemilut hesed*, is fundamentally focused on people. Mandated blessings accompany the performance of commandments "between man and God";

there are no blessings prescribed for giving *tzedakah* or performing acts of loving-kindness. Many have glossed this fact, but perhaps the most telling explanation is simple. One should not delay in bringing relief to a needy person, even to postpone the act long enough to say a blessing. "When the community is in trouble do not say, 'I will go home and eat and drink and all will be well with me.' . . . Rather, involve yourself in the community's distress . . . as was demonstrated by Moses" (Exod. 27:12). In this way Moses said, "Since Israel is in trouble, I will share their burden." Anyone who shares a community's distress will be rewarded and will witness the community's consolation (Mishnah *Ta'anit* 11a).

4. The dignity of the human being, poor though he may be, must be maintained and nurtured. The tradition is adamant with regard to *human dignity*. The Talmud states, "It is better to jump into a flaming furnace than to publicly embarrass somebody," and charity must be redeemed immediately because the poor are standing and waiting (Babylonian Talmud *Berakhot* 43b). In order to maintain their dignity, recipients of *tzedakah* are also obligated to give a percentage away (Babylonian Talmud *Gittin* 7b).

Clearly, the best way to offer a person a dignified life is to help him move toward being able to sustain himself. While not as potentially radical as the laws regarding the Sabbatical and Jubilee years,[48] having the poor person gather her own crops from those left behind affords her a role, and perhaps dignity, in the process.

As Leviticus 25:35 says, "And if your kinsman becomes poor and falters with you, you should strengthen him." And the Talmud continues the theme: "It is better to lend to a poor person than to give him alms, and best of all is to provide him with capital for business" (Babylonian Talmud *Shabbat* 63a). Maimonides famously established eight degrees of *tzedakah* and ranked them in order of superiority. The lowest level of *tzedakah* involved the begrudging giving of charity for others, while the highest degree "is one who upholds the hand of a Jew reduced to poverty by handing him a gift or a loan, or entering into a partnership with him, or finding work for him, in order to strengthen his hand, so that he will have no need to beg from other people."[49] In the early years of Jewish immigration to America, for example, Jews established Hebrew Free Loan Societies. In 1921, the president of the society in New York said, "Our aim is deeper than charity, better than asylums or almshouses, of more comfort than hospitals."[50]

Translation to a Globalized World

It is worthwhile to develop more explicitly the arguments to be found *within* the religious tradition for applying *tzedakah*. Too often, liberal Jews gloss over this matter, relying on vague references to "the prophetic tradition," or even more ambiguously to the "requirement of *tikkun olam*." At the same time, other Jews, studying and living by Jewish law, may rely upon narrow definitions of who is their "neighbor."

The theology and life work of Rabbi Abraham Joshua Heschel (1907–72) serves as an iconic example of the potential coming together of this split. Since the 1980s, that integration has grown apace with the development of organizations like Jewish Funds for Justice[51] and the American Jewish World Service,[52] both of which have Conservative rabbis on staff, and the Orthodox group Uri l'Tzedek.[53] Indeed, a growing number of Jews look within Jewish tradition to ground their concern with an obligation to social justice, broadly defined.

Created in God's Image

The Talmud famously records both sides of an argument. In a legal dispute, one is able to read the losing side's position as well as the winning side. Who knows when it may become relevant to know both? An oft-cited disagreement involves Rabbi Akiva (c. 50–135 CE) and Ben Azzai (c. 90–125 CE). Akiva says, "A great principle of the Torah is to love your neighbor as yourself." Ben Azzai, perhaps anticipating a time when the "neighbor" might be interpreted too narrowly, counters with an alternative verse: "These are the generations of Adam"(Gen. 5:1). His verse goes on to say, "When God created man he made him in the likeness of God." The likeness of God, *tzelem elohim,* is a phrase that appears only three times in the Hebrew Bible, all in the first chapters of Genesis, before Abraham's call. Nowhere in the Bible is "the image of God" offered as the reason for laws of justice and mercy.

The idea of creation in God's image—an idea rooted in the story of humanity rather than the particular story of the Jewish people, reappears in Christian and rabbinic literature. In the latter, it is brought to bear on laws of capital punishment and the duty to procreate but not related specifically to *tzedakah*. Nevertheless, it can provide powerful theological grounding for expanding the scope of the tradition, of broadening the obligation to turn one's wealth toward creating social justice.

Tzedakah through much of the Jewish past has been, for understandable reasons, a mostly Jewish affair. But not entirely. Jews are commanded to visit the non-Jewish sick and give to the non-Jewish poor. One reason offered is *mipineh darkhei shalom* (Babylonian Talmud *Gittin* 61a). Commentators differ in their understanding of that Hebrew phrase, translated "for the sake of the ways of peace."

Some interpret this phrase as representing practical, almost cynical, advice. Jews were a vulnerable minority, and they were advised to keep things "peaceful" with their hosts. Others read into it a more sublime and values-laden message: not only are Jews commanded to pursue justice, they are also commanded to pursue peace. The self-interested and the idealistic readings are both relevant today.

It was once possible to make an important distinction between people who lived in your city and people who did not. But today we are more aware of the interdependence of our shrinking globe. People living in the Southern Hemisphere are indeed our neighbors, more so than even a decade ago. The destruction of forests in Brazil will impact global warming in America, and angry people from across the world can drive airplanes into our buildings. Promoting just and sustainable economic development may be both a matter of bald self-interest *and* an expression of our faith in God and God's images on earth, including the factory workers whose Creator I bless each morning and whose welfare is my concern. It may also be among the most effective paths we pursue "for the sake of the ways of peace."

Conclusion

Taking care of the poor is a strong priority in Jewish, Muslim, and Christian perspectives. The challenge, from a Just Peace perspective, is translating this religious duty into contemporary economic contexts. Again, a practice norms approach is helpful, as no particular economy theory has ever produced a society where even the basic needs of every citizen are met. In practice, economic inequalities arise and must be dealt with in the real world. Religious traditions can do more, however, than be the voice of conscience in a society for taking care of the poor, as important as that role is. They need to be advocates for policies that regularly rein in the worst of economic abuses, protect vulnerable persons, and protect the environment from degradation and even destruction. The exact details of these polities can vary from society to society and from system to system, but the religious imperative to take care of the poor remains a clear challenge from religious leaders to political leaders. As Rev. William Sloane Coffin is reputed to have told President Ronald Reagan regarding budget priorities to protect the poor, "Mr. President, it is up to us as religious leaders to proclaim that 'justice shall roll down like waters, and righteousness like an ever flowing stream.' It is up to you to work out the details of the plumbing."

Notes

1. Commission on the Status of Women, "Governments Must Focus on Women as Economic Agents during Global Financial Crisis if Their Disproportionate Suffering Is to Be Adverted," news release, March 5, 2009, http://www.un.org/News/Press/docs/2009/wom1721.doc.htm, 1, 8.
2. Cedric De Coning, "Poverty and Terrorism: The Root Cause Debate?" *Conflict Trends* 3 (2004): 25.
3. New Revised Standard Version.
4. Martin Luther King Jr., "A Time to Break Silence," in *A Testament of Hope: The Essential Writings of and Speeches of Martin Luther King, Jr.,* ed. James M. Washington (New York: Harper Collins, 1992), 148.
5. Ched Myers has done extensive exegetical work on this, which I draw on in my discussion. Ched Myers, "The Biblical Vision of Sabbath Economics," Bartimaeus Cooperative Ministries, http://bcm-net.org/wordpress/resources.
6. World Council of Churches, "AGAPE: A Background Document," http://www.oikoumene.org/fileadmin/files/wcc-main/documents/p3/agape-new.pdf.
7. For a fuller discussion of this approach, see David Bronkema, David Lumsdaine, and Rodger A. Payne, "Foster Just and Sustainable Development," in *Just Peacemaking: The New Paradigm,* ed. Glen Stassen (Cleveland: Pilgrim Press, 2008), 132–52.
8. See their website, http://www.micahchallenge.org.
9. See their website, http://www.heifer.org. For an interesting description of gift economy, see Beverly Bell, "Mali's Gift Economy," *Yes! Magazine,* July 22, 2009, http://www.yesmagazine.org/new-economy/malis-gift-economy (accessed December 12, 2009).
10. The program, supported by the LWF Department for Mission and Development and coordinated locally, aims to raise awareness about illegitimate foreign debt at various church levels in countries of both the Northern and Southern hemispheres. Information at http://www.lutheranworld.org.
11. Lutheran World Federation, "LWF Latin America Churches Welcome Norway's Debt Cancellation" (Geneva: Lutheran World Federation, October 11, 2006).
12. David L. Johnston, "Rethinking Human Rights," in *Peace-Building by, between, and beyond Muslims and Evangelical Christians,* ed. Mohammed Abu-Nimer and David Augsburger (Lanham, MD: Lexington Books, 2009), 226–27. Roman Catholic social teaching advocates for inclusion of social, cultural, and economic rights; see U.S. Catholic Bishops, *Economic Justice for All: Pastoral Letter on Catholic Social Teaching and the U.S. Economy* (Washington, DC: U.S. Catholic Bishops, 1986), http://www.usccb.org/sdwp/international/EconomicJusticeforAll.pdf; and Pope Benedict XVI, *Caritas in Veritate,* The Vatican, http://www.vatican.va/holy_father/benedict_xvi/encyclicals/documents/hf_ben-xvi_enc_20090629_caritas-in-veritate_en.html.
13. Douglas L. Chigal, "Covenanting for Justice in the Economy and the Earth," *Reformed World* 55 (2004): 6.
14. "Alternative Globalization Addressing People and Earth—AGAPE: A Call to Love and Action," World Council of Churches, 2006, http://www.oikoumene.org/fileadmin/files/wccassembly/documents/english/pb-06-agape.pdf.

15. Ibid.
16. These statements are available at the World Council of Churches Web site, http://www.oikoumene.org.
17. Athena Peralta, *A Caring Economy: A Feminist Contribution to the Agape Process* (Geneva: World Council of Churches, 2005), 3.
18. The statement also makes specific recommendations to churches, governments, and the international community about reducing CO_2 levels, negotiating a binding treaty in this regard, and other relevant actions.
19. Rogate M. Mshana, *Poverty, Wealth and Ecology: The Impact of Economic Globalization* (Geneva: World Council of Churches, 2008), 13–14, http://www.oikoumene.org/fileadmin/files/wcc-main/documents/p3/poverty_24p.pdf.
20. Shaykh Ali Goma'a, *Environmentalism: An Islamic Perspective* (Cairo: Al-Wabel Al-Sayyeb, 2009), 44. For the original Arabic, see *al-Biy'ah: wa'l-Hifaz Alayha min Manzur Islami* (Cairo: Al-Wabel Al-Sayyeb, 2009), 68.
21. Ibid.
22. Ibid., 29.
23. See, for instance, even the shortest chapter of the Qur'an, *al-'Asr* (ch. 103).
24. Adam Smith, as cited in E. F. Schumacher, *This I Believe* (Foxhole, Dartington, UK: Green Books, 1997), 99–100.
25. See, for instance, Seyyed Hossein Nasr, *Islamic Art and Spirituality* (Albany: State University of New York Press, 1987); and Seyyed Hossein Nasr, *Traditional Islam in the Modern World* (San Francisco: HarperOne, 2011), particularly the chapters on Islamic work ethics and development.
26. Rama Coomaraswamy, ed., *The Essential Ananda K. Coomaraswamy* (Bloomington, IN: World Wisdom, 2004), 124.
27. Ibid.
28. Ibn Majah *Kitab al-Rahun*—Bab al-Muslimun Shuraka' fil Thalah.
29. Sahih al-Bukhari *Kitab al-Hiyal*—Bab Ma Yukrahu min al-Ihtiyal fi'l-Buyu'.
30. Shaykh Ali Goma'a, *Environmentalism*, 57.
31. For example, the Prophet also mentions salt in certain narrations.
32. Shaykh Ali Goma'a, *Environmentalism*, 57.
33. Sahih al-Bukhari *Kitab al-Musqat*—Bab Ith Man Man'a Ibn al-Sabil min al-Ma'.
34. For an in-depth analysis, see Abbas Mirakhor and Idris Samawi Hamid, *Islam and Development: The Institutional Framework* (New York: Global Scholarly Publications, 2010), ch. 5.
35. Shaykh Ali Goma'a, *Environmentalism*, 58.
36. Abu Dawud *Kitab al-Kharaj*—Bab fi Ihya' al-Mawat.
37. For an Islamic approach to environmental economics, see, for instance, Waleed El-Ansary, "Islamic Environmental Economics and the Three Dimensions of Islam: *A Common Word* on the Environment as Neighbor," in *Muslim and Christian Understanding: Theory and Application of A Common Word*, ed. Waleed El-Ansary and David Linnan (New York: Palgrave Macmillan, 2010).
38. Shaykh Ali Goma'a, *Environmentalism*, 59.
39. Ibid.
40. Ibid.
41. Ibid., 60.

42. Ibid., 60–61.

43. Ibid., 61.

44. "When you reap the harvest of your land, you shall not reap all the way to the edges of your field, or gather the gleanings of your harvest. You shall not pick your vineyard bare, or gather the fallen fruit of your vineyard; you shall leave them for the poor and the stranger: I the Lord am your God" (Lev. 19:9–10).

45. Moshe ben Maimon (Maimonides), *Mishneh Torah* (Cairo: c. 1175), "Gifts to the Poor," 9:3.

46. Joseph B. Soloveitchik, *Halackhic Man* (Philadelphia: Jewish Publication Society, 1983), 91.

47. Annette Aronowicz, *Nine Talmudic Readings by Emmanuel Levinas* (Bloomington: Indiana University Press, 1990), 99–100. (This statement is often attributed to Salanter directly, but it is not clear if it actually appears in his writings.)

48. The laws regarding the seventh and forty-ninth years would require at least another five pages.

49. *Mishneh Torah*, "Laws Concerning Gifts to the Poor," 7:7.

50. David G. Dalin, "Judaism's War on Poverty," Policy Review, #85, (September 1, 1997). http.hoover.org/publications/policy-review/article/6899.

51. Jewish Funds for Justice was founded in 1984 to fill a crucial void in Jewish philanthropy. Although Jews as individuals had been leading supporters of efforts to end the injustice of poverty in America, no national grant-making institution existed whereby Jews could express their commitment to advancing social and economic justice for all Americans. See http://www.jewishjustice.org.

52. American Jewish World Service was founded in 1985 by a group of rabbis, Jewish communal leaders, activists, businesspeople, scholars, and others as the first American Jewish organization dedicated to alleviating poverty, hunger, and disease among people across the globe. See http://www.ajws.org.

53. Uri L'Tzedek is an Orthodox social justice organization guided by Torah values and dedicated to combating suffering and oppression through community-based education, leadership development, and action. See http://www.utzedek.org.

CHAPTER 7

Practice Norm 7

Work with Emerging Cooperative Forces in the International System

Definition

*W*hile the dynamic relation between international actors, mainly independent states, is replete with tensions and accounts for much international conflict and war, it also stimulates international cooperation and peace. Increasingly since the early nineteenth century the international system has shifted upon the recognition of the decline of the utility of war, the rise of international trade, the dramatic increase of global exchanges and communications, and the ascendancy of democracy as the dominant form of government. In seeking to avert conflict and war, governments should look to those bodies that emerge from and represent international cooperation for guidance and mediating help. In working toward peace we must strengthen these global networks and associations, particularly when they can contribute to practical problem solving.*

Introduction

The age of the Internet has made working with emerging forces in the international community easier, while at the same time making the work of peacemaking more challenging. Facebook has been shown to work well for social justice organizing; Iranians used Twitter to organize nonviolent protests against what they considered an unjust and un-Islamic electoral process in their country. Cell phones and computers provide access for networking to individuals and organizations around the world. Yet this very connectivity also carries information promoting violent extremism, bomb making, and socially corrosive half-truths and outright lies. Social activists seeking to create greater justice and peace use these networking tools; so do those who oppose them. In addition, those who seek such technological connectivity are sometimes denied access to these tools by repressive governments who fear the free flow of information and human networking.

This practice norm is related to the communications revolution around the world but not exclusively defined by it. "Emerging cooperative forces" that are rapidly increasing today are nongovernmental agencies around the world and within nation-states. The twentieth century saw an unprecedented explosion of nongovernmental organizations (NGOs). Many of the most severe problems around the world, such as poverty, disease, and conflict, are transnational in scope. NGOs have developed with a humanitarian focus to address these needs, and many today are faith based in origin and mission. Not all NGOs are regarded as beneficial and benign, but they are a resource for international networking in the work of Just Peacemaking. Whether faith based such as World Vision, or more secular such as Médecins Sans Frontières, these kinds of "emerging forces within the international system" are a large and increasing force in the international system that can be engaged from a Just Peace perspective.

International cooperation through treaties to address vast problems such as the threat of climate change is another "emerging international force," but cooperation, as the difficulties at the United Nations (UN) Climate Change Conference in Copenhagen illustrated, can be frustratingly slow and partial. This is an arena where religious support for such cooperative efforts can be particularly helpful. While there has been much public discussion of the shortcomings of the Copenhagen conference, there has been little mention of the conference's positive outcomes: widespread recognition that a sustainable response to climate change is a moral imperative and the shared commitment of faith communities to take up this challenge and build interfaith cooperation toward this end. As Jewish United Nations Delegate Rabbi Warren Stone noted, "In a world where matters of faith seem so often and so tragically to divide us, there is no issue which aligns us more deeply than our shared dependence upon and sacred responsibility to this tiny planet, enfolded within its fragile atmosphere, spinning in the vastness of time and space."[1]

Jewish Reflection

Robert Eisen

Historical and Biblical Sources

On one level, the question of whether Judaism supports cooperative forces in the international system is easy to answer. Given the strong emphasis that Judaism places on the value of peace in general, it stands to reason that Judaism would support the notion that nations should work with international bodies in order to foster peace among them.[2] Yet if we are to seek more specific endorsements within Judaism for this type of activity, we encounter several obstacles. First, there is the problem that one always runs up against in Jewish political ethics, which is that Jews did not have political sovereignty for the majority of their history, and therefore there is little in classical Jewish sources that speaks about this branch of ethics. Second, the idea and practice of creating international bodies to safeguard peace throughout the world are relatively recent; the first serious proposals for this notion occur no earlier than the nineteenth century. Therefore, if the classical sources on Jewish politics are relatively meager, they will be even more meager on this particular issue. Nonetheless, Jewish sources are rich enough to provide some guidance here if we are willing to use a little creativity.

The first place one might look for a Jewish position on cooperation with international bodies for the sake of peace is the messianic doctrine. From the Bible onward, the messianic period is envisioned as an era of peace among nations. One of the earliest precedents for this idea is the celebrated and moving passage that appears in the second chapter of Isaiah and the fourth chapter of Micah in which the prophets predict that in the messianic era the Gentile nations will stream to the Mount of the Lord, beat their swords into plowshares and spears into pruning hooks, and never again wage war.[3] Later Jewish sources reflecting on the messianic period would support and expand upon this vision of the end of days. Given that in Judaism peace among nations is the end toward which history is moving, it would seem that Jews should certainly support cooperation with international bodies that are working for a more peaceful world.

The notion that such cooperation in the modern period is a harbinger of the messianic era was already suggested in the nineteenth century by Reform theologians, most notably Hermann Cohen (1842–1918), perhaps the greatest of them.[4] Yet we have to be cautious here. Associating international cooperation with messianism runs the danger of equating the present era with the messianic period, and messianism is a potent and dangerous force of which we must be very wary. It can excite the passion for peace but also violence. A case in point is the settlement movement on the West Bank, which was spawned by the messianic theology of Rabbi Abraham Isaac Kook (1865–1935). Kook's messianism was mostly benevolent on issues of peace and violence, but it was transformed into a malevolent ideology by his son Rabbi Tsevi Yehudah Kook (1891–1982) and his followers, who used it as a source of inspiration to settle the territories captured in the Six-Day War (1967) in anticipation of the messianic period. I would therefore argue that we think of cooperation among international bodies for the sake of peace as a valuable goal because it *resembles* what we hope for in the messianic period, but that there be no equation between our present era and the era of the messiah.[5]

An even more promising Jewish source in support of cooperation with international bodies for the purposes of peace can be found in the Noahide Code. This tradition dates back to early rabbinic Judaism (c. second century CE) and claims that before the revelation of the Torah on Mount Sinai God gave all human beings seven basic commandments to govern their religious and ethical behavior. There is some disagreement among the early rabbis about when these commandments were issued; one opinion claims they were given to Adam, while another claims they were given to Noah. (The term "Noahide" Code is in accordance with the second view.) There is also some disagreement about which laws were included in these seven, but a common list contains the following imperatives: prohibitions against idolatry, blasphemy, forbidden sexual relations, murder, theft, and tearing off a limb from a live animal and eating it, and a positive command to establish courts of law to enforce these regulations.[6]

It is the last of these commandments that is of greatest interest to us. The commandment that requires non-Jews to establish courts of law is referred to in rabbinic discourse by the term *dinim*—literally, "laws."[7] There are no lengthy theoretical discussions in classical Jewish sources about *dinim*, but in a detailed and marvelous study of this concept, Suzanne Last Stone demonstrates that in a number of these sources the primary justification for *dinim* is to ensure that Gentile societies be just and peaceful.[8] Evidence for this is the fact in a number of Jewish sources that the commandment of *dinim* is justified on the basis of the concept of *tikkun 'olam* ("fixing the world"), a phrase that in rabbinic law refers to the imperative to adjust laws to contingent, historical circumstances so that people can live in harmony. The rabbis also adduce support for *dinim* from God's statement to Abraham that he expects the patriarch to teach his children and posterity—both Jews and non-Jews—to do "what is just and right" (Gen. 18:19). The message of both justifications for *dinim* is that non-Jews must create just and peaceful societies.[9]

It is not too much of a stretch to infer from these observations that Jews should regard non-Jewish efforts to form international bodies for fostering peace as a fulfillment of a divine mandate and that cooperation with such bodies is not only desirable, but required. Certainly, when early and medieval rabbinic authorities spoke about *dinim*, they had in mind governments and court systems for individual non-Jewish kingdoms or countries, not international bodies representing a global community. The latter, as we have already noted, is a recent development. Still, the whole notion of *dinim*, which is an imperative designed to create peace *within* non-Jewish societies, can easily be extrapolated to include international bodies fostering cooperation *among* those societies, seeing as they serve the purpose of peace as well.[10]

Living in Modernity

There is debate in medieval Jewish sources about whether the courts of law that non-Jews are expected to set up are meant merely to enforce the other six Noahide prescriptions as defined by the rabbis, or whether non-Jewish courts have the right to promulgate their own legislation regarding these prescriptions in accordance with local mores and customs and judicial creativity. Clearly, the latter viewpoint is best suited to today's international community since there is widespread recognition today that we live in a multicultural world in which just and peaceful societies may take different forms depending on local culture.[11]

Another concept in Jewish law that can help us here is *dina de-malkhuta dina*, "the law of the kingdom is the law." This principle originates in the Talmud with the third-century rabbinic sage Samuel and dictates that Jews are required to observe the civil laws of the country in which they reside, and that in some cases those laws even override the strictures of Jewish law. *Dina de-malkhuta dina* becomes particularly important in the medieval period when all Jews lived under the rule of non-Jews, but it is also quite relevant in the modern period given that over half the population of Jews in the world live in non-Jewish countries.[12]

Modern academic scholars often attribute *dina de-malkhuta dina* to political practicality. The rabbis recognized that the Jews, for the sake of survival, had to obey the laws of the land in which they lived, and they therefore bowed to practical necessity. However, traditional rabbinic sources offer an array of other explanations for *dina de-malkhuta dina*, and one of these ties in directly with our discussion of *dinim*. Rashi, the famous eleventh-century commentator, justifies this principle on the basis of the imperative of *dinim*. Because non-Jews are mandated by God to establish legal systems so as to create just and peaceful societies, Jews are required to obey those laws.[13] Rashi's position is significant for our purposes because it gives further endorsement to what we have already inferred from the concept of *dinim* in our earlier discussion: non-Jewish law systems have a respected status in Jewish law when they foster justice and peace.[14] And once again we can extend that respect to international bodies that are formed for the same purpose.[15]

Examples of Jewish cooperation with international bodies abound in many spheres. Let us look, for instance, at Jewish groups that have cooperated with international initiatives regarding the environment, most notably the recommendations that emerged from the Copenhagen conference on climate change in December of 2009. One Jewish group that has become an important player on this issue is the Coalition on the Environment and Jewish Life, founded in 1993. It is made up of 29 national Jewish organizations spanning the full spectrum of religious views in Jewish communal life, and it has attempted to serve as the voice for the Jewish community on environmental issues in Washington, DC, and the United States in general. A similar group is Hazon, founded in 2000, which is the largest environmental organization in the American Jewish community and does a wide range of programs. There is also the Shalom Center, founded in 1983, which among its many initiatives has been active on environmental issues. These groups and others have sought to engage the Jewish community in the United States and other countries to make concerns about the environment more central to Jewish life. They have attempted to mobilize Jewish people and institutions to commit themselves to study Jewish perspectives on the environment; to effect change on environmental issues in the Jewish community itself, such as improving the sustainability of buildings operated by Jewish communal institutions; and to ensure a more secure and less carbon-based energy policy for the world as a whole.[16]

Christian Reflection

Matthew Hamsher and Glen H. Stassen

Biblical Sources Supporting International Cooperation

The strongest support for working with emerging forces in the international system as a Just Peacemaking practice can be found in Jesus's teaching on how we should treat one another. In Matthew 20:25–28 (Mark 10:35–45; Luke 22:24–27), Jesus advocates mutual servanthood. The early church plainly learned this lesson on cooperation from following the teaching of Jesus. Acts 2:44–45 speaks of the practice of mutual aid—giving to all as they have need. Galatians 3:28 and Colossians 3:11 say we are no longer Jew or Greek, barbarian or Scythian, but all are one in Christ. Revelation 7:9 prophesies the age of fulfillment when a great multitude from every tribe, nation, people, and language will gather and praise God. And Revelation 22:2 says the tree of life is "for the healing of the nations."

The prophet Isaiah brings another theme for supporting international cooperation. He speaks often of the nations coming to the mountain of Zion; of Judah not only being for itself, but being a blessing to the nations and a light to the nations; of God delivering the nations and bringing justice to them; of hoping the nations will see God's righteousness and repent; and of all the nations being gathered in justice and peace. And in Isaiah 56, God calls us to welcome the Gentiles (nations) to the temple. Isaiah knew himself to be a man of unclean lips among a people of unclean lips, and God sent the seraphim to redeem and deliver him. His message was not self-righteous exclusion of other nations. His message was of God not as the Holy One, high and separate from the nations, but as the Holy One, our Redeemer, who reaches out even to other nations. God's work is to redeem the nations and the outcasts. In that delivering, we see what God's holiness is.

Jesus cited Isaiah and Isaiah's words more than any other book of the Hebrew scriptures, and worked to make peace with a Roman centurion, a Canaanite woman, a Samaritan woman, and other Gentiles. In Luke 4, his first sermon in Nazareth, when he announced that the reign of God is happening in our midst, he said Elijah was not sent to his own country, but to the territory of Sidon, and Elisha was sent first not to Israel, but to a Syrian. He was announcing that God intends to include other nations, as the prophet Isaiah had already announced. Much of the New Testament may be read as the spread of the gospel to the nations. If Christians are to be followers of Jesus rather than followers of nationalism, this suggests they too have a sense of inclusion of the nations.

Both individuals and nations are tempted, of course, *not* to act cooperatively, but instead to try to dominate others and rule over them. The prophet Amos begins his prophecy by expressing God's judgment on the various neighboring nations for violating international law and God's law. So Christians have a solid basis for knowing the temptation to try to be like a god, ruling over others. That is the temptation that the devil offered to Jesus: you can rule all the kingdoms of the world if you just bow down and worship him. That looks very much like the temptation of power. Jesus answered, not by ducking his own responsibility, but by committing himself to the responsibility to serve God and not his own power. He quoted Deuteronomy: "Worship the Lord your God and serve him only."

Christian Models for Working with International Cooperative Forces

While it is by no means the case that all Christians have related to other nations by mutual servanthood and mutual aid, or have been internationalists, there are current models that support this practice norm. Many Christians have great respect for those who have devoted themselves to medical service, agricultural service, aid for the poor, education for the needy, or service for children at risk, in other nations. And many Christians have donated to World Vision, Bread for the World, Church World Service, the Heifer Project, Mennonite Disaster Service, or their denomination's international service organization, and have revered those Christians who have carried out these projects in other nations.

World Vision, for example, has a reputation for working cooperatively with Muslims to focus on aid to people in need. Peter Sensenig, the administrator of Fuller Theological Seminary's Just Peacemaking Initiative, writes, "The government of Somalia pushed out all foreign workers in 1976, but the Mennonites were invited to return in 1980 [because of their reputation for service and peacemaking]. The 1980s saw 1.7 million refugees from droughts, floods, and wars; in response Mennonite Central Committee brought food, water, sanitation, medicine, and craft programs. In 1982 MCC chartered an entire cargo ship for a delivery of corn during a food shortage. [Mennonites] sent many teachers, agricultural workers, health workers to Somalia in the 1980s, including my parents."[17]

Christians think of the church as a worldwide Christian church—as one international body, connecting and transcending many national borders. Surely this suggests that Christians want their nation to be of some service to other nations and to cooperate where possible. It suggests that we want a world of peaceful order in which nations respect international law and find ways to cooperate with each other for the common good.

A Good Practice for International Politics

Empirical political science indicates that nations that engage in international cooperation make fewer wars and have fewer wars made against them.

Conversely, the failure to engage in international cooperation has produced more conflict. When the United States shifted toward greater unilateralism and away from international cooperation in the first decade of the twenty-first century, it then soon declared three controversial wars—what it called the "War on Terrorism," and the war on Afghanistan, and the war on Iraq. The result was many thousands of deaths, much destruction in Iraq and Afghanistan, greatly increased hostility toward the United States, greatly increased numbers of angry persons recruited to terrorism,[18] and a cost soon to exceed $1 trillion—money much needed for investing in jobs of teachers, health-care workers, and police; infrastructure repair; and increased efficiency in the environment—and that would have produced far more teachers' jobs than when invested in the $1 million required per soldier in Afghanistan. It also caused a huge increase in the national debt. One million dollars per year pays for one soldier in Afghanistan or for jobs for 17 teachers. The large amounts invested in these wars have sucked jobs out of the domestic economy.

Muslim Reflection

Zeenat Rahman

Qur'anic and Prophetic Sources for Cooperation

There are strong sources for support of cooperative forces in the international system in both the Qur'an and the Prophetic examples.

Treaties and international covenants remain the traditional means by which nation-states (and de facto, their citizens) maintain and enforce peace. During his lifetime, the Prophet entered into no fewer than 23 treaties with other groups, tribes, and religions.[19] The Qur'an sets clear guidance on the obligation of individuals to honor their agreements. The Qur'an says, "O People who Believe! Fulfill your words *(agreements)"* (Qur'an 5:1) and "fulfill the promise; indeed the promise will be asked about" (Qur'an 17:34).

Peace in the context of treaties and international covenants has mainly referred to peace as the absence of war and the agreement to not engage in warfare. While this is necessary to a certain degree, it has its limits in terms of practical methods to advance international cooperation. As S. Ayse Kadayifci-Orellana points out in a recently published book on peacemaking, the "Islamic concept of peace is wider than absence of war, oppression, and tyranny." She also states, "The Quran refers to peace as the greeting, language, and condition of Paradise and God calls believers to the 'abode of Peace.'"[20]

Witnessing for peace is a way to make peace, as in the Qur'an, "O you who believe! Stand out firmly for justice, as witnesses to Allah, even though it be against yourselves, or your parents, or your kin, be he rich or poor, Allah is a Better Protector to both (than you). So follow not the lusts (of your hearts), lest you may avoid justice, and if you distort your witness or refuse to give it, verily, Allah is Ever Well-Acquainted with what you do"[21] (Qur'an 4:135). Also,

> It is not righteousness that ye turn your faces to the East and the West; but righteous is he who believeth in Allah and the Last Day and the angels and the Scripture and the prophets; and giveth wealth, for love of Him, to kinsfolk and to orphans and the needy and the wayfarer and to those who ask, and to set slaves free; and observeth proper worship and payeth the poor-due. And those who keep their treaty when they make one, and the patient in tribulation and adversity and time of stress. Such are they who are sincere. Such are the Allah-fearing. (Qur'an 2:177)[22]

These teachings of the Qur'an are shown in practice in the many contemporary examples of international cooperative work by Muslim countries. All Muslim countries are members of the United Nations. Muslim nations have also formed the Organization of Islamic Conference (OIC), which consists of 57 states, is spread over four continents, and is the second largest intergovernmental organization after the U.N.[23] Egypt and Jordan have signed peace treaties with Israel, and Muslim nations have joined organizations like the World Trade Organization (WTO) and signed on to the Geneva Conventions (1949), the Treaty on the Non-Proliferation of Nuclear Weapons (NPT; 1970), the Biological Weapons Convention (BWC; 1975), and the United Nations Framework Convention on Climate Change (1992).

This perspective applies not only to the traditional understanding of this practice norm as entering into treaties and international cooperative work, but also to the ways in which youth movements especially, through the Internet and through international youth work in conferences and service projects, are the new face of this norm.

The advent of the Internet has led to greater interaction than ever before by and among people from different nations. Instead of interacting nation to nation, interactions are more than ever conducted person to person. One does not have to look very hard for examples of how individuals online are affecting world dialog and discourse. This broader understanding of peace in Islam, combined with the changing dynamic and definition of international actors, calls for a new reading into Qur'anic sources for support of international cooperation, with special attention to the responsibility of the individual. Technology and globalization have changed the way that communities have interacted globally with one another and have given a great deal of ascendance to the individual. The Qur'an provides many points of guidance to direct individuals on how to enforce peace.

Until recently, the main mechanism to enforce international peace relied heavily on the actions of nation-states. These modern phenomena—the Internet, social movements, and the growth and prominence of international NGOs—can, however, contribute to a broader understanding of peacemaking in this norm.

International Youth Work as a Critical and Increasingly Important Part of This Norm

A social movement is defined as a network of individuals and institutions that work toward making an idea a reality. A movement of Just Peacemaking must involve all sectors of society, with special attention to groups that often get overlooked, such as youth and women's groups. Several factors underscore the importance of engaging with youth in particular. Young adults today are connected to their peers through technology in ways heretofore unknown by their predecessors.

Globalization has given rise to unprecedented interaction among diverse religious communities around the world. Ultimately, it is young people, as they in particular have embraced new forms of global communication, who will decide how these interactions tend. This increased communication has led to new forms of identity engagement among youth that are less reliant on traditional nation-state boundaries and more likely to be influenced by transnational factors. This interaction can lead toward conflict or cooperation. The dominant theory that outlines this interaction is the "clash of civilizations" as outlined by Samuel Huntington, which states that there is an irreconcilable division between Islam and the West. Alternately, many see the world through a different paradigm, separating not civilizations but, in the words of Dr. Martin Luther King Jr., those who choose to live together as brothers or perish as fools.

We live in a young world, evidenced by a youth bulge in volatile regions of the world. In Afghanistan and the Gaza Strip, the median age is about 17 years; in Iraq and Pakistan it is barely 20; and in Syria and Saudi Arabia the median is about 21.5 years. This trend extends all over the Middle East and North Africa—the median age is under 27 in Algeria, Morocco, Egypt, and Jordan.[24] How these youth express and engage their religious identities has influence far beyond their individual reach. Religion remains a primary source of identification for many and is a robust transnational identifier. Groups that promote intolerance, violence, and segregation have used religious identification in young people to actively promote division and mistrust. The power of religion, however, can be used by youth to build peace and productive engagement.

Just Peacemaking tools can give young people the ability to understand their faith as a bridge to promote equal dignity and mutual loyalty among diverse religious communities. Interfaith action counters the clash of civilizations and is an alternative way to engage young people of faith. It focuses not on our differences, but on our shared potential. Instead of pitting people of different religions against one another in an endless war, interfaith action builds mutual respect and understanding through cooperative service and constructive dialog.

There are numerous models for how young people of faith can positively engage a religiously diverse world. Consider the young Martin Luther King Jr., a devout Christian who worked with Jewish leaders and used the methods of Mahatma Gandhi, an Indian Hindu, to build a more just and equitable America. The tradition of Islam teaches the importance of interfaith cooperation, and a central tenet of the tradition is one that embraces diversity and promotes pluralism. The Qur'an states, "O Mankind, We created you from a single (pair) of a male and a female and made you into nations and tribes, that you may know each other. Verily the most honored of you in the sight of God is he who is the most righteous of you" (Qur'an 49:13). There are many modern examples of Muslims who have promoted pluralism, from the Muslims in South Africa who joined the struggle against apartheid to Badshah Khan, a Pashtun who was inspired by Gandhi's nonviolent approach and recruited thousands of young Muslims to rally for a free subcontinent.

Many NGOs around the world are working toward building international cooperation. An example of an NGO that seeks to make interfaith cooperation a social norm, with young people as the leaders of this movement, is the Interfaith Youth Core, which brings young people of different faiths together to serve others by building houses, serving the poor, or restoring the environment.

From this shared service experience, Interfaith Youth Core helps young people realize the shared values of all religions, such as compassion, mercy, and peace. Service to others and a shared-values dialog help young people understand how they can maintain their own faith identity while working together with those from different faiths to create not a clash of civilizations, but a more peaceful and just world.

Conclusion

Whereas treaties have been the predominant mechanism for Just Peacemaking among nations and their citizens, recent developments in technology, social movements, and the NGO world highlight the importance of establishing Just Peacemaking norms on an individual-to-individual basis. Increased person-to-person communication through technology and globalization offers opportunities to advance international cooperation. The growth in the world's youth population necessitates the development of new platforms of interaction, and NGOs today need to be skilled not just at the use of technology, but also in ways of bringing young people together. Just Peacemaking principles must be applied at both the national and individual levels with the realization that the paradigm is changing.

Notes

1. "North American Jewish Organizations Call for Action at UN Climate Change Conference" news release, December 4, 2009, http://sites.google.com/site/rabbiwarrenstone/rabbiwarrenstone/in-the-media/copenhagen-un-rabbi-warren-stone/climate-change-press-releases-media/north-american-jewish-organizations-call-for-action-at-un-climate-change-conference.

2. For instance, the rabbis inform us that "great is peace for all blessings are contained in it . . . Great is peace for God's name is peace" (Midrash *Numbers Rabbah* 11:7). Many of the major prayers in the liturgy fashioned by the rabbis end with a prayer for peace, including grace after meals, the *'amidah*, the priestly blessing, and the *kaddish*. A number of volumes in the Talmud conclude with a dictum by Rabbi Hanina bar Hama, who praises the students of Torah because they bring peace to the world. These volumes include *Berakhot, Yevamot, Nazir, Tamid,* and *Keritot.*

3. Isaiah 2:1–4; Micah 4:1–5.

4. David Novak, "Judaism and Cosmopolitanism," in *Law, Politics, and Morality in Judaism*, ed. Michael Walzer (Princeton, NJ: Princeton University Press, 2006), 130–31.

5. Novak, "Judaism," 131–32, rejects the messianic period as a model for international cooperation because it assumes a gradualistic and progressive messianism, when, in fact, Jewish views of messianism tend to view the messianic process in apocalyptic terms. Furthermore, progressive messianism expresses too much confidence in human beings and their ability to improve the world on their own. In

our own era, we have discovered that this is not the case. We need divine help to create a more peaceful world. The second point brings Novak close to Christian realists, most notably Reinhold Niebuhr, who took a similarly pessimistic view of the potential for human beings to create a peaceful world.

6. The earliest reference to this tradition is Tosefta, *'Avodah Zarah* 8:4. The central discussion of these laws in the Babylonian Talmud is found in *Sanhedrin* 56a–60b.

7. Tosefta, *'Avodah Zarah* 8:4; Babylonian Talmud *Sanhedrin* 57b.

8. Suzanne Last Stone, "Sinaitic and Noahide Law: Legal Pluralism in Jewish Law," *Cardozo Law Review* 12 (1990–91): 1157–1214.

9. Stone, "Sinaitic and Noahide Law," 1185–87. For the general notion that imperative of *dinim* is for the purpose of creating just and peaceful societies, see Maimonides, *Mishneh Torah, Hilkhot Melakhim* 10:11. The concept of *tikkun'olam* is dealt with in Mishnah *Gittin* 4:2–5:3. The first justification for *dinim* is espoused by Rabbi Nissim of Gerona, *Derashot ha-Ran*, the eleventh homily. The second justification is adduced by Rabbi Moses Isserles (Rema) in *Teshuvot Rema*, no. 10.

10. My argument is based on the observations of Jeremy Wieder, "International Law and Halakhah," in *War and Peace in the Jewish Tradition*, ed. Lawrence Schiffman and Joel B. Wolowelsky (New York: Yeshiva University Press, 2007), 224–25.

11. The two opinions grow out of alternative readings of two sources: Maimonides, *Mishneh Torah, Hilkhot Melakhim* 9:14, and Nahmanides, *Commentary on the Torah* on Genesis 34:13. See Stone, "Sinaitic and Noahide Law," 1172–75.

12. The principle of *dina de-malkhuta dina* appears in Babylonian Talmud *Nedarim* 28a, *Gittin* 10b, *Bava Kamma* 113a, *Bava Batra* 54b, 55a. A thorough study of this concept was done by Shmuel Shilo, *Dina De-Malkhuta Dina* (in Hebrew; Jerusalem: Academic Press, 1974).

13. Rashi on Babylonian Talmud *Gittin* 9b, s.v. *huts*. See also Shilo, *Dina De-Malkhuta Dina*, 83–84.

14. Stone, "Sinaitic and Noahide Law," 1208–12.

15. This position is argued by Wieder, *International Law*, 246–48, and Novak, "Judaism," 137.

16. Information about the organizations mentioned here can be found at the following websites: Coalition on the Environmental and Jewish Life, http://www.coejl .org; Hazon, http://www.hazon.org; the Shalom Center, http://www.shalomctr .org. For a general article outlining the reactions of Jewish groups to the Copenhagen conference, see Mirele B. Goldsmith, "The Environment in Spiritual Crisis? Jewish Grass-Roots Activism on the Rise," *The Forward*, February 5, 2010; also available at http://www.forward.com/articles/124440.

17. Peter Sensenig, Director of Just Peacemaking Initiative, Fuller Theological Seminary (http://www.justpeacemaking.org).

18. The official report of the United States Department of State on international terrorism shows the astounding increase in terrorist incidents (from increased recruits to terrorism) since these three wars were declared:

> 208 terrorist attacks caused 625 deaths in 2003;
> 3,168 attacks caused 1,907 deaths in 2004;
> 11,111 attacks caused 14,602 deaths in 2005;

14,500 attacks caused 20,745 deaths in 2006;
14,506 attacks caused 22,508 deaths in 2007;
11,770 attacks caused 15,765 deaths in 2008.

19. S. Ayse Kadayifci-Orellana, "Muslim Perspectives on War and Peace," in *Peace-Building by, between, and beyond Muslims and Evangelical Christians*, ed. Mohammed Abu-Nimer and David Augsburger (New York: Lexington Books, 2009), 19–47.
20. Ibid.
21. Qur'an 4:135.
22. Qur'an 2:177.
23. Organization of the Islamic Conference, "About OIC," http://www.oic-oci.org/page_detail.asp?p_id=52.
24. Central Intelligence Agency, "CIA World Factbook," https://www.cia.gov/library/publications/the-world-factbook.

CHAPTER 8

Practice Norm 8

Strengthen the United Nations and International Efforts for Cooperation and Human Rights

Definition

*I*t is necessary to strengthen the United Nations (U.N.) and other such organizations so that these groups can develop the capacity to identify, prevent, and, if necessary, intervene in situations of conflict within and between nations. Once conflict is stopped, these organizations must also work to ensure peace and reconciliation. In the twenty-first century, security concerns of states are simultaneously internal, regional, and transnational. At the same time, the evolution of the idea of human rights has also given these international efforts a vital role. As U.N. Secretary-General Kofi Annan has stated, state sovereignty necessitates responsibility, first to prevent internal conflict and human rights abuses, second to respond to such situations with appropriate measures, and finally to rebuild areas that have been harmed by such clashes. Empirical data show that the more nations are engaged in supporting U.N. actions, the fewer wars they experience.

Introduction

On the evening of November 13, 2008, the United Nations General Assembly unanimously adopted a consensus resolution reaffirming the world body's firm commitment to promote universal respect for all fundamental freedoms and human rights. In adopting the "Promotion of Interreligious and Intercultural Dialogue, Understanding and Cooperation for Peace" resolution, the General Assembly affirmed the right to freedom of thought, conscience, and religion as a central element of the establishment of tolerant societies and durable peace. More than 80 member-states cosponsored the 2008 resolution, which calls on member-states to establish initiatives that identify practical actions for promoting interreligious and intercultural dialog, tolerance, and understanding at all levels of society. The vote was ironic because many of the nations that voted for it are hardly noted for their own respect for human rights, but their vote signals the worldwide pressure to avoid being known for opposing U.N. work for human rights, and this in turn adds persuasion power to those who prod governments to support U.N. and international efforts for human rights.

Humankind is called to work for understanding and peace not despite our various religious traditions, but because of our traditions. Asif Ali Zardari, president of Pakistan, which cosponsored the text, said that, as the chosen representative of 180 million Pakistanis who were suffering from "the menace of hatred," he rejected those who promoted division and rallied around those who would unite the creations of the one and only God.

The U.N. recognizes that faith can motivate people to work for peace and that developing religious tolerance across lines of difference may go a long way toward establishing such peace. People of faith must also acknowledge that the U.N. is a valuable world body, necessary for the mediation of global conflict and postconflict development. If our faith mandates that we work for peace, the U.N. should be a central means by which we conduct this work.

Yet it is also important to realize that the United Nations is a human institution that badly needs reform in a number of ways, as contributors to this chapter argue.

Muslim Reflection

Najeeba Syeed-Miller

Rule of Law in Primary Texts

While there are diverse schools of thought that relate to both law and politics within the Muslim tradition, Islam gives a clear deference to the notion that a society should be ruled by some form of authority that has a method of integrating citizen engagement into its governance. At the very inception of the Prophet Muhammad's mission, the Qur'an commanded him to utilize sound methodology for governance, and even though he was in possession of a divine message, he should reach out to others for consultation. Thus his authority could not be unchecked.

And their rule is by counsel among themselves. (Qur'an 42:38)

Allah commands you to make trusts to those worthy of them, and that when you judge between people you judge with justice. (Qur'an 4:58)

In these two verses, we see the early formations of the rule of law that was paramount over the Prophet's personal preferences. His mission was a complex one that included community governance and faith-based guidance of his flock. From these verses and many other traditions, the impending separation (after the death of the Prophet) of the leader of faith and of government was being set so that the rule of law would guide decisions of future leaders. Many scholars have commented on the fact that the religious leadership and state leadership have been throughout many periods of Islam separate entities; the scholars were not the ones making political decisions, nor vice versa. This was a form of checks and balances for one authority upon the other. Khaled Abou El Fadl discusses the fact that "political legitimacy" was not a legal issue, and jurists, we will see, were willing to concede this point to the rulers.[1]

Prophet Muhammad designated others as leaders, anticipating perhaps the need for Muslims to choose leaders and establish the rule of law with the understanding that order must be developed by mechanisms of government. Abu Burdah said, "The Messenger of Allah sent Abu Musa and Muadh Ibn Jabal to Yaman, and he appointed each one of them to govern a part of Yaman, and he said, 'Yaman is divided into two parts,' then he said, 'Be gentle to the people, be not hard on them, make them rejoice and do not incite them to aversion.'"[2]

The rule of law of a state should be challenged not by violence, but by discourse and discussion. Ibn Abbas cites the Prophet as saying, "He who dislikes the order of his amir should withhold himself from opposition for he who rebels against the rule by a span dies in the state of jahiliyyah [ignorance]."[3] Clearly, the obedience to rule of law was paramount in the discourse of the Prophet's own rhetoric. However, if one does disagree and obedience to injustice is being called for, then there should be ways to respond to those in authority. According to Abu Said, the Prophet said, "The most excellent jihad is the uttering of truth in the presence of an unjust ruler."[4] Further, the government must be one that has an affirmative duty for benevolence and munificence. Ma'qil said, "I heard the Prophet say 'There is not a man whom Allah grants to rule people, then he does not manage their affairs for good, but he will not smell the sweet odour of Paradise.'"[5]

Further, there was a clear understanding that a "distinction among countries" would emerge.[6] As discussed by scholars, the "countries of Islam were divided into three categories, the Holy Precincts, the Hijaz, and everything else."[7] Different sets of rules that applied to each region regarding property bore witness to the fact of clarity that laws must be localized to the regions of the jurisdiction.

A system of governance that promoted mutual consultation, counsel, engagement of others, compacts for establishing justice, and methods for dissent that did not pose physical harm was clearly at the heart of the Muslim paradigm. Engaging with a transnational governance body is not a contradiction for followers of Islam. The body must typify the above stated norms: (1) affirmative duty for promoting positive rule of law, (2) norms for engagement that allow consultation between those within the system and acknowledgment of the need for political-jurists separation, and (3) allowance for dissenting within the discourse and clearly designated mechanisms for voicing the disagreement especially as it relates to those who feel that rulings are unjust.

Postconflict Humanitarianism

If one of the major functions of the U.N. is to *prevent* conflict and *provide* for postconflict needs of nation-states, then we must investigate the Muslim traditions to bring to light whether or not these are compatible goals. Peacemaking is explored to a great extent in other chapters of this book, so we will not expound upon this topic but to say that the prevention of conflict is key to the practice of Islam as enjoined by both the Qur'an and the Sunnah. For example, "The Believers are but brethren so make peace between your brethren" (Qur'an 49:10). In a *hadith*, Jarir said, "The Messenger of Allah said, Allah has no mercy on him who is not merciful to men." The notion of reconciliation is a way of life for those who follow the traditions of the Prophet and is built into the fabric of Muslim social and religious cultures.

The aspect of provision for those who are left without after a conflict is also integrated into the texts of Muslims: "Righteousness is this that one should believe in Allah and give away wealth out of love for Him to the near of kin, and the orphans and the needs and the wayfarers and the beggars and for the emancipation of captives" (Qur'an 2:17). The *hadith* literature reflects this form of altruism as well. "A man asked the Messenger of Allah, what Islam is the best one?" He said, "That thou feed (the poor) and offer salutation to whom thou knowest and whom thou dost not know."[8]

Modern Muslim scholars such as Muhammad Asad (*The Principles of State and Government in Islam*) recognize the theological basis for this notion. "If some readers suppose that the idea of such a social insurance scheme is an invention of the twentieth century, I would remind them that it was in full swing many centuries before the present name was coined, even before the need for it became apparent under the impact of modern industrial civilization: name the Islamic Commonwealth at the time of the Rightly Guided Caliphs."[9]

Charity extended to those who were not Muslim as well. "In the early years of *hijra* (the Hegira era, or Muslim calendar), there was a famine in Modar (Saudi Arabia). The Prophet organized a humanitarian convoy to help the inhabitants there who, at that time, were not converted to Islam."[10] There is a complex, healthy, and lively debate among Muslim scholars in the current era regarding the notion of what ethical obligations Muslims have toward those of other faiths. Ann Elizabeth Mayer in *Islam and Human Rights, Tradition and Politics* delineates the varying degrees to which modern Muslim scholars adhere to a view that international humanitarian law and Islamic principles are compatible or not. She outlines the example of Lebanese scholar Subhi Mahmassani who pulls on "tolerant and egalitarian strains" from early Islamic traditions and practices that discard "any features of Sharia that would be incongruous on the scheme of international human rights."[11] Certainly the ethical basis that calls for charity to non-Muslims encourages not only a commitment to international aid and support, but also a commitment to human rights for all people.

Certainly, there is much more to explore, and further questions to investigate might include the following: (1) What is the resolution of modern interpretations that have allowed Muslim scholars the right to engage in political rule, and how does this limit the ability of commitment to international law? (2) If scholars do draw on the interpretations that are seen as more related to peaceful coexistence that *do* exist within texts and practices, will such rulings be viewed as culturally relevant and indigenous to the Muslim community by the religion's own adherents? (3) What remains of the thrust by some Muslim scholars and movements that demand the existence of a Muslim state for the practice of Islam? Is it possible for the notion of civil religion to find space in the modern Muslim discourse that creates a venue within such regimes as the U.N. for Muslims to remain grounded in the values of their traditions while fully participating in the exercise of international human rights law and humanitarian actions?

Modern Responses to the United Nations

The Cairo Declaration was presented at the 1993 World Conference on Human Rights and was endorsed by the Organization of Islamic States.[12] There remain ongoing tensions regarding the Cairo Declaration of Human Rights in Islam (CDHRI) and the Universal Declaration of Human Rights (UDHR). In Mayer's estimation, the drafters of the CDHRI intentionally differed from the UDHR, which states (Article 7), "All are equal before the law and are entitled without any discrimination to equal protection of the law. All are guaranteed to equal protection against any discrimination in violation of this Declaration and against any incitement to such discrimination."[13] The UDHR functions in a landscape where rights are considered as equally protected and attainable as a basic factor of full participation in society. According to Mayer, in several provisions of the CDHRI, "sex and religion are not included in the categories on the basis of which it is impermissible to discriminate,"[14] thus limiting women and non-Muslim citizens in areas of leadership positions in government and family law.

Furthermore, the CDHRI has been roundly criticized for the distinction in the calculus of measuring equality for men and women and for lack of clarity about protection of minorities within Muslim majority rule. Mayer and others have acknowledged that "independent Muslim human rights advocacy," apart from that exercised by national governments, has been severely limited by governments.[15] Perhaps this is where the greatest hope lies, in the nongovernmental, civil-society tracks of diplomacy that Ambassador John McDonald and Louise Diamond identify in their eight tracks.[16]

Many organizations such as Islamic Relief—a U.S.-based agency—engaged in relief work in Haiti following the earthquake of January 2010, and performed humanitarian aid even when Muslims were not the recipients. Scores of organizations throughout the Muslim world are redefining the methodology by which human rights are defined, protected, and perpetuated. The relationship between these key agents of change and Muslim scholars must be fostered and nurtured. If the scholars function in absence from and without connection to the emerging practitioners, a vital key toward sustained peacebuilding will be lost. On a recent trip to Israel, I was privileged to be in the company of leading Muslim religious leaders, imams, Orthodox rabbis, and priests who were studying to be lawyers at Ono College. They did not come together to discuss the religious issues that divided them, but rather to become exposed to contemporary theory and practice of human rights jurisprudence. Many of those who had studied religious law were unexposed to basic theories of human rights law. The religious scholars saw great value in the knowledge that they were acquiring, both because of the increase in their own understanding of their traditions vis-à-vis human rights law and because there was a joint commitment to achieve some level of advocacy for whatever they identified as human rights issues between and within their communities.

This cross-pollination within the faith grouping and across the faith communities of academic and scholarly inquiry allows for the forging of ties between *legitimate, indigenous* scholarship and normative practices of human rights law. Too often, the exploration of Muslim traditions is done by those without a deep understanding of the heritage, and those within the religious realm are often underexposed to the scholarship of modern human rights theorists. Perhaps also considering interdisciplinary programs when one is being trained as a member of the clergy or as a lawyer in Muslim communities would allow for a depth of scholarship that is as yet unachievable because of the bifurcated systems of education between religious and secular legal training. More investment in such interdisciplinary endeavors will ensure that the values of religious communities are brought into the public sphere while connecting people across cultural, religious, and ethnic lines for lasting peace.

Jewish Reflection

Robert Eisen and Alvin K. Berkun

A Prophetic Vision for Disarmament and Peace

"Into the Bright Future,"[17] an article that appeared in the *Jerusalem Post* in April 2006, recalls an event before the delegates of the United Nations disarmament conference in 1982. It represents Yehuda Avner's retelling of then Prime Minister Menahem Begin's address, which was really a homily based on the words of Isaiah, *ve-hayah be-aharit ha-yamim*, "And it shall come to pass in the last of days" (Isa. 2:2).[18] The prime minister cited the famous passage introduced by this clause: "And it shall come to pass in the last days that the Mount of the Lord's House shall stand firm above the mountains and tower above the hills . . . And the many peoples shall go and say: 'Come, let us go up to the Mount of the Lord' . . . For instruction (Torah) shall come forth from Zion, the word of the Lord from Jerusalem . . . And they shall beat their swords into plowshares and their spears into pruning-hooks; nation shall not take up sword against nation; they shall never again know war" (Isa. 2:2–4).[19] The question is, however, whether this beautiful vision can be realized within history or must wait for realization beyond history. The prime minister acknowledged this dilemma. "'Honorable delegates: Please note that in the original Hebrew text, it is written, *ve-hayah be-aharit ha-yamim*, which in the traditional English translations is rendered, 'in the last of days,' or 'in the end of days.' Would this phrase then not imply that we shall have to wait until the last days—or the end of days—in order to merit universal peace and the tranquility of disarmament? . . . Well then, where is the blessed peace?"[20]

Neither Isaiah nor the Israeli prime minister quoting the prophet advocated waiting until the end of history. Such would be a counsel of despair and not consistent with the vision of the prophet Isaiah. In human history there has been war, and devastation, and the world has also seen peace. "Nearly three millennia have passed since Isaiah's immortal words were spoken—'*ve-hayah be-aharit ha-yamim*.' Thousands of wars have devastated lands and have destroyed countless millions of people. Whole nations have been on the brink of extermination, as manifested in the Shoah. Plowshares have been beaten into swords, pruning-hooks into spears."[21]

Begin concluded as follows: "Fellow delegates: There is one question we have to ask ourselves: Whatever our animosities, our recriminations, and our states of war, can we nations still talk to one another? Israel's answer is, 'Yes. We must. We can. We, Israel, have the experience.'"[22]

From Vision to Practice: The United Nations

But between vision and practice, between Jewish values as a broad interpretation of prophetic aims and the specific institution of the United Nations, there is a rising tension. Since the founding of the state of Israel in 1948, or even since Prime Minister Begin's stirring words in 1982, much has changed. Many Jews, not only those in Israel, now contend that the U.N. exhibits extreme bias against Israel, and they are therefore largely dismissive of its actions.

The charge certainly has merit. The bias against Israel in the U.N. has been especially evident since the mid 1970s. Since that time, there has been an increasing imbalance in the U.N.'s handling of the Middle East conflict, an imbalance that continues to the present day. For instance, since its founding in 2006, the U.N.'s Human Rights Council (HRC) has passed 79 resolutions, 33 of which have been for the purpose of censuring Israel—that is, almost half of its resolutions. While an argument can certainly be made that at times Israel has been guilty of violating human rights, the almost exclusive focus on Israel's record has been absurd. Human rights abuses are far worse and much more widespread in dozens of other countries around the globe—including those with representatives on the UNHRC itself. Yet Israel remains the focus of the UNHRC's criticisms. In 2007, the UNHRC passed no fewer than nine resolutions condemning Israel while in the same year expressing only "deep concern" on one occasion about the gross violations of human rights taking place in Darfur.[23]

In light of this imbalance, international law in recent years has been the subject of a lively discussion among a number of rabbis and academics who have debated whether the state of Israel is required to follow the regulations of international law governing war. The debate has included topics not just about the actual waging of war, but also about issues related to it, such as the right of a nation victorious in war to annex conquered territory and the status of peace treaties between a Jewish state and non-Jewish states. These latter topics are of obvious importance in light of the highly charged issue of Israel's conquest of the West Bank in the Six-Day War and its ongoing occupation of that territory.

Rabbi Shaul Yisraeli (1909–95) provided an early and highly influential treatment of whether Israel was required to adhere to international norms in matters of war.[24] In an essay composed in 1954, Yisraeli argued that Israel must indeed adhere to those norms.[25] He based his position on the principle of *dina de-malkhuta dina* in Jewish law—"the law of the kingdom is the law." As noted in chapter 7, this principle has roots in Talmudic literature and was formulated in order for Jews to deal with the inevitable conflicts that arose between the dictates of Jewish law and the laws of the countries in which they resided. This principle required that, in the area of civil law, Jews adhere to the laws and customs of their respective countries. Yisraeli argued that in war *dina de-malkhuta dina* applied in the international arena as well. Just as Jews had to obey the local laws of their non-Jewish rulers, they also had to abide by the laws of the international community.[26] Since the publication of Yisraeli's essay, a number of Jewish ethicists have endorsed his approach. Some have also expanded upon it and applied it to areas other than war.[27]

It should be pointed out that Yisraeli applied his ruling in a manner quite inimical to the spirit of Just Peacemaking that has been the focus of this volume. His essay was in response to an incident that occurred in 1953 in which the Israeli government had sent an elite army unit to attack an Arab village just across the Israeli-Jordanian border in reprisal for Arab violence against Jewish villages on the Israeli side of the border. Since the end of the 1948 war, armed groups from Jordanian border towns had been infiltrating into Israel and terrorizing its citizens, and in one such raid on the Israeli village of Yehud, a woman and her two young children were killed. The Israeli attack on Kibiyeh was in response to that incident, and Kibiyeh was chosen as the target because the perpetrators of the violence in Yehud had apparently come from there. In the attack on Kibiyeh, several dozen Arabs were killed, including women and children. The operation elicited international condemnation. Yisraeli's essay was devoted to the question of whether the attack was justified in Jewish law. He essentially answered in the affirmative, arguing that the Arab nations were technically at war with Israel, that Israel had a right to defend itself, and that the attack in Kibiyeh was one battle in that war. Yisraeli also justified the civilian casualties in the Kibiyeh operation on the premise that when it came to matters of war, Jews were to conduct themselves in accordance with the norms of international law because of the principle of *dina de-malkhuta dina*, and according to Yisraeli's understanding, international law recognized that in a defensive war civilian casualties were an inevitable, if unfortunate, result of military action. Yisraeli thus used the principle of *dina de-malkhuta dina* to support the right of Israel to take military action against its enemies despite civilian casualties—not to foster peacemaking.

Yet in light of the theme of this chapter, it is important to note that Yisraeli added a caveat to his ruling that could potentially support greater efforts toward Just Peacemaking in regard to the United Nations and international law. Yisraeli recognized that there were pacifist groups in the international arena working to abolish war, and he stated that if such groups were ever to succeed in changing international law to outlaw war, the state of Israel would have to abide by that decision. After all, the principle of *dina de-malkhuta dina* would require Jews to follow international law in this instance as well.[28] Thus, conceivably, *dina de-malkhuta dina* could just as easily be used as a vehicle for peace as for war. This principle specifies only that Jews follow the dictates of international law, not what those dictates should be. At least one commentator has pointed out that, in fact, international law has evolved precisely in the direction of Yisraeli's speculations here. While not outlawing war entirely, international law, especially as represented by the resolutions of the United Nations, at present does not look upon war favorably, and there are numerous regulations designed to strictly limit both its use and its violent consequences. One may also point out that this was largely true even in Yisraeli's own day.[29] Yet whatever the norms of international law may be, what is most important for our concerns is that Yisraeli set an important precedent in arguing that the state of Israel had to obey the regulations of international law in matters of war.

Yisraeli's position should require Jews to accept the resolutions of the U.N., seeing as those resolutions are also, in some sense, international norms that would be subject to the principle of *dina de-malkhuta dina*. In fact, in the early years of the state of Israel, prominent rabbis seemed to assume that this was the case. Rabbi Ben-Tsiyyon Uzi'el (1880–1953) and Rabbi Meshulam Roth (1875–1962) both ruled that land captured by Israel in the 1948 war located in territory designated as Palestinian by the U.N. could not be considered part of Israel until the U.N. had made a determination to that effect.[30] The views of these rabbis could not have been influenced by Yisraeli, since they slightly predated his essay on Kibiyeh, and neither of them specifically invoked the principle of *dina de-malkhuta dina*. Nonetheless, it can be argued that they effectively supported a position similar to his. Both assumed that the state of Israel was beholden to the decisions of the U.N. because Jews were required to abide by international norms.[31]

But since the 1970s and the frequency with which Israel is subject to an unequal critique by the United Nations, a number of Jewish ethicists have concluded that the decisions of the U.N. need not be heeded by Israel. They base their position on the fact that according to medieval Jewish law a king is forbidden to apply laws to his subjects in an unfair manner. Such laws must be instituted impartially and without bias toward any individual or group if they are to have standing in Jewish law. Because the resolutions of the U.N. against Israel fail this test, they too have no status in Jewish law.[32]

One rabbinic authority rejects the resolutions of the U.N. for another reason. Rabbi Avraham Sherman argues that in order for a non-Jewish law to be authoritative in accordance with the principle of *dina de-malkhuta dina*, it must be observed in a widespread manner among the people for whom the law is intended. A law that is not taken seriously by non-Jews need not be observed by Jews either. By this standard, the resolutions of the U.N. also fail to have authority. It is often the case that when a decision of the U.N. conflicts with a nation's interests, the nation simply ignores the decision. Israel, therefore, has no obligation to uphold the U.N.'s resolutions either.[33]

As is well known, there is considerable contemporary debate in the global community on the subject of Israel and the U.N. The weight of the debate still leans toward Israel respecting international law, and the United Nations as a representative of international law. However, Jews find it increasingly difficult to accept the U.N. as an authoritative body as long as it acts with bias against Israel. This is not to say that Israel is without flaw in regard to its treatment of the Palestinians. Our contention, however, is that Israel would be more responsive to the U.N.'s complaints about its human rights abuses if the U.N. would act in a manner that fosters trust and good will among Jews and Israelis and encourages a sense of duty on their part to adhere to the U.N.'s demands.

Broad Jewish values and principles favor the peaceful resolution of disputes and the kinds of human rights norms included in the founding charter of the U.N. There is significant tension, however, between Jewish values and practices and the U.N.'s values and practices. "Can nations still talk to one another?" Prime Minister Begin asked. Yes, but increasingly the conversation is almost unbearably strained when it comes to the U.N.

Christian Reflection

Andrew Sung Park and Katherine Schofield

The U.N. Combines and Strengthens Several Just Peacemaking Practices

The United Nations was organized and established by members of the great generation that fought and suffered in World War II. Those who established the United Nations were determined to do what they could to prevent that kind of devastation for succeeding generations, including our generation and our successors, and to prevent nuclear war. The preamble to the U.N. Charter was written by those who had suffered in that great war, including Glen Stassen's father, Harold Stassen.[34] It begins, We the peoples of the United Nations determined

- to save succeeding generations from the scourge of war, which twice in our lifetime has brought untold sorrow to mankind, and
- to reaffirm faith in fundamental human rights, in the dignity and worth of the human person, in the equal rights of men and women and of nations large and small, and
- to establish conditions under which justice and respect for the obligations arising from treaties and other sources of international law can be maintained, and
- to promote social progress and better standards of life in larger freedom

Saving succeeding generations from the scourge of war was the main motivation for creating the United Nations, whose founders lived through the devastation of two world wars. Since its creation, the U.N. has often been called upon to prevent disputes from escalating into war, or to help restore peace when armed conflict does break out, and to promote lasting peace in societies emerging from wars.

The U.N. has engaged in the following Just Peacemaking practices in more countries than most realize: conducting conflict resolution and war-halting negotiations; promoting democracy, human rights, sustainable economic development, and humanitarian aid; protecting the sustainability of the environment; preventing nuclear proliferation (via inspections in 90 countries by the International Atomic Energy Agency); and of course working with cooperative networks in the international system. The U.N. has enabled people in many countries to participate in free and fair elections. In addition, the U.N. welcomes observer status and influence from a rapidly increasing number of citizen peacemaking organizations, including church groups and faith groups, thus encouraging Just Peacemaking practice 10.

Disagreements and conflicts make news; most of the U.N.'s contribution is quieter and makes less news, so people are relatively unaware of its most important work. The U.N. has devoted more attention and resources to promoting economic development and local skill building than any other organization. Its annual disbursements, including loans and grants, amount to more than $10 billion. The U.N. Development Program supports more than five thousand projects with a budget of $1.3 billion. It is the largest multilateral source of grant development assistance. The World Bank has loaned approximately $400 billion for development projects in developing countries since 1946.

In addition, UNICEF spends more than $800 million a year, primarily on immunization, health care, nutrition, and basic education in 138 countries. A 13-year effort by the World Health Organization (WHO) resulted in the complete eradication of smallpox from the planet in 1980. This has saved an estimated $1 billion a year in vaccination and monitoring, almost three times the cost of eliminating the scourge itself. WHO also helped drastically reduce the incidence of polio. Through oral rehydration therapy, water and sanitation, and other health and nutrition measures undertaken by U.N. agencies, child mortality rates in the developing countries have been cut in half since 1960, increasing the life expectancy from 37 to 67 years. A WHO program also has saved seven million children from river blindness and rescued many others from guinea worm and other tropical diseases.

In approximately 40 wars, the U.N. has deployed peace-keeping forces to allow adversaries to prevent or halt wars and get to negotiations and conflict resolution. At the time of this writing, 16 active peace-keeping forces were in operation. The United Nations has negotiated 172 peaceful settlements that have ended regional conflicts, including an end to the Iran-Iraq War, the withdrawal of Soviet troops from Afghanistan, and an end to the civil war in El Salvador. The hope of the founders of the U.N. that we would avoid a third world war and the use of nuclear weapons has thus far been realized, although whether this hope will continue to be fulfilled depends on work by us and on God's grace. As chapter 9 states, the number of people killed in wars since the founding of the U.N. has been reduced to ¼ of what it was in the first half of the twentieth century.

By investigating individual complaints of human rights abuses, the U.N. Human Rights Commission has focused world attention on cases of torture, disappearance, and arbitrary detention and has generated international pressure to be brought on governments to improve their human rights records.

The main impact of the U.N. is its extensive work for world health, sustainable economic development, human rights, and democracy. The scriptural teachings of all three of our faiths strongly emphasize God's will that we work for the kind of justice that delivers the needy and oppressed. The four biblical words for justice—*mishpat, tzedakah, dike*, and *dikaiosyne*, occur 1,060 times in the Bible. In Christian Bibles unfortunately, these words are often translated "judgment" or "righteousness," so Christians do not see the meaning as clearly as they should. But the meaning is delivering justice, or community-restoring justice, and this is one of the most emphasized themes in the Bible. The work of the United Nations for the kind of justice that delivers the needy and the outcasts from their deprivation and oppression is essential implementation of God's will for justice.

Children's Rights and the United States

Christian teaching strongly emphasizes the human rights of children. Jesus said, "Let the little children come to me, and do not stop them; for it is to such as these that the kingdom of heaven belongs" (Matt. 19:14).[35] The Bible, Hebrew and Greek, is full of teachings emphasizing children. Yet the United States and Somalia are the only countries that have failed to endorse the U.N. Convention on the Rights of the Child, which was adopted on November 20, 1989.[36] Largely negotiated during the Reagan administration, the Convention emphasizes the rights of children to survival; to develop to their full potential; to protection from abuse, neglect, discrimination, and exploitation; and to participate in family, cultural, and social life. "The United States' failure to ratify the Convention on the Rights of the Child is an embarrassment," said Jo Becker, children's rights advocacy director for Human Rights Watch. "It damages the U.S. reputation as a human rights leader and undermines its ability to improve the lives of children around the globe . . . The Convention reflects what all Americans want for their children."[37] To support the U.N. and human rights of children, President Barack Obama and the U.S. Senate must act to ratify the treaty the United States labored very hard to shape. Christians deeply care about the well-being of children.

Reducing Violence against Women and Empowering Women

In 2009 we celebrated the tenth anniversary of the International Day for the Elimination of Violence Against Women. In his address marking the occasion, U.N. Secretary-General Ban Ki-moon noted that up to 70 percent of women experience physical or sexual violence by men.[38] At a U.N. event promoting gender equality, the secretary-general was joined by actress Geena Davis, Sweden's Princess Madeleine, Britain's Duchess of York, the head of the World Congress of Muslim Philanthropists, heads of foundations, corporate leaders, academics, diplomats, representatives of voluntary organizations, several other celebrities, and several hundred participants. "Our goal must be clear," Ban emphasized. "No tolerance of the use of rape as a weapon of war. No excuses for domestic violence. No looking the other way when it comes to sex trafficking, so-called 'honor killings' or female genital mutilation." He believes that "full empowerment requires more progress in two key areas: expanding economic opportunity and ending violence against women."[39] Christians believe that women and men are created in God's own image and equal before God (Gen. 1:27) and that the dignity of every person is divinely ordained.

The International Need for Checks and Balances and the Rule of Law

Christians have been much influenced by the Apostle Paul's teaching in the Epistle to the Romans that we are to respect the governing authorities. Paul says that Christians should "be subject to the governing authorities . . . For the same reason you also pay taxes, for the authorities are God's servants, busy with this very thing" (Rom. 13:1–7). Three German scholars, J. Friedrich, W. Pöhlmann, and P. Stuhlmacher, jointly published an authoritative article on the historical context and meaning of this influential passage.[40] When Paul was writing his letter to the Romans, Rome had recently experienced a major tax revolt by followers of one whom Latin historian Suetonius had called "Chrestus," apparently meaning either followers of Jesus or a Jewish Messiah figure. The result was that Jews were expelled from Rome, including Christians Priscilla and Aquila. Now as Paul was writing, another revolt was brewing against a new tax that Emperor Nero had declared. The Roman historian Tacitus reported in 58 CE that popular clamor against the new tax forced Nero to cancel the tax temporarily and then to publish the tax tables for the first time, thus making it more difficult for the tax collectors to overcharge and pocket the overage. So Paul's point was not that Christians should obey any order by any ruler (for example, a Hitler or a Gaddafi), but that Christians should not participate in another tax revolt. They should instead "pay all of them their dues, taxes to whom taxes are due, revenues to whom revenues are due . . . Owe no one anything except to love one another" (Rom. 13:7–8).

With Romans 13:1–7 and Colossians 1:15–20, Christians affirm that government was created for good, justice, peace, and reconciliation. "God has ordered human society with various institutions and set in place forms of government to maintain public order, to restrain human evil, and to promote the common good . . . We must support and pray for all those who shoulder the burdens of government (1 Tim. 2:1–2)."[41]

With Revelation 13 and Colossians 2:15, however, we also affirm that government and the powers and authorities are fallen. Revelation 13:1–10 describes the Roman government as a haughty and blasphemous beast that makes war on the saints. Colossians 2:15 says the Roman government crucified Jesus, and then God "disarmed the principalities and powers and made a public example of them, triumphing over them." The prophets of Israel frequently confronted governments for their injustice, and Jesus, in good prophetic tradition, confronted the reigning powers in Jerusalem for their injustice. Hence the apostles said that when the authorities command injustice, "we must obey God rather than human authority" (Acts 4 and 5). Although government provides important service, it also needs to be kept accountable to its God-given tasks of promoting justice and correcting wrongdoing. Since governments are not immune from the effects of human sinfulness, Christians will oppose any idolatrous claims to absolute authority made on behalf of the state and will criticize policies that do not adhere to biblical teaching of justice.

Therefore, the historic wisdom of the United States has been to build checks and balances wherever there is concentration of power. A profound biblical understanding that we all sin demands more than trust in particular rulers. "We thank God for a constitutional system that decentralizes power through the separation of powers, fair elections, limited terms of office, and division among national, state, and local authorities."[42] "As the founding fathers intended, we have checks and balances within our Constitution's framework" where Congress, the president, and the courts work to check and balance each other against domination by any one powerful ruler.[43]

In accordance with these teachings, both biblical and historical, we do not want a world of anarchy where any nation's government initiates war that is unwise and unjust without restraints, without checks and balances. Governments sometimes blunder into unwise or unJust Wars. Article 51 of the U.N. Charter states clearly, "Nothing in the present Charter shall impair the inherent right of individual or collective self-defense if an armed attack occurs against a member." But a war of initiation or intervention, such as the war against Iraq based on a false claim about weapons of mass destruction that were not there, or the more defensible recent intervention to protect citizens of Libya against an impending massacre by the forces of Muammar Gaddafi, needs approval by other nations—in the case of Libya including the Council of Arab Nations and the U.N. Security Council. Though the U.N. itself is not perfect, neither is any nation or leader. Just as President Obama has been criticized for failing to get congressional approval before joining the NATO coalition in the bombing of Libya,[44] bypassing the checks and balances built into the U.S. governmental system, so the world needs and should respect the checks and balances of consultation with the United Nations.

Furthermore, we do not want a world where nations lack a place where they regularly talk with each other and work out their conflicts and disagreements. The U.N. provides that regular interaction. This fits Jesus's teaching in Matthew 5:21–25 that when we have anger with a brother or with an adversary, we should go quickly to that other and work on making peace together.

The United States has enormous power economically, culturally, and militarily. U.S. military spending exceeds the combined military budgets of the next 16 countries. Moreover, there is no more Soviet Union to balance U.S. power. In light of the warnings of the Bible and the founders of our nation that concentrated power needs checks and balances, this enormous U.S. power argues that our nation needs the checks and balances of international cooperation.

In our globally interconnected world, this wisdom is spreading internationally: international organizations and the treaties to which America has added its name serve as checks and balances so that governments are less likely to act rashly or unjustly. The U.N. is no world government that replaces national governments; it actually makes the international system more orderly so national governments can be more effective in a more peaceful context. Realistic awareness that all sin and fall short of the glory of God (Rom. 3:23) tells us we all sometimes need checks and balances against rash action. Other nations do; so does the United States.

Historical wisdom and biblical teaching also include the principle of government as the rule of law rather than the whim of rulers. Repeatedly the Hebrew scriptures teach that kings are subject to the rule of law, and law is not merely the whim of the ruler but is based on God's will for justice, which is above all rulers. Hence the prophets of Israel had a strong basis for confronting unjust rulers.[45]

Furthermore, Jesus emphasized that God shines the sun and rains the rain on all people, just and unjust alike. Therefore we are to include all people in the community of neighbors to whom we are to show our love. In this Jesus is fulfilling the teaching of Leviticus 19:17 as well as the prophet Isaiah, who calls

Israel to be a light to the Gentiles. As Amy-Jill Levine points out, the Hebrew prophets also have a universal thrust of justice for all nations, so Jesus's teaching of love and justice for all nations should not be interpreted in a way that gets misused anti-Semitically.[46] What is clear is that Jesus's teaching emphasized that we are to include all people in the community of neighbors to whom we are to show our love. Therefore, there is a strong biblical call for doing our ethics internationally and not reducing our faith to narrow nationalism. And there is surely strong biblical basis for the rule of law, not merely the rule of power and greed.

Because of the dramatic increase in world trade; the internationalization of finance and economies; the dramatic increase in communication, media, email, and plane travel among nations; the increase of immigration and emigration; the spread of support for human rights; and awareness of the need to prevent war, nations have worked together to develop international law, especially in treaties, embedded by U.S. ratification as the law of our own land. The United States has often taken a lead in developing international law; we benefit greatly from a world of relative order and justice rather than anarchy and war.

When a powerful United States disrespects the limits of international law, others perceive it as dominating unfairly. According to the Pew Global Survey, international resentment against the United States increased dramatically during its time of more unilateral policymaking.[47] This resentment fuels recruitment to terrorism. According to U.S. State Department data, the number of reported terrorist incidents and deaths worldwide increased shockingly after the United States invaded Iraq and defended torture of defenseless prisoners. As was noted in Chapter 7, there were 208 terrorist attacks that caused 625 deaths in 2003, the year the War in Iraq began. The first year after the War in Iraq had begun, 3,168 attacks caused 1,907 deaths; 11,111 attacks caused 14,602 deaths in 2005; approximately 14,000 attacks caused more than 20,000 deaths in 2006, 14,506 attacks caused 22,508 deaths in 2007, and as the war was winding down, 11,770 attacks caused 15,765 deaths in 2008.

U.N. Reform

To strengthen the U.N., the U.N. Security Council needs to represent the geopolitical and economic dimensions of the world. Its permanent membership consists of the victors in World War II—the United States, the United Kingdom, Russia, China, and France. According to Archbishop Celestino Migliore, the Holy See's permanent observer to the U.N., it is necessary to curb the veto power of these members or to make permanent members of the world's largest democracy (India), the largest Muslim nation (Indonesia), and regional powerhouses such as Nigeria and Brazil, if the U.N. desires better participation of other members.[48] After World War II, the five permanent members once represented close to 40 percent of the world's population. They now make up only 29 percent.

The U.N. and the Church

According to theologian Robert McAfee Brown, Christians give primary loyalty to "the God who is above all other gods" like nation and race.[49] If we give our loyalty to America, our race, or our religion, our loyalty is partial, parochial, and sectarian. As Christians, we are the citizens of God's "Kin-dom"[50] first and then the citizens of our own nation. Christians in the world are a global force, giving their ultimate loyalties not to their own nations, religions, or races, but to God.

Article 6 of the U.S. Constitution specifies that the supreme law of the United States is all international treaties that the United States has signed and the Senate has ratified. The United States is one of the 51 original nations that signed the charter of the U.N. in 1945, and the Senate ratified it.[51] The United States has a constitutional obligation to uphold the U.N.

The World Council of Churches and the U.N.

Adopted at the founding conference in San Francisco in 1945, the preamble to the Charter of the United Nations remains one of the most influential public documents of human history.[52] Church representatives present at the San Francisco conference pressed for a preamble and other provisions. The conference adopted the preamble and other provisions for human rights and fundamental freedoms along the recommended lines. According to John Foster Dulles, a Presbyterian layman and later U.S. secretary of state, religious people took the lead in seeking that the U.N. should be dedicated not only to a peaceful world, but to a just order. It was they who inspired the General Assembly, the Social and Economic Council, and the Trusteeship Council to reflect on moral forces rather than on the power of a few militarily strong nations operating in the Security Council without commitment to any moral principles of law and justice.[53] Church representatives also played a significant part in the discussion that bore the fruit of the inclusion of Article 71, which provides for an enduring structure of consultation between the United Nations and nongovernmental organizations—as emphasized by Just Peacemaking practice 10.[54]

In 1946, a postwar meeting of the World Council of Churches (WCC) decided to form a Commission of the Churches on International Affairs (CCIA). The WCC cooperated with the International Missionary Council in the effort of creating the CCIA to ensure an effective relationship between the WCC and the leadership of the United Nations. The U.N. recognized the CCIA as one of the first nongovernmental organizations in 1946. Since that time, on behalf of the WCC, the CCIA has worked to advance peace with justice and freedom and to promote respect for and observation of human rights and fundamental rights such as religious liberty and self-determination.[55]

The Work of the CCIA

The Commission of the Churches on International Affairs of the World Council of Churches has contributed to new standards of human rights, antimilitarism, and people's rights to peace and social development and to new enforceable standards in the fields of religious freedom and tolerance. It played a key role in drafting Article 18 on religious freedom and liberty of the Universal Declaration of Human Rights.[56]

The WCC further assisted in laying down important new international principles of human rights, such as victim support and the prohibition of torture, initiating the installation of a working group on torture within the U.N. Commission on Human Rights. Furthermore, it has made possible the testimony of victims themselves, human rights defenders, and church leaders. The CCIA of the WCC has carried out its mission by monitoring human rights violations, promoting awareness of human rights mechanisms, strengthening international solidarity and advocacy for them, educating peoples on respecting human rights and justice through churches, convening human rights experts and officials in member churches, and visiting critically significant human rights sites. Through its extensive network of churches around the world, the WCC exposes the reality of specific human rights violations, calls the root causes of such violations to global attention, and provides international forums for discussing these issues.[57]

The WCC Church and Society conference in 1966 said, "The U.N. is the best structure now available through which to pursue the goals of international peace and justice. Like all institutions it is not sacrosanct and many changes are necessary in its Charter to meet the needs of the world today. Nevertheless we call upon the churches of the world to defend it against all attacks which would weaken or destroy it and to seek out and advocate ways in which it can be transformed into an instrument fully capable of ensuring the peace and guaranteeing justice on a world-wide scale."[58]

The theologian Reinhold Niebuhr thought that the United Nations was a necessary experiment, although he warned that human nature was too perverse to sustain idealistic hopes for the U.N. premises.[59] Instead of utopian hopes, we need step-by-step affirmation of the U.N. by regular policy decisions that work along with the U.N., showing respect for its purposes. So it calls for our support as well as our constructive criticism.

The Need Continues to Grow

As Secretary-General Ban Ki-moon puts it, "Every day we are reminded of the need for a strengthened United Nations, as we face a growing array of new challenges, including humanitarian crises, human rights violations, armed conflicts and important health and environmental concerns. Seldom has the United Nations been called upon to do so much for so many. I am determined to breathe new life and inject renewed confidence into a strengthened United Nations firmly anchored in the twenty-first century, and which is effective, efficient, coherent and accountable."[60] With the U.N. secretary-general, we need to seek a world of justice, peace, and care by strengthening the U.N. Above nationalities, religions, and races, we must rise and work together to build up the one human family. We need the U.N. to help the world see the common good, not only narrow Ayn Rand–style atheism and individualistic greed.

Conclusion

In our increasingly interconnected world, the United Nations plays a vital role by drawing attention to global injustice, intervening in situations of conflict, and building peace through dialog and economic initiatives. The teachings of Islam, Judaism, and Christianity each emphasize the blessedness of reconciliation and the imperative to care for those who live in fear and poverty. In this way these traditions support the work of the U.N. Yet it is clear that the U.N. is not flawless in its handling of worldwide conflict and does not have all the answers when it comes to Just Peacemaking. Muslims, Jews, and Christians must continue to envision a more peaceful world than the one we presently know and speak out of their traditions to strengthen and reform the United Nations, as the authors of this chapter have done.

Notes

1. Khaled Abu El Fadl, *Rebellion and Violence in Islamic Law* (Cambridge: Cambridge University Press, 2001), 158.
2. Muhammad Maulana Ali, *A Manual of Hadith* (London: Curzon Press, 1977), 404.
3. Ibid., 397.
4. Ibid., 398.
5. Ibid., 403.
6. Al-Mawardi, *The Ordinances of Government*, trans. Wafaa H. Wahba (Berkshire, UK: Ithaca Press, 1997).
7. Ibid., 172.
8. Ibid., 389.

9. Muhammad Asad, *The Principles of State and Government in Islam* (Selangor, Malaysia: Islamic Book Trust, 1980), 92.

10. Jamal Krafess, "The Influence of the Muslim Religion in Humanitarian Aid," *International Review of the Red Cross*, http://www.hhh.umn.edu/humanitarianisms/ readings/Islam%20and%20Humanitarianism.pdf.

11. Ann Elizabeth Mayer, *Islam and Human Rights, Tradition and Politics* (Boulder, CO: Westview Press, 2006), 128.

12. Ibid., 40.

13. Ibid., 83.

14. Ibid., 84.

15. Ibid., 138.

16. Louise Diamond and John McDonald, *Multi-Track Diplomacy: A Systems Approach to Peace* (West Hartford, CT: Kumarian Press, 1996).

17. Yehuda Avner, "Into the Bright Future," *Jerusalem Post*, April 2006, http://www .jpost.com/Israel/Article.aspx?id=18859.

18. Diamond and McDonald, *Multi-Track Diplomacy*.

19. Ibid.

20. Ibid.

21. Ibid.

22. Ibid.

23. The difficulties that Israel has experienced in the U.N. are discussed in Michla Pomerance, "International Law, Israel, and the Use of Force: Historic Perspectives/ Current Perplexities," in *War and Peace in Jewish Tradition*, ed. Lawrence Schiffman and Joel B. Wolowelsky (New York: Yeshiva University Press, 2007), 265–312. For the imbalanced record of the UNHRC regarding Israel, see http://www.eyeontheun .org/browse-un.asp?ya=1&sa=1&u=344&un_s=0&ul=1&tp=1&tpn=Resolution.

24. Yisraeli was a major Orthodox Israeli rabbi and authority on Jewish law in the religious Zionist camp during the first decades of the state of Israel. He would later become the head of Mercaz ha-Rav, the flagship rabbinic institution in Israel for religious Zionism.

25. The essay was first published in Hebrew under the title "Military Operations for the Defense of the State" in *Ha-Torah ve-ha-Medinah* 5–6 (1953–4): 71–113. A slightly expanded version appeared in the collection *'Amud ha-Yemini* (Tel Aviv: Moreshet, 1966), 168–205. It has since been reprinted several times. I will be citing from the 1992 edition published by Erets Hemdah, Jerusalem.

26. *'Amud ha-Yemini*, 191–5 (sections 5:8–16).

27. See, for example, Michael J. Broyde, "A Jewish View of World Law," *Emory Law Journal* 54 (2005: Special Edition): 79–97; Michael J. Broyde, "Just Wars, Just Battles and Just Conduct in Jewish Law: Jewish Law Is Not a Suicide Pact!" in *War and Peace in Jewish Tradition*, ed. Lawrence Schiffman and Joel B. Wolowelsky (New York: Yeshiva University Press, 2007), 7; R. Avraham Sherman, "The International Law (of War) in Light of the Laws of the Torah" (in Hebrew), *Torah she-be-'al-Peh* 44 (2004): 59–78; R. Neriah Gutel, "Warfare in an Area Full of Civilians" (in Hebrew), in *Ha-Milhamah ba-Teror*, ed. Ya'ir Halevi (Kiryat Araba, Israel: Makhon Le-Rabaney Yishuvim, 2006), 102; Jeremy Wieder, "International Law and Halakhah," in *War and Peace in the Jewish Tradition*, ed. Lawrence

Schiffman and Joel B. Wolowelsky (New York: Yeshiva University Press, 2007), 239–64. Some of the insights of Broyde and Wieder were incorporated into Eisen's discussion in chapter 7.

28. *Amud ha-Yemini*, 195 (section 5:15). Here I take issue with Rabbi Neriah Gutel and others who claim that, according to Yisraeli, Jews should follow what nations do in war, not what international law dictates (Gutel, "Warfare," 94–95). The international norms governing war of which Yisraeli speaks are those of international law. In his discussion, Yisraeli frequently refers to these norms as *hok*, which can only mean law. He also adduces examples of the types of norms that govern war, such as the rules that regulate the proper declaration of war and those that determine what types of weapons may be used, and these are clearly references to international law.

29. R. Yehudah Shaviv, "'You Will Never Think of Battle Again': The Validity of War Between Nations" (in Hebrew), *Tehumin* 9 (1988), 225–27.

30. Uzi'el was the Sephardic Chief Rabbi in the first years of the state of Israel. Roth was an important and respected Orthodox rabbi in Israel during the same period.

31. R. Avraham Sherman, "The Wars of Israel: Their Legitimacy in Determining Sovereignty in the Territories of Israel" (in Hebrew), *Tehumin* 15 (1993): 23–30; Sherman, "International Law," 60–76.

32. Maimonides, *Mishneh Torah*, "Laws of Theft," 5:13–14; *Shulhan Arukh, Hoshen Mishpat*, 369:8; *Rosh* on Babylonian Talmud, *Nedarim* 28a; Sherman, "Wars of Israel," 29–30; Sherman, "International Law," 74–76; and Wieder, "International Law," 248. Broyde also notes that for international law to have standing in Jewish law, it must be just and fair, though he does not elaborate on this point. See Broyde, "Jewish View," 96.

33. Sherman, "International Law," 64–68, 72–74.

34. Harold Stassen was a devout Christian and was elected president of the American Baptist Convention. He resigned as governor of Minnesota to fight in the Navy in the South Pacific as Admiral Halsey's chief of staff, and by war's end had earned the rank of captain. He came home saying, "Glen, war is so horrible that we need to do all we can to prevent World War III and a war with nuclear weapons." Prior to World War II, President Roosevelt had heard him advocating the need for a United Nations, and appointed him as a U.S. delegate to the U.N. Charter-writing assembly in San Francisco in 1945. When that assembly concluded, the reporters from the many nations that covered the assembly "voted Stassen one of the two delegates who made the most effective contributions to the development of the U.N. Charter; the other was Australian Foreign Minister Herbert Evatt." Marshall Houts, introduction to *Eisenhower: Turning the World Toward Peace*, ed. Marshall Houts and Glen Stassen (St. Paul, MN: Merrill/Magnus Publisher, 1990), xii.

35. New Revised Standard Version.

36. Human Rights Watch, "US: Ratify Children's Treaty," http://www.hrw.org/en/news/2009/11/18/us-ratify-children-s-treaty.

37. Ibid.

38. Sojourner, "Eliminating Violence against Women," *SojoMail*, November 26, 2009, http://mail.united.edu/exchange/aspark/Inbox/This%20Thanksgiving%20

Remember%20the%20Immigrant,%20Pilgrim%20-%20SojoMail%2011.26.09. EML?Cmd=open.

39. Associated Press, "Actress and Muslim Philanthropist Promote Women," *The New York Times* (February 22, 2010), http://www.nytimes.com/aponline/2010/02/22/world/AP-UN-UN-Empowering-Women.html?_r=1.

40. Johannes Friedrich, Wolfgang Pöhlmann, and Peter Stuhlmacher, "Zur historischen Situation von Römerbrief 13.1–7," *Zeitschrift für Theologie und Kirche* 73 (1976): 131–66.

41. National Association of Evangelicals, *For the Health of the Nation* (Washington, DC: National Association of Evangelicals, 2006), 5.

42. Ronald J. Sider and Diane Knippers, eds., *Toward an Evangelical Public Policy* (Grand Rapids, MI: Baker, 2005), 367.

43. National Association of Evangelicals, *An Evangelical Declaration against Torture: Protecting Human Rights in an Age of Terror* (Washington, DC: National Association of Evangelicals, 2009), § 5.11.

44. http://www.nytimes.com/2011/03/22/world/africa/22powers.html.

45. Sider and Knippers, *Evangelical Public Policy*, 157–58.

46. Amy-Jill Levine, *The Misunderstood Jew: The Church and the Scandal of the Jewish Jesus* (New York: HarperOne, 2006).

47. Pew Survey, March 2004, http://www.people-press.org: "An important factor in world opinion about America is the perception that the U.S. acts internationally without taking account of the interests of other nations. Large majorities in every nation surveyed (except the U.S.) believe that America pays little or no attention to their country's interests in making its foreign policy decisions. This opinion is most prevalent in France (84%), Turkey (79%) and Jordan (77%), but even in Great Britain 61% say the U.S. pays little or no attention to British interests."

48. The Archbishop Celestino Migliore spoke on October 4, 2004, at a session of the U.N. General Assembly held to discuss ways to revitalize and *strengthen* the United Nations. Archbishop Migliore stopped short of suggesting that the veto power of the Security Council members over decisions be ended. "Vatican Favors Reform of U.N. Security Council," *America* 12 (2004): 6.

49. Robert McAfee Brown, *Making Peace in the Global Village* (Philadelphia: Westminster Press, 1981), 31.

50. To avoid the sexist language of "kingdom," Isasi-Diaz coined the term *kin-dom*. Ada Maria Isasi-Diaz, "Solidarity," in *Lift Every Voice: Constructing Christian Theologies from the Underside,* ed. Susan B. Thistlethwaite and Mary Potter Engel (Maryknoll, NY: Orbis Books, 1998), 39.

51. United Nations, *The United Nations Charter*, http://www.un.org/en/documents/charter/intro.shtml.

52. Konrad Raiser, "The United Nation and the WCC: Rights and Justice," *Ecumenical Review* 3 (1995): 278.

53. Ibid., 280.

54. Ibid.

55. The World Council of Churches, "History and Overview of WCC Relations with the United Nations," http://www.wcc-coe.org/wcc/what/international/un-hist.html.

56. World Council of Churches, "International Affairs, Peace and Human Security," http://www.wcc-coe.org/wcc/what/international/humrts.html.

57. Ibid.

58. World Council of Churches, "United Nations Advocacy," http://www.wcc-coe .org/wcc/what/international/un-advocacy.html, italics original.

59. Walter Lippmann, *U.S. War Aims* (Boston: Little, Brown, 1944), 129.

60. Ban Ki-moon, "Reform Under Ban Ki-moon: A Stronger United Nations for a Better World," *Reform at the United Nations*, http://www.un.org/reform.

CHAPTER 9

Practice Norm 9

Reduce Offensive Weapons
and the Weapons Trade

Definition

A reduction of offensive weapons and the weapons trade frees money to support sustainable development and reduce poverty. Such a reduction also reduces the risk of war and the destructiveness of wars. The amassing of weapons is in opposition to what has proven effective for Just Peacemaking. In reducing the number of offensive weapons in the world, it becomes possible to create an environment in which talk and cooperative conflict resolution are more likely to occur, and peace is given the chance to blossom. Indeed, as we lessen our trade and sale of weapons to other countries we begin to construct an international community where the ability to trust one another becomes a more attainable possibility.

Introduction

In the 1980s faith communities began to take the lead in antinuclear protests throughout the United States. Beginning with the American Catholic Bishops' powerful pastoral letter, "The Challenge of Peace: God's Promise and Our Response," and building momentum with the support of many Protestant denominations, the Central Conference of American Rabbis, and other faith groups including the Buddhist Soka Gakkai International, a movement emerged in which rejection of the development, trade, and use of nuclear weapons became a central conviction across faith traditions. Although the 1990s saw a relative decline in antinuclear protest, after the attacks of September 11, 2001, the topic reemerged as a central concern for faith communities. Muslim voices joined the opposition to nuclear weapons in June 2000 as the "Joint Nuclear Reduction/Disarmament Statement" by religious and military leaders was issued in Washington, DC. At the release of the statement, Dr. Muzammil Siddiqi of the Islamic Society of North America noted, "We must say to ourselves first and then to the world that we want a total and universal ban on the possession and production of nuclear weapons"[1] and argued for Islamic support of this view.

These faith communities' denunciation of nuclear weapons is so strong and far reaching that the argument has been made that nuclear opposition is one of the most widely shared convictions across faith traditions.[2] But these faith groups do more than issue statements. From the 1970s to today faith-based antinuclear marches—many of them interfaith—have drawn thousands of supporters in dozens of countries around the world. These marches bring attention to the importance of the issue while helping faith communities reflect on the spiritual reasoning behind their convictions.

All three Abrahamic traditions offer clear guidelines to limit the horror of war. Understanding and applying traditional texts in the current historical and political context requires a careful analysis (what Glen Stassen calls "analogical contextualization"), but the mandate to reduce weapons that cause unwanted destruction remains clear and compelling. This chapter provides three complementary views. Stassen connects biblical cautions against reliance on weapons with current efforts to reduce offensive weapons, and suggests specific applications to the "War on Terror" and nuclear abolition. Patricia Anton explores Qur'anic and *hadith* texts that balance the need for defense (deterrence) with the core Islamic principle that calls for the primacy of saving lives; in her essay, she also explores a peacemaking approach to jihad. Finally, Reuven Kimelman explores the traditional biblical texts that proscribe the limits of war—especially its impact on civilians and the earth—and provides contemporary examples of Jewish writing on weapons of mass destruction.

Christian Reflection

Glen H. Stassen

Scripture in Our Time

Two errors of interpretation need to be avoided, both based on unimaginative literalism. One is to read straight from biblical teaching in its particular context to our particular context with no attention to differences in context, and with no attention to how our perception of biblical contexts and our context can be biased by our own loyalties and ideologies. The second error is to say the contexts are different and then conclude that means the biblical teachings do not apply to us. That sweeps the Bible out of our ethics and gives our own loyalties and ideologies free rein without correction by biblical witness. Instead, I commend a version of the method of William Spohn (1944–2005), which I call "analogical contextualization," for interpreting how biblical teachings guide us.[3] Unimaginative and literalistic substitution is anachronistic. But an allegedly Christian ethic that evades the way of Jesus is hardly Christian.[4] Neither legalistic rules nor reducing Jesus's way to an abstract principle or doctrine is faithful to the richness of biblical guidance. So Spohn asks us to immerse ourselves imaginatively into the narratives of Jesus in the Gospels, as in his own Jesuit training in Ignatius's *Spiritual Exercises*, and then ask how the narratives apply *analogously* to us in our context.

Spohn pays attention to social context in his most salient example: foot washing was carried out by "a Gentile slave, someone who would not be contaminated by the impurity that clung to bare feet." With his compassionate love, Jesus took the role of a slave and washed his disciples' feet. He taught the disciples to serve the needs of others, with humility. Spohn points to an analogous act in our social context: an Irish-American pastor in an inner-city parish in Baltimore, in a "foot-washing" worship ceremony, shined the shoes of 12 elderly African American men. "The message was not democratic equality but the last becoming first and the first becoming last, the kingdom of God's reparation of justice long delayed."[5]

I call Spohn's method "analogical contextualization" because we need careful study of the meaning in the original context, and critical study of our present social context, so we can envision how the teaching applies analogously in our context. So when Jesus calls on his disciple to "Put up your sword. All who take the sword die by the sword" (Matt. 26:52), his teaching applies by analogy to us and asks us to cease putting our trust and our actions in demonstrations of offensive military power. A contemporary example of putting our trust in offensive military power is declaring a "war on terror" and also declaring war on Afghanistan and Iraq, two predominantly Muslim nations, as a response to the reprehensible actions of some Muslim extremists, as happened during the Presidency of George W. Bush. This response using "the sword" only served to feed the Muslim extremist narrative that the United States is out to make war on Islam. Those who take up war in this way will become the objects of war by additional numbers of recruits to that very extremism. Instead, we need to prove untrue the claim that the United States is out to attack Islam. We need to work for justice for people oppressed, including Muslims who are oppressed.

Weapons and the Bible

The Bible has very specific warnings against putting trust for security in our weapons. Like addiction, placing our trust in weapons leads us to depend on them and to exaggerate what they can do for us. This makes us foolish, and we end up with destruction. Jeremiah 2:13 warns, "Two sins have my people committed: they have forsaken me, a spring of living water, and they have hewn out for themselves cisterns, cracked cisterns that can hold no water."[6] Four verses later, the specific idolatrous trust that holds no water is named: seeking military alliances with Egypt and Assyria, trusting in their many war chariots and war horses. Isaiah 30 and 31 prophesy similarly: "Shame on those who go down to Egypt for help and rely on horses, putting their trust in chariots many in number, and in horsemen in their thousands, but do not look to the Holy One of Israel or seek guidance of the LORD!" The prophet Hosea, in chapters 10 and 11, makes the same point about putting trust in military weapons and the armies of Egypt and Assyria: it will lead to destruction or exile. Idolatrous trust in military weapons leads us to exaggerate what the weapons will do for us, to utter lies in defense of our false trust, and to engage foolishly in war, which brings about the horror of war and exile: "Ephraim is like a silly senseless pigeon, now calling upon Egypt, now turning to Assyria for help . . . I will take Ephraim [Israel] captive as soon as I hear them flocking. Woe betide them, for they have strayed from me! . . . Like a bow gone slack, they relapse into the worship of their high god; their talk is all lies, and so their princes shall fall by the sword" (Hosea 7).

The prophets' message is clear: putting trust in military weapons *instead of trusting in God's will for practices of justice and repentance from idolatry* leads to foolish wars and terrible destruction. And that, sadly, is what happened to both Judah and Israel.

This was theological truth then, and it was also practical for survival. Norman Gottwald's book, *All the Kingdoms of the Earth*, places the foreign policies of the prophets in context.[7] Israel lived in a threatening context: large empires came and went. The prophets were saying Israel needed to focus on obeying God and practicing justice. Failing that, the nation became disunited and therefore more tempting as a potential victim. When they put their trust in horses and chariots, they got entangled in wars. They overestimated what the weapons they were trusting in could do for them, and they ventured into foolish alliances and battles. Sadly, they were driven into exile. When Jesus said a king should not march to battle without first sitting down to assess the likely outcome, he was calling for counting the cost, just as the prophets had (Luke 14:31–32).

Jesus identified with Israel's prophetic tradition and especially with the prophet Isaiah. He lived in a time when every now and then someone would claim to be the Messiah and lead a rebellion against Rome. Each time, Rome would massacre them. These small rebellions were building toward a major, climactic rebellion. Jesus wept over Jerusalem because they did not know the practices that make for peace. And then he prophesied, "But no; it is hidden from your sight. For a time will come upon you, when your enemies will set up siege-works against you; they will encircle you and hem you in at every point; they will bring you to the ground, you and your children within your walls, and not leave you one stone standing on another, because you did not recognize God's moment when it came" (Luke 19:41–44).

Jesus prophesied five times in the Synoptic Gospels, and once in the Gospel of Thomas, that war (with Rome) would bring about the destruction of the temple and Jerusalem. He saw it coming. And his prophecy came true in 66 CE: the small "messianic" rebellions led to a major revolt. Rome responded as Jesus prophesied, destroying Jerusalem and the temple and sending Judah into exile, tragically, for 20 centuries. Jesus's warning was no Platonic idealism; it was practical realism based on God's reality as discerned before him by the prophets.

When Jesus's disciple nevertheless took up the sword against those who came to arrest him, Jesus said to him, "Put up your sword. All who take the sword die by the sword" (Matt. 26:52). Jesus was telling him to cease placing his trust in offensive weapons.

Practical Realities in Our Time

As was noted in the introduction, careful attention to context and interpretation is very important in dealing faithfully and creatively with biblical texts in regard to ethics. In our time, the biblical warning pertains all the more. Putting trust in military weapons can tempt a nation to foolish wars, and wars in our time can be enormously destructive because weapons are so much more lethal. When Yugoslavia split into separate countries, Serbia inherited its military and its military weapons. Serbia had far more offensive weapons than its neighbors. In the 1990s its demagogic dictator, Slobodan Milosevic, succumbed to the temptation that comes with possession of large quantities of offensive weapons and initiated three wars—against Bosnia, Croatia, and then Kosovo. The rest of the world saw this as terribly unjust. They joined together and defeated Serbia. The people of Serbia then deposed their militaristic demagogue in a democratic election. Milosevic was put on trial for war crimes before the International Criminal Court. He died in ignominy before the court could reach its verdict.

The United States spends as much to build up its military might as all other countries in the world combined. The temptation to put our trust in military weapons for our security, and to neglect God's call for justice and peacemaking, permeates the air waves. The United States also initiated three wars in one year, as was noted above, the war against Afghanistan, against Iraq, and the permanent "War on Terror" aimed mostly at Muslim extremists. The world switched from sympathetic support after 9/11 to seeing the United States as a bully. We are still digging our way out.

Around the world, the same patterns are clear. North Korea has 69 mobile army regiments to South Korea's 15; it has 260 landing craft to South Korea's 10. It invests its trust in military force while its people live in poverty and hunger and its economy sinks into despair. Investing in military weapons rather than factories wastes precious money that could produce far more jobs if invested usefully. Iran has a military that greatly worries its neighbors, has rockets, and is enriching uranium; other nations are intensifying sanctions against Iran. On the day of this writing, Israel has used its military to kill civilians on a flotilla of six ships bringing needed food and medical supplies to Gaza. Although opinions on the justification of military force in this instance vary, worldwide anger is clear and deep, in part because people know Israel has a powerful army and the Palestinians have none.

Many perceive that each of the above nations could have greater security if it would emphasize human rights and Just Peacemaking toward other nations more and would put its trust in offensive weapons less.

Reducing Offensive Weapons Reduces War Making and Terrorism

As international relations scholars point out, most nations now realize that making war does not pay.[8] Today's weapons are so devastating that the opponent will do too much damage in retaliation. Even if "we" "win," the net result is a loss for both sides. Placing our trust in offensive weapons is not working. As a result, most nations have decreased their investments in weapons. In the seven years from 1988 to 1995, "the developing world's arms imports dropped to just one-quarter of their peak in 1988."[9] And most nations are not making wars. Because of the realization that war does not pay, along with the nine other Just Peacemaking practices developed since World War II, the number and extent of international wars is decreasing dramatically. Most of what remains are civil wars, rebellions, and terrorism—although these examples of systematic violence bring horrendous suffering to innocent civilians.

Milton Leitenberg of the University of Maryland's School for International and Security Studies has estimated that war and state-sponsored genocide in the first half of the twentieth century killed as many as 190 million people, both directly and indirectly. That comes to an average of 3.8 million deaths per year. His analysis found that wars killed fewer than one-quarter of that total in the second half of the twentieth century—40 million altogether, or 800,000 per year.[10] The exception occurs when one nation arms itself excessively in offensive weapons and convinces itself that it can get away with war without much damage to itself. This is the idolatrous trust about which the prophets and Jesus warned.

The official report of the United States Department of State on international terrorism shows the astounding increase in terrorist incidents since the declarations of war against terrorists, against Afghanistan, and against Iraq (all mostly Muslim) and the torture of (Muslim) prisoners:

- 208 terrorist attacks caused 625 deaths in 2003.
- 3,168 attacks caused 1,907 deaths in 2004.
- 11,111 attacks caused 14,602 deaths in 2005.
- 14,500 attacks caused 20,745 deaths in 2006.
- 14,506 attacks caused 22,508 deaths in 2007.
- 11,770 attacks caused 15,765 deaths in 2008.

Placing trust in offensive weapons to create safety from terrorism has backfired; it has increased the number of recruits to terrorism. In their joint assessment, the 16 U.S. intelligence organizations concluded that making war against Muslim nations has caused increased anger and increased recruitment of terrorists.

By contrast, in recent years Great Britain in its struggle with Irish Republican Army terrorism in Northern Ireland, and Turkey in its struggle with the PKK (Kurdistan Workers' Party) terrorist movement in which thirty thousand people were killed, both adopted a strategy of working for human rights and economic development in Ireland and in the Kurdish areas of Turkey. Great Britain involved Irish Catholics extensively in the political process, and Turkey ensured that Kurds were well represented in Turkey's parliament. Instead of placing their trust in offensive military attacks, they engaged in Just Peacemaking practices of justice and human rights. Both Irish and Kurdish terrorist movements have essentially ceased.

David Cortright has pointed out that a recent RAND Corporation study shows that terrorist groups usually end through political processes and effective law enforcement, not the use of military force. An examination of 268 terrorist organizations that ended during a period of nearly 40 years found that the primary factors accounting for the end of terrorist tactics were participation in political processes (43 percent) and effective policing (40 percent). Military force accounted for the end of terrorist groups in only 7 percent of the cases examined.[11] This suggests that the United States will be much safer from terrorism when it shifts its trust from military attacks (Al Qaeda is in about 60 countries; military attacks won't work) to working for human rights for all and justice for the oppressed. A nation seen as working sincerely and consistently for justice and human rights is far less likely to be the object of recruitment of terrorists for attacks against it. Skilled police work will still be needed. Focusing on human rights and justice will not stop all terrorism, but it will reduce the motivation that drives people to the desperate and despairing evil of terrorism.

Dealing with the Nuclear Threat

Influential editorials in *The Wall Street Journal* (January 4 and 13, 2007) by 17 conservative U.S. former national security policy makers, including George P. Shultz, William J. Perry, Henry A. Kissinger, James Goodby, and Sam Nunn, declared that the existence of large numbers of nuclear weapons in the world threatens to destroy untold numbers of humankind, *and* it decreases U.S. security. Today's problem is not deterring Russia, but preventing both proliferation of nuclear weapons and their falling into more dangerous hands. Therefore, continuing Cold War reliance on nuclear weapons is a grave danger to U.S. security as well as world security. It produces more nuclear weapons and enriched uranium and plutonium around the world that can be stolen or taken over by terrorists. These policy makers agree that the United States would be far more secure in a nuclear-free world. The power of the U.S. military to deter a conventional attack is far more effective than nuclear weapons are against a nuclear attack—especially by terrorists. These conservative national security experts advocate specific steps that include treaties, policy changes, export of nuclear fuels, and mutual verification. These national leaders, formerly known as hawks who advocated military buildups, are now saying that reducing offensive nuclear weapons multilaterally is crucial for national security.

President Obama has affirmed these steps and has begun to implement them, though cautiously and with increases in spending for nuclear weapons because of the partisan nature of the Senate and the need for 67 votes to ratify treaties. The President and his allies need citizen support to get these critical changes in offensive weapons policies implemented. Citizen support can be coordinated and informed by connecting with the largest grassroots U.S. peace organization, Peace Action, or the movement for nuclear abolition, the Two Futures Project.[12]

Reducing offensive weapons and reducing our trust in them not only is biblically faithful, it decreases wars and terrorism and makes us more secure. It does not require complete disarmament, and it can be accomplished by international agreement with inspections and verification. Each step in this direction makes us safer and decreases the waste of money and the buildup of deficits.

Muslim Reflection

Patricia Anton

In the classic articulation, developed by Imam Al-Shatibi (d. 1388), of what constitutes the higher objectives of Islamic law (*maqasid al-shari'ah*), the preservation of life is generally listed as the first of these aims.[13] In Just Peacemaking, the strategy of reducing offensive weapons argues that such reduction results in fewer wars, less destructiveness within wars, and lower expenditures on warfare—saving money that could be allocated to efforts in poverty reduction.[14] In short, the purpose is saving lives. As Muslims we understand the gravity of efforts to reduce offensive weapons in light of the verse from the Qur'an that establishes the primacy of saving lives: "We ordained . . . that if anyone saved a life it would be as if he saved the life of the whole people."[15] When faced with the reality of modern weaponry, weapons of mass destruction (WMD), and nuclear weapons, there is often a sense of overwhelming fatalism that infects communities, causing them to block out the situation and resign from acting in response to combating the proliferation of these weapons. When viewing the impacts of war as statistics or passing scenes on the television or computer screen, it is easy to round it off to a lot or just too much. However, when "somewhat less killing" can mean hundreds of thousands of lives,[16] as Muslims we must remember the pasasge about the significance of saving even one life, the prohibition against despair among believers,[17] and the reminder that even in the last hour on the earth, we should persist in planting seeds for better tomorrows.[18]

The Limitations of War

Within the period of revelation, after years of enduring persecution, the Muslim community received permission to fight back against those who attacked them and committed oppression. This permission came explicitly with the condition that recognized limits should not be transgressed.[19] No revelation given sanctioned unprovoked military aggression.[20] From revelation and the example of the Prophet Muhammad (pbuh), the traditional Islamic parameters of warfare developed regulations prohibiting actions that would be considered unnecessary transgression and that open the door for oppression and bloodshed. Included in the commonly cited prohibitions are the killing of noncombatants, specifically inclusive of women, children, elderly, and religious people; killing of livestock; poisoning of wells; burning of trees; destruction of crops; and mutilation or burning of those killed. Additionally, hostility should cease when the enemy inclines toward peace. Qur'an 8:61. Not surprisingly, these guidelines are mirrored in the biblical texts cited by Reuven Kimelman in his essay in this chapter.

Modern weaponry has completely changed the reality of warfare, such that international scholars argue war is too costly to pursue when considering the scope of retaliation.[21] The discussion of what constitutes legitimate methods for warfare in this context is a challenge that Islamic scholars have not yet been able to comprehensively address in a way that provides clear guidance. The questions are relatively new, and they do not lend themselves to simple analogies with prophetic times.

The Dilemma of Deterrence

Few Muslims would disagree with the problematic nature of modern weaponry, yet obstacles do exist in pursuing conversation about reducing weapons. The first is the argument of the necessity of deterrence. The general nature of modern offensive weaponry is that it violates what is Islamically acceptable in warfare because of its indiscriminate nature and the horrific kinds of damage it can inflict. However, faced with enemies who utilized, or are capable of utilizing, these weapons, Muslims have felt the need to adopt the methodologies of the modern world to guard against having enemies who believe that they are unchecked in their ability to exploit and oppress. The Islamic argument of necessity (durur) has been enacted by many scholars to make offensive weapons not only permissible, but necessary. These scholars cite the following verse to argue that deterrence is obligatory while maintaining the normative preference for peace and restraint:

> Let not the unbelievers think they can get the better (of the godly): They will never frustrate (them). Against them make ready your strength to the utmost of your power, including the steeds of war, to strike fear into (the hearts of) the enemies of God and your enemies, and others besides who you may not know, but who God doth know. Whatever ye shall spend in the cause of God, shall be repaid to you and you shall not be treated unjustly. But if the enemy inclines towards peace, do thou also incline towards peace, and trust in God for He is the One who Heareth and Knoweth (all things). (Qur'an 8:59–61)

The commonly used example of the argument of necessity in Islamic law is that pork is prohibited, but if other food is not available and survival is at risk then it becomes not only permissible, but obligatory to eat it. What is added and generally understood in this example is that (1) the nature of the thing remains prohibited and the condition of necessity disliked, (2) consumption should be of the minimum necessary for survival, and (3) one should be eager to return to generally permissible food. These same conditions must also accompany the resort to necessity when taken on other issues, including the acquisition and use of modern weaponry whose nature must continue to be recognized as Islamically prohibited. Most Muslims would instinctively recoil at the mere thought of being forced to eat pork, yet how much more disgusting is the nature of weapons that kill indiscriminately, maim horrifically, and destroy and pollute the environment in catastrophic ways.

Practical Realities in Our Time

The well-known *hadith*, found in Imam Al-Nawawi's (1234–78) Forty Hadith, on enjoining good and forbidding evil says, "Whosoever of you sees an evil action, let him change it with his hand; and if he is not able to do so, then with his tongue; and if he is not able to do so, then with his heart; and that is the weakest of faith."[22] Within the Muslim world, there is apparent skepticism that the threat of these weapons by enemies, and the related call to necessity, will end anytime soon. However, the believers should be wary about acceptance of these things as if their nature were permissible, and maintain the dislike within their hearts as a minimum and advocate for their reduction to whatever extent is possible. Public pressure is the only force in the past century that has been able to reduce weaponization in the face of forces supporting escalation.[23] Therefore, it is important that discussion of these issues, particularly among religious leadership, not brush over the problematic nature of these weapons so that public mentality does not distinguish between horses, which the Qur'an says to have as a deterrent against military aggression, and the reality of nuclear weapons, WMD, and other modern offensive weaponry.

As Reuven Kimelman points out in his essay, one problematic dynamic about the modern use of the deterrence argument is that deterrence is only effective if the enemy believes that the willingness to use the weapons is real. Part of the reality of the modern world is that these conversations are public, so bluffing is problematic. In convincing your enemy of your willingness to use weapons such as WMD and nuclear weapons, you will consequently create within your own populace people who feel that their use is legitimate and who will then be willing to use them. Considering the contemporary technological ability afforded to nonstate actors, this is a very dangerous line to pursue. Creating ambiguity about the willingness to use these weapons creates confusion about the nature of Islamic teachings and in turn adversely impacts the Islamic invitation to God's path both within the Muslim community and within the wider global community. As another well-known *hadith* from Imam Al-Nawawi's Forty Hadith states, "That which is lawful (*halal*) is plain and that which is unlawful is plain (*haram*) and between the two of them are doubtful matters about which not many people know. Thus he who avoids doubtful matters clears himself in regard to this religion and his honor, but he who falls into doubtful matters falls into that which is unlawful."[24]

The call to enjoin good and forbid evil, inwardly and outwardly, should be to the abandonment of that which transgresses the limits, and there should be no ambiguity that modern offensive weaponry is beyond the limits.

Unequal Power and the Threat of Offensive Weapons

The second source of resistance to discussing weapons reduction among Muslims focuses on what is perceived as discrimination and exploitation by more powerful nations. There is a natural human tendency to want to point out what the other guy is doing. The Muslim world feels extreme frustration with the demonization of their religion and culture and is naturally inclined to argue that others need to be looking at their own records and stop pointing fingers at the Muslims. It is unfortunate that this feeling of being under attack creates a defensive posture among Muslims that can subvert discussion of Islamic moral leadership on these issues. Because of this dynamic, the mutual emphasis on an international reductions approach[25] and creating partnerships across boundaries of faith and culture is important to engaging the Muslim world in reduction efforts.

The Just Peacemaking practice argues that if offensive weapons are not able to eliminate the defensive response, then initiating war ceases to be an attractive option, so war is reduced and lives are saved. This practice entails a spiritual jihad combating forces that pull decisions and resources away from the benefit of society and into areas that feed spirals of conflict, exploitation, and destruction. Political dynamics often use security concerns to bolster support through stimulating the public's legitimate sense of justice, leading to policies that appease anger and the inclination for revenge and retaliatory punishment. In the face of the forces that feed militarization, there is a need for an informed scholarly voice that will advocate for policies that promote better actual security and well-being of our societies.

The first step in the process for reaching an Islamic legal ruling (*usul al-fiqh*) on an issue is to understand the question being asked. In this environment, where political rhetoric often prejudices the public against what works, it is important that religious scholars maintain dialog with academics in other fields to understand the broader facts and context related to a particular situation. Another principle in *fiqh* methodology is that decisions are made upon certainties and not upon ambiguities. With regard to weapons of mass destruction and nuclear weapons, there is the certainty of the toxic threat of their production, the dangers related to their possession and maintenance, and the horrific results of their use. The assumption that is being called into question is their actual effectiveness in creating deterrence in our post–Cold War context; this is an area that needs to be given careful attention by religious scholars whose decisions are used in supporting policies.

Jihad, Just Peacemaking, and Social Justice

The glory and essence of jihad have never been in killing, as some rhetoric indicates, but in the devotion to struggle with one's entire being to that which is pleasing to God, and to establish that which is most consistent with the well-being of God's creation to which humanity is entrusted on this earth. True jihad is not a simplistic rhetorical exercise, but requires vigilance inwardly and outwardly by the individual who proposes to undertake it. Large amounts of money being spent on weapons that exceed the necessity of deterrence—while the needs that are obligatory in Muslim society (*fard al-kifayyah*), such as food, health care, and education, are not being met—amounts to oppression and social injustice. The neglect of these areas of social welfare is something that the entire Muslim community will be asked about on the Day of Judgment, if no one steps forward to fulfill them. This makes the concern with misappropriation of large amounts of unnecessary weapons an area that more Muslims should be addressing, particularly those who have the ability to advocate on these issues.

Advocacy and working toward the eradication of nuclear weapons is one example of where Muslim scholars and activists have been able to work toward the reduction of offensive weapons technologies. While these efforts need further circulation and support, the points of agreement are consistent, as is clear in the report from the World Muslim Congress (1984)[26] or the statement given by Muslim scholars participating in the Muslim-Christian Initiative Against the Nuclear Weapons Danger (2005).[27] The core arguments persist:

- "There is no room in Islam for indiscriminate killing and destruction."[28]
- "Nuclear weapons are not included in the scope of legitimate self-defense."[29]
- The production of these weapons is a huge waste of resources that should be better spent in eliminating human suffering.
- Muslims must support all efforts to reduce the development and production of these weapons and work toward their elimination.

Jewish Reflection

Reuven Kimelman

This study of the Jewish attitude toward weapons of mass destruction presents the classical sources and principles on war, its conduct and limitations followed by a sample of contemporary applications on the subject of WMD in the United States and Israel.[30] Traditional (classical) Jewish texts speak to the limitations of warfare, especially in terms of protecting innocent lives and respecting the earth. Contemporary Jewish texts build on these traditions, applying core principles to the new challenges of weapons of mass destruction—especially nuclear weapons—and the concurrent challenges of balancing self-defense and deterrence with the protection of all life on earth.

Types of War

Jewish tradition classifies wars according to their source of legitimization. Biblically mandated wars are termed mandatory. Wars undertaken at the discretion of the Sanhedrin are termed discretionary. Wars "to expand the border of Israel" are designated as discretionary.[31] Intermediate wars such as preventive, anticipatory, or preemptive wars defy neat classification. The assumption is that national self-defense is as much a moral right as is personal self-preservation. The question is whether the moral category of self-defense is limited to an already launched attack. The majority position answers in the affirmative. (This position is seconded by Article 51 of the United Nations Charter: "Nothing in the present Charter shall impair the inherent right of individual or collective self-defense if an armed attack occurs against a member.") The minority position holds that a preemptive strike against an enemy amassing for attack is close enough to a defensive counterattack to be categorized as mandatory.

The Ethical Conduct of War

In the Jewish interpretations of the biblical text, the estimation of one's own losses and one's own interest is insufficient for validating discretionary war. The "good" must appear achievable and the "evil" reducible. For example, before laying siege to a city, a determination must be made whether it can be captured without destroying it.[32] There is no warrant for destroying a town for the purpose of "saving" it. The other rules for sieges follow similar lines of thought: indefensible villages may not be subjected to siege; negotiations with the enemy must precede subjecting a city to hunger, thirst, or disease for the purpose of exacting a settlement; and emissaries of peace must be sent to a hostile city for three days. If the terms are accepted, no harm may befall any inhabitants of the city. If the terms are not accepted, the siege is still not to begin until the enemy has commenced hostilities. Even after the siege is laid, no direct cruelties against noncombatant inhabitants may be inflicted, and a side must be left open as an escape route.[33]

Much of the moral discussion of the conduct of the war derives from the prohibition in Deuteronomy 20:19–20 against axing fruit-bearing trees in the environs of the besieged city. The principal points deal with the issues of wanton destruction and the protection of the noncombatant.[34] With regard to wanton destruction, already in the first century BCE the Hellenistic Jewish biblical philosopher Philo (20 BCE–50 CE) extended the prohibition against axing fruit-bearing trees to include vandalizing the environs of the besieged city: "Indeed, so great a love for justice does the law instill in those who live under its constitution that it does not even permit the fertile soil of a hostile city to be outraged by devastation or by cutting down trees to destroy the fruits."[35] A century later, the Romano-Jewish historian Josephus (37–c. 100 CE) prohibited incinerating the enemy's country and killing beasts employed in labor.[36] Despoiling the countryside without direct military advantage comes under the proscription of profligate destruction.

A millennium later, Rabbi Abraham Ibn Ezra (1089–c. 1164) explained that fruit trees are singled out as a major source of life. War is no license for destroying what is needed for human life. A century later, Maimonides extended the prohibition to exclude all wanton destruction. The assumption is that if the destructive urges provoked by war against nonhuman objects can be controlled, there is a chance of controlling the destructive urge against humans.[37]

The protection of the noncombatant is rooted in the ruling that a fourth side of a besieged city be left open.[38] Whether the motive is humanitarian or tactical,[39] the principle is no harm to those who intend no harm. As Philo notes, "The Jewish nation, when it takes up arms, distinguishes between those whose life is one of hostility, and the reverse. For to breathe slaughter against all, even those who have done very little or nothing amiss, shows what I should call a savage and brutal soul."[40]

These rules on the limitations of sieges formed the basis for proscribing directing offensive weapons primarily at civilian targets. This precludes the military option of counterpeople warfare in conventional war as well as mutually assured destruction (MAD) in nuclear warfare. Thus multimegaton weapons, whose primary goal is civilian slaughter and only secondarily military targets, are out of the question. We should thus seek to eliminate unacceptable weapons along with unacceptable targets.

These ethical intrusions in waging war have two major foci: safeguarding the moral character of the soldier and maintaining the human image of the enemy. Any system that appreciates the realities of both the moral life and the military task faces a dilemma in promoting the moral perfection of the individual while allowing for military involvement. Some systems forswear war as the price of moral excellence. Others apportion the moral life and the military life to different segments of the population. Neither alternative is totally acceptable in Jewish ethical theory. Indeed, as mentioned, Philo explained the prohibition against slaying the defenseless out of concern with the savagery of the soul of the soldier; whereas the *Midrash* even condemned a king for the ruthless slaying of an enemy.[41] This concern for the ethical quotient of the would-be killer engaged Jewish ethical thought throughout the centuries. Salient contributions were made by Nahmanides in the thirteenth century, Isaac Arama and *Sefer Ha-Hinukh* in the fourteenth century, Hayyim Attar in the eighteenth century, and Samuel David Luzzato in the nineteenth century. Such agonizing over the moral stature of the soldier is summed up in the twentieth century in the words of former Justice Haim Cohen of the Israeli Supreme Court: "It seems that constant violence, even in self-defense, is not easily compatible with moral sensitivity."[42]

With regard to maintaining the human image of the enemy, referring to Deuteronomy 21:10–14, Josephus says the legislator of the Jews commands "showing consideration even to declared enemies. He . . . forbids even the spoiling of fallen combatants; he has taken measures to prevent outrage to prisoners of war, especially women."[43] Since there are times when evil has to be used to hold evil in check, the problem, as the chief rabbi of prestate Palestine Abraham Kook (1865–1935) noted, is how to engage in evil without becoming so. His solution requires all to be constantly involved in repentance.[44]

Since there is no war without evil—either because killing can never be deemed a good, or because war inevitably entails unnecessary killing—there is no war that does not require penance. The ongoing dialectic between the demands of conscience and the exigencies of the hour was caught by Kook's younger contemporary Martin Buber in the following words: "It is true that we are not able to live in perfect justice, and in order to preserve the community of man, we are often compelled to accept wrongs in decisions concerning the community. But what matters is that in every hour of decision we are aware of our responsibility and summon our conscience to weigh exactly how much is necessary to preserve the community."[45]

Reflection on Weapons of Mass Destruction

The modern discussion of weapons of mass destruction has two foci: among the superpowers and among Israel and her neighboring enemies. What combines the two is the perception that the Jewish experience ominously foreshadows the human experience. As lawyer, author, and Holocaust survivor Samuel Pisar (b. 1929) stated, "Standing in the shadow of the crematoria, we wish to give witness to humanity that it is possible to turn the whole world into a crematorium by the use of nuclear weapons."[46] The one event that ties both together is the Holocaust. The common lesson is "never again." With regard to the superpower conflict "never again" means let not genocide become the model for omnicide, or the destruction of all people. With regard to Israel it means let not the Holocaust happen again. These two are in tension when contemporary Jewish leaders consider nuclear abolition and the issue of deterrence.

In *Confronting Omnicide: Jewish Reflections on Weapons of Mass Destruction*, contemporary Jewish thinkers wrestle with the legitimacy of WMD.[47] One of the central issues in the application of traditional teachings to the reality of WMD is the awareness that the exponential growth in human power has upset the balance between its constructive and destructive use. Whereas the crowning achievement of human power—civilization—takes a concerted effort of multitudes over many generations, its destruction can be perpetrated by a few in an instant. In the past, it took many a considerable time to bring about mass evil; now a few can bring about unlimited evil almost instantaneously. According to Rabbi Irving Greenberg, this new reality has to lead to the "demythologization" of power. He writes, "The glorification of power and the deification of human sovereignty must be reversed. When one glorifies power one makes it absolute . . . The loss of the sense of divine partnership and of being accountable to a covenantal standard has intensified the tendency to be corrupted by power."[48]

Greenberg also learned from the Holocaust that the Nazis were most successful in implementing their murderous policy toward the Jews when the local population stood by because they saw the Jews as outside their moral universe. It is imperative thus that no power claiming a moral basis place any foreign population outside that power's moral universe. Indeed, as our power for destruction grows, so must grow our efforts to maintain our sense of universal humanity. As the Exodus is used by the Bible to demand of the liberated Jews—having experienced the vulnerability of slaves in Egypt—that they not oppress society's most vulnerable, so must the Holocaust teach Jews never to inflict on others what was inflicted on them.

Greenberg also argues that all power must be subject to checks. This can be derived from the experience of the biblical flood. Post-Holocaust humanity is like postdiluvian God. After the flood, even the Divine realized that unleashing the power to destroy humanity was unacceptable. Thus God initiated a covenant with creation to limit his destructive power. Whatever policy is adopted, concludes Greenberg, any worthy response to the Holocaust has to include working for the elimination of WMD. Eliminating WMD is a key part of the Just Peacemaking practice of reducing offensive weapons.

Rabbi David Novak's opposition to any use of nuclear weapons is based on the prohibition against wanton destruction. He follows the interpretation of Abraham Ibn Ezra (1089–c. 1164), who argues that fruit trees are emblematic of what is humanly necessary. Thus destruction of what is necessary to human survival is prohibited. Anything like a scorched earth policy would be prohibited regardless of its military advantage. For Americans especially, this means working to eliminate the aggressive rhetoric too often used by our leaders, rhetoric that exacerbates international tensions and makes disarmament ever more remote.[49]

Deterrence

Deterrence uncovers one important tension on the issue of WMD in contemporary Jewish writing. Whereas all decry the use of nuclear weapons, most find advantages in their possession. For example, Rabbi Lord Immanuel Jakobovits

(1921–99) lists five nuclear paradoxes, in which it appears that nuclear weapons have contributed to world peace and stabilization in the post–World War II era.[50] For Rabbi Greenberg, it is wrong—indeed, evil—for good people to appear to lack power. The weakness of the good tempts bullies, especially in the international scene. Even a balance of terror among the superpowers is preferable. Indeed, he argues that it may have already saved millions of lives.[51] Rabbi Walter Wurzburger (1920–2002) has weighed in on the dilemma of having a nonusable deterrent. The dilemma is that the nuclear arsenal is an effective deterrent only if the adversary is persuaded of its potential retaliatory use. Still, for him a MAD strategy cannot be countenanced in Judaism: "On the one hand, the actual use of nuclear weapons must be ruled out, for it is inconceivable to sanction the very extinction of the human species. On the other hand, a total ban on the use of nuclear weapons would be tantamount to unconditional surrender not only of a national self-interest but of our entire value system."[52]

Weapons of mass destruction also threaten the Jewish tradition of a covenant with the earth. Rabbi Bradley Artson argues that Judaism presents "a flat refusal to countenance the use of nuclear weapons even as tools of defense. The scope of their devastation, the inability to provide for the immunity of noncombatants, and the meaninglessness of dividing defense from offense in a nuclear war propels this weapon beyond the pale of acceptability."[53]

He goes on to argue that a nuclear holocaust represents a rejection of divinely created order, for the prophet Isaiah says, "The Creator of heaven Who alone is God, Who formed the earth and made it, Who alone established it, did not create it for a waste, but formed it for habitation" (Isa. 45:18). God's covenant is not just with humanity, but with all life on earth, as Genesis says at the end of the first worldwide destruction through water. Since the rainbow serves as a reminder of the covenant of life, it has been adopted as the emblem of the Jewish nuclear freeze movement.

Resolutions of Jewish Organizations

In response to the Reagan nuclear buildup, almost every national Jewish organization during 1981 and 1982 took a position on nuclear weapons.[54] Many of the above considerations were digested in these resolutions. For example, the Central Conference of American Rabbis called on the United States and the Soviet Union to freeze and reduce nuclear testing, production, and deployment.[55] The Holocaust figured prominently in statements by the Council of Jewish Federations and Welfare Funds, and the Women's League for Conservative Judaism. The flood also came into play in statements by the Federation of Reconstructionist Congregations and Havurot, which stated in part, "Choose life that you may live" (Deut. 30:19).[56] Similarly, the Rabbinic Council of

America stated, "We affirm the responsibility of mankind to preserve life on earth." Some extended their concern to chemical and biological weapons. The National Council of Jewish Women resolved to urge the United States "to support national and international efforts which advance the cause of world peace and human welfare."[57]

In sum, the consensus is that just as there are unacceptable targets, there are unacceptable weapons. From the limitations of sieges in the classical sources, it can be extrapolated that weapons directed primarily at civilian targets would be proscribed. This prohibits the military option of counterpeople warfare in conventional war, as well as a policy of mutual assured destruction. Multimegaton weapons whose primary goal is civilian slaughter and only secondarily military targets would be totally proscribed, which is not the case with weapons that may be used in a discriminating fashion on military targets.[58]

Modern Israel

The concern for the moral quotient of the soldier and the life of the enemy constitutes the "purity of arms" doctrine of the Israel Defense Forces. The doctrine limits killing to necessary and unavoidable situations.[59] It was the former prime minister of Israel, David Ben-Gurion (1886–1973), who made it a principle of the Israel Defense Forces.[60] There has been considerable debate in Israel on the extent of the gap between the real and the ideal on this issue.[61]

Strangely, the moral issue of Israel and WMD, especially nuclear weapons, is not much discussed in Israel. This is probably due to two factors. The first is the widespread belief that Israel's neighbors would destroy it if they could. The second is Israel's policy of nuclear opacity, a policy—much like that of Pakistan until recently—that is intended to minimize its visibility and thus minimize the pressure on Arab governments to acquire a nuclear option. Still, there exists an extensive treatment of Israel's development of its nuclear deterrent by Avner Cohen[62] and a helpful recent article by Louis Beres.[63] Because of this policy of opacity there has not been a public discussion of the utility or utilization of nuclear weapons. According to Cohen, "From the outset, Israeli thinking about the unthinkable has been linked with the concept of last resort. That is, the defense of Israel must not rely on the threat or use of nuclear weapons as long as its enemies have no nuclear weapons, except in cases of extreme national emergency when the survival of the state as a political entity is threatened."

Cohen goes on to claim that "the 1973 war provided Israel a great lesson in what constituted a last resort, and the extent to which Israeli leaders were committed to the principle of nonuse and were aware of the nuclear taboo."[64] He concludes that Prime Minister Golda Meir's (1898–1978) "reluctance to consider use of nuclear weapons raised the bar for what constitutes a true dire moment in which the use of nuclear weapons is justified."[65] Indeed, he generalizes, "the instinctive reluctance of Israeli leaders to consider seriously the use of nuclear weapon in these two crises (The Six-Day and The Yom Kippur War) is rooted in a double sense of prohibition: the evolving global normative prohibition against the use of nuclear weapons and Israel's own code and culture of nuclear opacity."[66]

This raises the question of its utility as a weapon of last resort. If a successful Syrian-Egyptian two-pronged attack in which the supply of planes, tanks, and ammunition was rapidly being depleted was not considered such, what would constitute a last-resort threat to Israel? Apparently, a last resort would be used only if the enemy encroached upon Israel's major urban areas. But by then it would be too late to use nuclear weapons, for if the enemy were already entrenched in Israeli territory Israel would not nuke its own population centers and it would be too late to nuke the enemy's city if the function is deterrent as opposed to revenge. Thus it would seem that nuclear weapons may prove to be dinosaurs in a war between Israel and its neighbors as opposed to, say, Iran.

Is there a Jewish justification for Israel's possession of nuclear weapons? Among the respondents in *Confronting Omnicide* Israeli Rabbi Pinchas Peli (1930–89) guardedly uses the Holocaust to justify Israel's possession of nuclear weapons: "If anyone has the right to possess nuclear weapons in order to deter murderous aggression, Israel is the country that irrefutably should have such a right. It is, after all, the only state in the world that is threatened openly and constantly with total destruction . . . Auschwitz and Treblinka are still with us. To the Jewish people 'Final Solutions' through annihilation are not a nightmarish fairy tale."[67]

Peli does not outright permit WMD. Rather he states that if anyone has the right it is Israel and then only in order to deter murderous aggression.

Policy

Of course, the more countries that go nuclear, the greater the possibility of intentional or mistaken use. On the principle that you stop what is stoppable, no nonnuclear country should be allowed to acquire nuclear weapons. Indeed, the present nuclear club should join forces and bully other countries into compliance with the Chemical Weapons Convention, the Biological Weapons Convention, the Nuclear Nonproliferation Treaty, and the Comprehensive Nuclear Test-Ban Treaty. Once all countries that previously sought the destruction of Israel comply, then Israel should be similarly bullied into compliance. Of course, Israel could not be asked to forgo its nuclear option without Iran and Pakistan also doing so. It is unlikely that Pakistan would comply without the compliance of its nuclear neighbor, India, which in turn would probably not comply without the compliance of its nuclear neighbor, China, which of course would need the compliance of Russia, which of course would need the compliance of the United States. Yet nothing could be more salutary for the Jewish vision of world peace than to have the goal of eliminating Israel's nuclear arsenal trigger the worldwide elimination of nuclear weapons.

This strategy coheres with it a classic vision of world peace with its own measure of *realpolitik* or political practicality. Before the prophet Isaiah envisages nations beating their swords into plowshares and their spears into pruning hooks, he foresees, "In the days to come . . . many peoples shall come and say, 'Come, let us go up to the mountain of the Lord . . . that He may teach us His ways . . . for out of Zion shall go forth teaching and the word of the Lord from Jerusalem. He shall judge between the nations, and arbitrate for many peoples'" (Isa. 2:2–3).

Isaiah's vision of universal disarmament is predicated on the existence of a universal house of prayer (see Isa. 56:7) that will function both as a locus of moral instruction and as a court for the arbitration of national conflict. When national conflicts can be adjudicated fairly by an international tribunal, then and only then will "nation not lift up sword against nation nor learn war anymore" (Isa. 2:4). For Isaiah, it is not enough to desist from going to war; nations must also cease educating for war. Training for war itself can prove an irresistible temptation. The policy of beating swords into plowshares, however, entails not just the replacement of the sword with the plowshare, but the beating of the sword into a plowshare; that is, the conversion of the means of destruction into the means of construction. Creating an economic alternative to the arms industry is thus an imperative of realistic disarmament, as is its universalization.

Conclusion

This chapter suggests that there are some important agreements between Muslim and Jewish teaching on weapons and the limits of war. Both traditions seem to preserve the right of individuals and nations or groups to self-defense. Both traditions wrestle with the implications of this right in the current context—where nuclear and other weapons of mass destruction pose unheard-of threats to all life on earth. Kimelman and Anton both point to the need for contemporary religious and political leaders to revisit their traditional texts for guidance about how to maintain political rights as well as moral rights in the current historical context where weapons are more powerful than our ancestors could have imagined.

All three traditions share a fundamental commitment to "preserve life"—especially the lives of innocents and the life of earth itself. The Jewish and Muslim essays focus on this ethical principle, while the Christian essay makes reference to it in Stassen's exploration of justice and peacemaking. Because of this shared foundation, all three essays point to the importance of reducing our contemporary reliance on war and weapons. Stassen points to contemporary political science evidence that war is no longer an effective political strategy. Kimelman underscores this point in his exploration of the limitations of nuclear reprisal (and thereby deterrence) in a geographical context like the Middle East. Anton makes a similar point in her call for contemporary Muslim leaders to seek new strategies for dealing with inequitable international power relations.

The three essays move beyond questions of effectiveness and *realpolitik* in rejecting weapons of mass destruction. They make the moral point that many other scholars in this book identify as core to the three traditions. We must reduce offensive weapons and the weapons trade because all human life is sacred: this includes the life of the tax collector and the infidel, the enemy and the innocent.

Notes

1. http://www.icpj.net/2006/muslim-statement-on-nuclear-disarmament/.
2. Susan Brooks Thistlethwaite, "Let's Take Religious Nuclear Opposition to the Next Level," Center for American Progress, April 12, 2010, http://www.american progress.org/issues/2010/04/religious_nuclear.html.
3. William C. Spohn, *Go and Do Likewise: Jesus and Ethics* (New York: Continuum, 1999), ch. 3.
4. John H. Yoder, *The Politics of Jesus* (1972; repr., Grand Rapids, MI: Eerdmans, 1994), ch. 1.
5. Spohn, *Go and Do Likewise*, 52–54.
6. New English Bible.
7. Norman Gottwald, *All the Kingdoms of the Earth* (New York: Harper & Row, 1964).
8. Paul Schroeder, "Work with Emerging Cooperative Forces in the International System," in *Just Peacemaking: The New Paradigm*, ed. Glen Stassen (Cleveland: Pilgrim Press, 2008), 159; John Mueller, *Retreat from Doomsday: The Obsolescence of Major War* (New York: Basic Books, 1989); Robert Jervis, *The Meaning of the Nuclear Revolution* (Ithaca, NY: Cornell University, 1989), ch. 1 et passim, and especially p. 38; Richard Rosecrance, *The Rise of the Trading State* (New York: Basic Books, 1985).
9. Glen Stassen, ed., *Just Peacemaking: The New Paradigm for the Ethics of Peace and War* (Cleveland: Pilgrim Press, 2008), 186.
10. See John Horgan, "Does Peace Have a Chance?" *Slate*, August 4, 2009, http://www.slate.com/id/2224275.
11. Seth G. Jones and Martin C. Libicki, *How Terrorist Groups End: Lessons for Countering al Qa'ida* (Santa Monica, CA: RAND Corporation, 2008), xiii–xiv.
12. See http://www.peace-action.org and http://twofuturesproject.org. [0]

13. Ahmad Al-Raysuni, *Imam Al-Shatibi's Theory of the Higher Objectives and Intents of Islamic Law* (Herndon, VA: International Institute of Islamic Thought, 2005), 137.
14. Stassen, *Just Peacemaking*, 177.
15. Qur'an 5:32, Abdullah Yusuf 'Ali, *The Meaning of the Holy Qur'an* (Brentwood, MD: Amana, 1993), 257.
16. Stassen, *Just Peacemaking*, 180.
17. Qur'an 3:139, "Lose not heart, nor fall into despair: for ye must gain mastery if ye are true in faith" ('Ali, *Meaning*, 163).
18. Yusuf Talal DeLorenzo, trans., *Imam Bukhari's Book of Muslim Morals and Manners* (Alexandria, VA: Al-Saadawi Publications, 1997), 204.
19. Qur'an 2:190, "Fight in the cause of God those who fight you, but do not transgress limits; for God loveth not transgressors" ('Ali, *Meaning*, 76). Qur'an 22:39–40, "To those against whom war is made, permission is given (to fight), because they are wronged—and verily, God is Most Powerful for their aid—They are those who have been expelled from their homes in defiance of right—(For no cause) except that they say, 'Our Lord is God'. Had not God checked one set of people by means of another there would surely have been pulled down monasteries, churches, synagogues, and mosques in which the name of God is commemorated in abundant measure. God will certainly aid those who aid His (cause)—for verily God is Full of Strength, Exalted in Might" ('Ali, *Meaning*, 832–33).
20. Qur'an 60:7–9, "It may be that Allah will grant love (and friendship) between you and those whom ye (now) hold as enemies. For Allah has power (over all things); And Allah is Oft-Forgiving, Most Merciful. Allah forbids you not, with regard to those who fight you not for (your) faith nor drive you out of your homes, from dealing kindly and justly with them: For Allah loveth those who are just. Allah only forbids you, with regard to those who fight you for (your) faith, and drive you out, of your homes, and support in driving you out, from turning to them (for friendship and protection)" ('Ali, *Meaning*, 1454–55).
21. Stassen, *Just Peacemaking*, 177.
22. Ezzeddin Ibrahim (Translator), Denys Johnson-Davies (Translator), An-Nawawi's Forty Hadith (Chicago: Kazi Publications, 1995), Hadith #34.
23. Stassen, *Just Peacemaking*, 181.
24. An-Nawawi's *Forty Hadith*, 6.
25. Stassen, *Just Peacemaking*, 181.
26. Sohail H. Hashmi and Steven P. Lee, eds., *Ethics and Weapons of Mass Destruction* (Cambridge: Cambridge University Press, 2004), 344.
27. Muslim-Christian Initiative on the Nuclear Weapons Danger, *Muslim-Christian Study and Action Guide on the Nuclear Weapons Danger* (Washington, DC: Islamic Society of North America and the Churches' Center for Theology and Public Policy, 2007), 26.
28. Hashmi and Lee, *Ethics*, 344, and Muslim-Christian Study, 26.
29. Muslim-Christian Initiative, *Muslim-Christian Study,* 26
30. For more extensive treatment of the subject, see Reuven Kimelman, "Judaism and Weapons of Mass Destruction," in *Ethics and Weapons of Mass Destruction: Religious and Secular Perspectives,* ed. Sohail H. Hashmi and Steven P. Lee (Cambridge, UK: Cambridge University Press, 2004), 363–84; and Reuven Kimelman, "War," in

Frontiers of Jewish Thought, ed. Steven Katz (Washington, DC: B'nai Brith Books, 1992), 309–32.

31. *Midrash Lekah Tov to Deuteronomy, ed. S. Buber* (Vilna: Almanah & Brothers, 1884), 35a. Midrash *Leviticus Rabbah* 1:4 draws the distinction between David's wars "for Israel" and those "for himself."

32. Midrash *Sifre Deuteronomy* 203, ed. Finkelstein (Berlin: Gesellschaft zur Föderung der Wissenschaft des Judentums, 1939), 239; with S. Fish, *Midrash Haggadol on the Pentateuch: Numbers* (London: Manchester University Press, 1940), 451.

33. Sifre Numbers 157, ed. H. S. Horovitz, (Jerusalem: Wahrmann Books, 1966), 210, and Z. M. Rabinowitz, *Midrash Haggadol on the Pentateuch Numbers* (Jerusalem: Mossad Harav Kook, 1967), 538n17. See Saul Lieberman, *Tosefta Ki-fshutah*, 10 vols. (New York: Jewish Theological Seminary of America, 1955–88), 8:989; and Radbaz (R. David b. Zimra) to Maimonides, "The Laws of Kings and Their Wars," 6:7 (cited in n38).

34. On the issue of wanton destruction, see David Novak, *Jewish Social Ethics* (New York: Oxford University, 1992), 118–32.

35. Philo, The Special Laws 4, 226, Loeb Classical Library (Cambridge, MA: Harvard University Press, 1939) 7:149.

36. Josephus, *Against Apion II*, trans. H. St. J. Thackeray, Loeb Classical Library vol. 1 (Cambridge, MA: Harvard University Press, 1912), 212–14.

37. Moses Maimonides, *Mishneh Torah, Book of Judges* "The Laws of Kings and Their Wars," 6:10. See also Moses Maimonides, *Sefer Ha-Mitzvot*, negative mitzvah no. 57.

38. See *Sifre Numbers* 157, , ed. H. S. Horovitz, (Jerusalem: Wahrmann Books, 1966), 210; and S. Fish, *Midrash Haggadol on the Pentateuch: Deuteronomy* (London: Manchester University Press, 1940), 450.

39. See Saul Lieberman, *Tosefta Ki-fshutah*, 10 vols. (New York: Jewish Theological Seminary of America, 1955–88), 8:989; and Radbaz (R. David b. Zimra) to Maimonides, "The Laws of Kings and Their Wars," 6:7.

40. Philo, The Special Laws 4, 224–25, Loeb Classical Library (Cambridge, MA: Harvard University Press, 1939) 7:149.

41. *Lamentations Rabbah*, introduction, section 14. See 2 Kgs. 6:22 with 1 Kgs. 20:31.

42. Haim Cohen, "Law and Reality in Israel Today," in *Violence and Defense in the Jewish Experience,* ed. Y. Aharoni, L. Goodman, S. Baron, and G. Wise (Philadelphia: Jewish Publication Society of America, 1977), 332.

43. Josephus, *Against Apion II*, 212–13.

44. See his *Orot Ha-Torah* 11 (Jerusalem: Mossad HaRav Kook, 1985), 34–35.

45. Martin Buber, *Israel and the World: Essays in a Time of Crisis* (New York: Syracuse University Press, 1997), 246–47. The reluctance to attribute evil, however politically necessary, to divine command apparently lies behind the refusal to ascribe to God the Mosaic command of the Levites to slay their brethren. See Midrash *Seder Eliahu Rabbah* 4, ed. M. Friedmann, (Jerusalem, Israel: Bamberger and Wahrman, 1960), 17.

46. Samuel Pisar, *Of Blood and Hope* (Boston: Little, Brown, 1980), 306.

47. Daniel Landes, ed., *Confronting Omnicide: Jewish Reflections on Weapons of Mass Destruction* (Northvale, NJ: Jacob Aronson, 1991).

48. Irving Greenberg, "The Dialectics of Power: Reflections in the Light of the Holocaust," in *Confronting Omnicide: Jewish Reflections on Weapons of Mass Destruction*, ed. Daniel Landes (Northvale, NJ: Jacob Aronson, 1991), 27.

49. David Novak, "Nuclear War and the Prohibition of Wanton Destruction," *Confronting Omnicide: Jewish Reflections on Weapons of Mass Destruction*, ed. Daniel Landes (Northvale, NJ: Jacob Aronson, 1991), 100–120.

50. Immanuel Jakobovits, "Confronting Omnicide," in *Confronting Omnicide: Jewish Reflections on Weapons of Mass Destruction*, ed. Daniel Landes (Northvale, NJ: Jacob Aronson, 1991), 199–208. In the same vein, Henry Kissinger has noted that "all wars in the postwar period have occurred where there were no American forces and no nuclear weapons, while Europe under American nuclear protection has enjoyed the longest period of peace in its history" (Henry A. Kissinger, "Nuclear Weapons and the Peace Movement" [Washington, DC: Ethics and Public Policy Center, 1982], 32.)

51. See *B. Sanhedrin* 72a, 74a with Reuven Kimelman, "Terror, Political Murder, and Judaism," *Journal of Jewish Education Review* 62, no. 2 (1996): 6–11.

52. Walter S. Wurzburger, "Nuclear Deterrence and Nuclear War," in *Confronting Omnicide: Jewish Reflections on Weapons of Mass Destruction*, ed. Daniel Landes (Northvale, NJ: Jacob Aronson, 1991), 230.

53. Bradley Shavit Artson, *Love Peace and Pursue Peace: A Jewish Response to War and Nuclear Annihilation* (New York: United Synagogue of America, 1988), 221.

54. The following resolutions are assembled in *Preventing the Nuclear Holocaust: A Jewish Response*, ed. David Saperstein (New York: UAHC, 1983), 49–63.

55. *Ibid.*, 51.

56. *Ibid.*, 53.

57. Preventing the Nuclear Holocaust: a Jewish Response, ed., David Saperstein (UAHC, 1983), 54.

58. See Marc Gopin, *Between Eden and Armageddon: The Future of World Religions, Violence, and Peacemaking* (New York: Oxford University Press, 2000), 70.

59. See Ehud Luz, "The Moral Price of Sovereignty: The Dispute about the Use of Military Power within Zionism," *Modern Judaism* 7 (1987): 51–98. For Israel's experience in maintaining these standards under war conditions, see Meir Pa'il, "The Dynamics of Power: Morality in Armed Conflict after the Six Day War," in *Modern Jewish Ethics: Theory and Practice,* ed. Marvin Fox (Columbus: Ohio State University, 1975), 215; and Avraham Shapira, *The Seventh Day: Soldiers Talk about the Six-Day War* (New York: Scribner, 1971), 132.

60. See Cohen, "Law and Reality," 332.

61. See Luz, "Moral Price , 51–98, 76. For Israel's experience in maintaining these standards under war conditions, see Pa'il, "Dynamics of Power," 215; and Shapira, *Seventh Day*, 132.

62. Avner Cohen, *Israel and the Bomb* (New York: Columbia University Press, 1998).

63. Louis René Beres, "Israeli Nuclear Deterrence," *Midstream* 47, no. 2 (February/March 2001): 10–12.

64. Avner Cohen, "Nuclear Arms in Crisis under Secrecy: Israel and the Lessons of the 1967 and 1973 Wars," in *Planning the Unthinkable*: *How New Powers Will Use*

Nuclear, Biological, and Chemical Weapons, ed. Peter R. Lavoy, Scott D. Sagan, and James J. Wirtz (Ithaca, NY: Cornell University Press, 2000), 120.

65. Ibid., 121.

66. Ibid., 123.

67. Pinchas Peli, "Torah and Weapons of Mass Destruction: A View from Israel," in *Confronting Omnicide: Jewish Reflections on Weapons of Mass Destruction*, ed. Daniel Landes (Northvale, NJ: Jacob Aronson, 1991), 80.

CHAPTER 10

Practice Norm 10

Encourage Grassroots Peacemaking Groups and Voluntary Associations

Definition

*J*ust Peacemaking necessitates not only the participation of individual peace-makers, but also the combined efforts of peacemaker communities. These groups and associations provide a framework for the development of individuals who work for increased cooperation and peacemaking action in the world. A transnational network of people who open themselves up to learn from one another partially transcends the dominant norm of self-interest and encourages an environment of advocacy for the voiceless and powerless. Peacemaking groups are also able to focus attention on particular concerns and maintain the kind of perseverance and foresight necessary for a movement to emerge over generations. Grassroots organizations are inherently focused on transformation and do not easily become entrenched in cycles that perpetuate conflict and injustice. Just Peacemaking relies not only on the actions of nations or heads of state, but also on ordinary people who are empowered through cooperative action.*

Introduction

Dressed in their finest brightly colored outfits a parade of children and teachers walks slowly, carrying peace candles through the streets of Lahore, Pakistan. At the end of their peace walk the children give presentations, recite peace poems, sing songs of peace, and distribute handmade placards declaring, "We want Love. We want Peace. We want Education." In a country where the literacy rate is 57 percent, and considerably less in disadvantaged communities, these children represent hope for the adults of their city. They attend the ABC4All School, an education project of A Better Community for All,

Pakistan. ABC4All was launched in May 2008 and is a "Cooperation Circle" of the United Religions Initiative. This grassroots organization, composed of 45 Muslims, Hindus, and Christians, is committed to promoting interfaith dialog for peace and reconciliation and works to create sustainability and development in suffering communities. They assert that all children have the right to health and education. In a letter reporting on ABC4ALL's 2010 International Day of Peace celebration, Program Coordinator Yuel Bhatti noted, "We are facing so many challenges to providing facilities to these innocent underprivileged students, those who don't have the means to have education. As education is the way to peace, I am so glad that a number of Christian and Muslim children, youth and women are in this program."[1]

Thousands of grassroots organizations like this one are at work around the world to combat poverty, violence, illness, oppression, and other evils that impact people of all ages, nations, and faiths. These organizations stimulate solidarity within the local community, inspire participants to visualize a better world, and provide the resources and training necessary to make actual sustainable change in society. Often grassroots organizations have links to faith communities, whether they are initiated by religious bodies or simply draw support from people of faith. Islam, Judaism, and Christianity each support the development of grassroots organizations, sometimes explicitly through sacred word or historical example, but also implicitly in their teachings about empowerment, justice, and the importance of interpersonal relationships.

Muslim Reflection

Rabia Terri Harris

When God created the creation, He inscribed upon the Throne: My mercy overpowers My wrath.

—hadith qudsi

Revitalization Heals Reaction

Revitalization through returning to the source is a constant theme in Muslim life. The source we seek is first of all God, and next God's greatest gifts: the Book, and Prophetic example, through which God may be known. But if what we are seeking when we return to the source is not what the source is seeking, then we will misread our texts. The Qur'an terrifyingly says of itself, "By it He causes many to stray, and many He leads into the right path" (Qur'an 2:26). What makes the difference? Getting the point of God's work.

We misunderstand God's work when we misunderstand power. One of the most tragic and widespread of errors is to equate power with abuse. Having suffered abuse, we invent an abusive deity, then try to please that deity through hurting ourselves and others. But the God of the Qur'an is far exalted above that. That God lays down the tremendous law "Let there be no compulsion in religion" (Qur'an 2:256). That God disavows all oppression justified by invoking God: "I do not tyrannize them, but they tyrannize themselves" (Qur'an 11:101). That God has sent forth all the profound and transformative grassroots peace and justice movements we are accustomed to misconstrue as private clubs for ritual and belief.

Muhammad, (s)[2] like all the prophets who preceded him, was the messenger of *that* God. "We have not sent you," God told him, "save as a mercy to the worlds" (Qur'an 21:107). Muslims who take on the Prophetic mission of universal mercy hold one of the great keys to peacemaking in our time. There are many such people, and their moment is arriving. But first, let us briefly examine how we got to where we are.

The most influential movement in the Muslim world today is the Salafi movement, which began and grew as an anti-imperial movement. Its theology is intolerant and severe because the first empire against which it pitted itself, the Ottoman Empire, was the political instrument of other Muslims. The Ottomans were Turks; their subjects were Arabs, who roused themselves toward freedom by dreaming of lost empires of their own. To legitimate armed revolt against the Ottomans, internal Arab opponents had first to invalidate Ottoman Islam. Then in large part through alliances of convenience between domestic rebels and rival empires (see *Lawrence of Arabia*), the Ottomans fell. Arab allies of the West disillusioned their followers by accepting puppet status, and with this last blow, from Morocco to Indonesia, Europeans attained overlordship of the entire Muslim world.

Muslims were appalled. Many felt that such a situation could never have developed if "Muslims were really Muslims." A few then took up the Salafist theological tool of *takfir*, declaring others apostate, and directed it against every Muslim who accepted Western rule. Western governments themselves were simply abominations to be driven from Muslim lands. This is the thinking that has given us Al-Qaeda, the Taliban, and many other reactionary groups whose members incline to violence. These groups are, one and all, utopians. But the utopias they visualize must be secured by force because they are structured upon force; they have an eerie lack of positive content. And they are structured that way because they are the offspring of trauma.

The solution to trauma is not more trauma; it is healing. The solution to traumatized Islam is not further attacks on Islam; it is supporting natural regeneration from within. In theological terms, this requires preferring what the Prophet tells us God prefers, which is the control of wrath through mercy. And in social terms, it requires freeing ourselves from the illusions of coercion, and instead tracing power back to where it really lies, in the act of free consent.

The great Syrian nonviolence theorist Jawdat Said (b. 1931) has written, "The greatest truth that the prophets learnt and endeavoured to teach mankind is that a human being cannot be exploited or humiliated except with his consent and through his ignorance. Once he is enlightened with knowledge, no one can exploit or humiliate him—he would not tolerate that. That is why the dissemination of knowledge and not holding it back is the task of the prophets and their legacy."[3]

He also wrote, "Those who come after us to solve these problems will come up with new ways and means—without feeling that they are defying God, His Book and His Prophet. They will not feel that they are annulling God's Scripture; on the contrary, they will feel they are glorifying God and His Book and His shari'ah. They will have great peace of mind, and they will feel that they have released themselves from the heavy burdens and the yokes, not that they are rebelling against God and His Messenger."[4]

Thus the essential underpinning for successful grassroots peacebuilding in the Muslim world, Said suggests, is a growing clarity that what these groups are pursuing *is Islam itself.*

Theory Is Necessary

Grassroots work is challenging in much of the Muslim world. In *Who Speaks for Islam?* (2008), John Esposito and Dahlia Mogahed reported that although the great majority of Muslims polled by Gallup across six years and 35 countries hope for increased political freedoms, "A majority of Muslim governments control or severely limit opposition to political parties and non-governmental organizations (NGOs). They have the power to license and ban or dissolve them, as well as to control their ability to hold public meetings and to access the media."[5] Esposito and Mogahed explain that after the European colonial powers withdrew, they left a mess behind.

Arbitrary borders and nonrepresentative rulers produced weak nation-states with nondemocratic governments that perpetuated a culture of authoritarianism. Nongovernment organizations that are key to supporting democracy (political parties, trade unions, educational and social services, professional and human rights organizations, and the media) were state controlled or nonexistent.[6]

Yet they report "few respondents associate 'adopting Western values' with Muslim political and economic progress."[7] What is strongly desired across the board is "a new model of government—one that is democratic yet embraces religious values."[8] The same desire will necessarily shape the reestablishment of civil society.

It is not so easy to pick up the threads, but it is important to recognize that there are threads to be picked up. European rulers of Muslim countries generally overthrew not only the preexisting political order, but the indigenous civil order as well. Western governments treated the ancient guilds, schools, charitable foundations, and Sufi communities they encountered exactly as their successor regimes now treat the embryonic new civil sector.

If the peacebuilding web of civil society is ever to spread through Muslim countries on a large scale, it must draw together the old and the new. And everywhere, the work is already under way.

Muslim grassroots peacemakers confound Western expectations in numerous ways. For one thing, they are likely to appear progressive and conservative at the same time. Serious Muslims regulate their lives by the Sunnah, the Prophetic example—a deeply conservative strategy. Yet all the historical precedents a progressive social movement could hope for can be derived from that example. To give an indication of the wealth of case studies available, we have the following:

- Muhammad's prerevelation involvement in the Hilf al-Fada'il, the League of the Virtuous, a group founded to protect the rights of unaffiliated travelers in Mecca.
- His cooperative solution, from the same period, to the volatile argument among the Meccan tribes over who should place the cornerstone of the Kaaba.
- The motive behind his annual retreat on Mount Hira, which led to his reception of revelation. (It was a deep sense of personal responsibility for social change.)
- The 13 years of nonviolent resistance practiced by the new Muslim community in Mecca after revelation began.
- Muhammad's summons to Medina to serve as arbitrator in a divided city, and the Pact of Medina he instituted, the first secular constitution in the world.
- His principle of holding each community accountable to its own law.
- His clear insistence on equality of persons before the law.
- His personal practice of redistribution of wealth, and the community rules he instituted to support economic justice.
- The immense importance he attached to keeping promises.
- The deep respect he showed to ordinary persons, and his particular concern for the welfare of women and children.
- The rigorous limits he placed on the conduct of war, once it began.

- The bloodless Conquest of Mecca, one of the greatest triumphs of nonviolence history.
- In his Farewell Sermon, an assertion that he feared the use of nonviolence was still most fragile, and might slip from community practice after his death. Much of it has.

All this material has long been accessible to any educated Muslim. However, it takes a *theoretical* transformation—the case study method—to begin to put it to new dynamic use. Without a careful examination of the *point* of the Prophet's actions, as illuminated by our own experience of how the world really works, students of the Sunnah can squander their intellectual energy in futile arguments over irrelevant details. As Jawdat Said observed about the Qur'an, "Unless we realize and acknowledge that relationship between the revealed text . . . and the world of matter, which is the referent of the Scripture, we shall continue to dwell in the wilderness and to charge each other with blasphemy."[9]

Once *personal experience attains spiritual dignity*, empowerment is possible. Civil institutions are built of empowered people. Major Muslim intellectuals devoted to this revivifying religious impulse have included Muhammad Iqbal (1877–1938), the great poet of Pakistan; Muhammad Hamidullah (1908–2002), incisive historian and last citizen of Hyderabad; and Ayatullah Ali Montazeri (1922–2009) and Ali Shariati (1933–77), champions of Islamic democracy in Iran. Still among us are the magisterial nonviolence theorists Jawdat Said of Syria and Wahiduddin Khan of India; liberation theologian Farid Esack of South Africa; feminist theologians Riffat Hassan of Pakistan and Amina Wadud of the United States and Indonesia; and many others. Their writings motivate thousands across the globe.

On the Front Lines of the Nonviolent Jihad

There is no space in this brief survey to mention even a fraction of the vital peacebuilding initiatives undertaken by Muslims in recent years. However, we can take the first steps toward establishing a typology of such ventures.

Nonviolent revolution. Today the world is watching the prospects of the Iranian opposition movement, which accuses the current regime of betraying the founding ideals of the Islamic Republic. Whether this struggle succeeds or fails in overturning authoritarian rule, it should remind us that the Islamic Republic was founded through an extraordinary nonviolent success. Neither residual outrage at the American hostage-taking episode, nor distaste for the subsequent hardening of the country's rulers, should distract us from reflecting on the bloodless overthrow of the shah in 1979. Weakness toppled strength in Iran through a classic nonviolent campaign. It could happen again.

Nor is this the only such campaign the Muslim world has seen. Abdul Ghaffar Khan's army of 100,000 weaponless mujahidin, the Khudai Khidmatgar, were essential to chasing the British from the Indian subcontinent. Though Gandhi could not have succeeded without him, Khan's work has been shamefully neglected. His only guidebook for this achievement was the Qur'an. Palestinians are beginning to develop a similar reading.

Transitional revival movements. These are movements whose internal structure is pietistic and authoritarian but not coercive, and which cultivate a principled commitment to peace. Tablighi Jamaat is the foremost of these. The largest mass movement among subcontinental Muslims and the busiest Islamic missionary force in the world (active primarily in Africa), the Jamaat is ultra-traditional but explicitly nonviolent. Among peaceful transitional movements one might also mention Senegal, which, when Europe threatened, took a position against armed struggle. A Sufi order run as a state, it is the only traditional African polity to survive colonization essentially intact.

Charismatic social reform movements. These are change organizations formed around the vision and presence of a gifted individual. Strangely little known outside his own country is the legendary Abdul Sattar Edhi, whose foundation has built or inspired much of the social service network of Pakistan. More visible in the West is the movement of Turkish preacher, teacher, and writer Fethullah Gülen, whose emphases on service to humanity and interfaith understanding have drawn thousands of highly educated followers in Turkey, Central Asia, and North America.

Muslim interreligious initiatives. Interfaith peace and justice collaborations are a growing phenomenon in high-diversity countries and a crucial dimension of the peacebuilding web. Muslims are now included in such collaborations across the United States, and have taken significant leading roles in a number of instances. Examples are the Muslim Peace Fellowship and the Interfaith Youth Core.

Muslim minority institutions. These are bulwarks against alienation and laboratories of the possible that may eventually export their models to Muslim-majority lands. Of particular interest for its reconciling and mediating potential is the growth of Islamic chaplaincy in North America, Britain, and Australia.

Women's movements. There are so many outstanding grassroots Muslim women's movements that it is difficult to count them all. An American organization, the Women's Islamic Initiative in Spirituality and Equality, has collected background information on more than 260 Muslim women organizers around the world, and these represent just a fraction of the people in the field. Taking one as a representative of many, we call attention to the pioneering Malaysian organization Sisters in Islam, which for years has taken courageous high-profile positions against dogmatism, social exploitation, and spiritual inertia.

Other social-justice movements. Again, there are more than are countable. Positive Muslims, a faith-based South African organization focusing on reducing the stigmatization of victims of the HIV/AIDS epidemic, is one example. The Mosque Cares, centering its work on African American community development in the United States, is another.

Grassroots peace education. These activities are probably underreported. One program that has made it onto the radar is the Aceh Peace Project, an ambitious peace education program created by a group of academics and activists under the leadership of Dr. Asna Husin. According to the Canadian International Development Agency, one of the program's funders, "Training in conflict transformation, facilitation, and mediation skills has been provided to 244 individuals. A specialized library with Indonesian and English materials on peacebuilding and trauma healing has been established . . . Approximately 40 Dayahs (Islamic Boarding Schools) were trained to teach peace education using the peace manual and curriculum, and approximately 30 Dayahs continue to use these tools while teaching peace education. 1,700 students (576 of whom are women) are actively learning from the new peace curriculum."[10]

Mutual aid. Arguably the greatest contribution from the Muslim world to the century just past was Bangladeshi economist Dr. Muhammad Yunus's invention of microfinance. While sustainable economics as a peacebuilding factor is the subject of another chapter, it is important to note that the basic mechanism of microcredit, solidarity lending, is also a powerful teacher of social cooperation.

Serving the Cherisher of the Worlds

Ibn Khaldun (1332–1406), the father of sociology, long ago observed that the glue that holds empires together and the acid that dissolves them are both brewed from a single political substance: `asabiyya, perhaps best translated as "pride in group identity." History is moved by galvanizing loyalties. Whoever or whatever can command the strongest loyalty will eventually prevail, and will remain in power for as long as that loyalty prevails. Therefore the true locus of power in this world is not force, but consent of the will to something beyond itself. And the most enduring and reliable type of consent is uncoerced. This is the reason why freedom of association, through which people exercise the power of consent, is a challenge to tyranny, and why grassroots groups bonded by affinity can serve to check unjust concentrations of force.

Islam entered history in order to replace narrow, savage, and rapacious forms of `asabiyya with an overarching sense of human community based on mutual aid and individual accountability before God. Now we need to do it again. Every conscientious Muslim declares, every day, that "praise belongs to God, Cherisher of the Worlds." Every society, large or small, is just such a world, and every group committed to cherishing what God cherishes is performing an act of praise. Our work is before us.

Do good without looking down on anything involved with it. For the small is great, and little is much. And let no one say that someone else is fitter to act than oneself, for by God it will then be so.

—Hadrat 'Ali

Jewish Reflection

Peter S. Knobel

Peacemaking is a *mitzvah* (commandment). Much of the Jewish literature discusses the role of the mediator. Mediation can take place only when an appropriate ground has been established to make it possible. Therefore it is essential to develop groups that will pursue peacemaking as their primary objective.

The creation of a climate for peacemaking often relies on the development of voluntary associations and grassroots pressure. Leaders need the support of enough of their constituency to make change possible. In the late twentieth century the rise of feminist grassroots pressure led to the ordination of women as rabbis in the Reform, Conservative, and Reconstructionist movements. Another development in the same movements is the ceremony bat mitzvah, a rite of passage for girls to be recognized as women, which now stands parallel to bar mitzvah, the classic rite of passage to adulthood for boys. While Orthodox Judaism does not ordain women as rabbis, they are now being trained as experts in Jewish law (*halacha*) to serve in a quasi-rabbinical role. In some Orthodox congregations there are special ceremonies recognizing girls as women. A further innovation created by feminism with the full inclusion of women in non-Orthodox Judaism is women-only prayer groups, which are parallel to male worship services. In addition there are even a few Orthodox synagogues that, while maintaining the separation of men and women, allow Torah to be read by both men and women. Changing knowledge and changing social conditions create grassroots pressure to change or modify Jewish law or custom. Ultimately within Orthodoxy these changes will be sanctioned by rabbinic authorities. Another example was the unwillingness of most Orthodox authorities to ban smoking until a social climate was developed that would ensure their edict was followed. While these examples do not relate directly to peacemaking, they make clear that voluntary associations and grassroots groups have the power to alter practice.

The Jewish burial society (Chevra Kadisha) provides an interesting model for establishing a voluntary grassroots organization. Burying the dead in a proper manner is an important *mitzvah* within Judaism. In addition to being a *mitzvah* it constitutes an act of loving-kindness. The people who prepare the bodies of the deceased for burial themselves require proper preparation and an attitude that the work they are performing is a sacred obligation. While the Jewish burial society is not an example of a peacemaking group per se, it was the obligation of Jews to bury the deceased of non-Jews, as the tradition tells us, *mipnei darchei shalom* (because of the ways of peace). The history of this concept is born of a concern to maintain good relations with non-Jews, who were the majority. It may have been born of a fear of persecution. However, especially in the twentieth century, it has been used homiletically and rhetorically to justify acts of peacemaking. If one looks at the history of the opposition in the United States to the Vietnam War, it was grassroots organizations that ultimately came together as a movement. The creation of voluntary associations to do good works is part of Jewish tradition. For example, the Hebrew Free Loan societies provide interest-free loans to help individuals develop self-sufficiency. One can imagine creating similar organizations to support peacemaking activities.

Historically, but especially in the United States, Jews have been disproportionately involved in the development of the labor movement, the civil rights movement, and the anti-Vietnam War movement. All of these involvements derived from a prophetic ethic as well as a deeply ingrained concept of justice built into Jewish law (*halacha*). The power of collective responses to injustice has been amply demonstrated. Most social change comes about when sufficient numbers of people protest the inequalities they perceive.

Voluntary associations and grassroots groups are about capacity building. In Judaism when two study Torah together God is present. The Divine inhabits the space created by relationships. The *Targum* (Aramaic translation) to Ecclesiastes interprets 4:12, "A cord of three strands is not easily broken," to mean that two or three righteous people who come together have the ability to annul the consequences of the behavior of a corrupt and evil ruler. The power of righteous people is inestimable. The concept of the *minyan* (the ten people necessary for communal prayer) also suggests that the power of piety rests in the hands of a group.

Jewish faith-based communal organizing begins with the development of relationships with members of the religious community. It is the sharing of individual stories and the eliciting of individual concerns. Then it involves connecting those stories and concerns to concerns and stories embedded in the Jewish tradition. The group that emerges from this relationship building is then called to confront the issue collectively. Only through relationship building and careful listening do these grassroots associations gain traction and power. Judaism teaches that we are our brothers' and sisters' keepers. It teaches that each human being is created in the image of God.

There is a Hasidic story told by Rabbi Moshe of Sasov (1745–1807) about how he learned true love from a peasant in a tavern. He saw the peasant put his arm around a fellow peasant, and in a drunken tone of voice say, "Ivan, do you love me?" "Of course I love you." "Ivan, do you know what gives me pain?" "No, I do not know what gives you pain." "If you do not know what gives me pain, how can you say you love me?" Knowing where the other hurts is essential for the work of joining together in peacemaking. Community organizing through relationship building emphasizes the communality and mutuality of concerns that are rooted in our shared humanity, and provides the possibility for collective action.

One example is Just Congregations, a community organizing program of Union for Reform Judaism, which set the following goals for its community organizing program:

- Significantly increase meaningful social justice engagement by congregations (increasing both the number of congregations involved and the number of people involved within them).
- Foster a synagogue culture that fully integrates social justice into congregational life, ensuring that the pursuit of justice is at the center of congregational life alongside learning and worship.
- Enable synagogues to join with neighboring religious congregations of all faiths, recognizing and developing their capacity to be agents of effective social change for the common good.
- Connect congregations to each other and to congregation-based community organizing (CBCO) networks in their local community; increasingly train leading congregations to mentor others in CBCO.
- Strengthen the relationships of synagogues to non-Jewish congregations, building an effective context for coalitions to address issues of particular Jewish concern (e.g., Israel and anti-Semitism).
- Strengthen the Reform Jewish Movement's impact on critical social justice issues.[11]

While at the moment this project is spreading across the North American Reform Jewish community, the model is applicable broadly. In fact, it is simply a formulaic way of understanding how grassroots voluntary organizations come into being.

Today countless grassroots groups dedicate themselves to peacemaking and the defense of human rights. One can point to organizations such as Rabbis for

Human Rights, which describes itself as a rabbinic voice of conscience in Israel. Its members come from all streams of Judaism.

Rabbis for Human Rights (RHR) was established with the purpose of giving voice to the Zionist ideal and the Jewish religious tradition of human rights. Since its inception in 1988, RHR has championed the cause of the poor in Israel, supported the rights of Israel's minorities and Palestinians, worked to stop the abuse of foreign workers, endeavored to guarantee the upkeep of Israel's public health-care system, promoted the equal status of women, helped Ethiopian Jews, battled trafficking in women, and more.

RHR seeks to prevent human rights violations in Israel and in areas for which Israel has taken responsibility, and to bring specific human rights grievances to the attention of the Israeli public while pressuring the appropriate authorities for their redress.[12]

Rabbis for Human Rights derives its mission from a series of Jewish texts, including Genesis 1:27; Leviticus 19:33-34; Deuteronomy 16:20; Mishnah *Avot* 1:12; and Babylonian Talmud *Shabbat* 10a, 119b; which affirm the blessedness of humankind and encourage the pursuit of peace and justice.

In addition, B'tselem was established in 1989 by a group of prominent academics, attorneys, journalists, and Knesset members. It endeavors to document and educate the Israeli public and policymakers about human rights violations in the Occupied Territories, combat the phenomenon of denial prevalent among the Israeli public regarding these violations, and help create a human rights culture in Israel. It derives its name from Genesis 1:27, which, as mentioned above, declares that human beings are created *be-tselem elohim*, in the image of God.

Another powerful example of grassroots peacemaking is the Parents Circle-Families Forum, made up of Israelis and Palestinians who have lost immediate family members due to the violence in the region. Their mission statement is the following:

> To prevent further bereavement, in the absence of peace
> To influence the public and the policy makers—to prefer the way of peace over the way of war
> To educate for peace and reconciliation
> To promote the cessation of acts of hostility and the achievement of a political agreement
> To prevent the usage of bereavement as a means of expanding enmity between our peoples
> To uphold mutual support between our members
> We strive to offer a breakthrough in people's frame of mind, to allow a change of perception, a chance to re-consider one's views and attitudes towards the conflict and the other side. The Forum activities are a unique phenomenon, in that

they continue during all political circumstances and in spite of all tensions and violence in our region. Our members initiate and lead projects throughout the Israeli and Palestinian communities.[13]

Often loss and grief can lead to greater enmity or it can become the catalyst for peace and reconciliation. In this instance, it is the latter option that has prevailed.

American Jewish World Service offers another model of a grassroots organization, rooted in Jewish values, working to create a climate for peacemaking. Its mission statement is as follows: "American Jewish World Service (AJWS) is an international development organization motivated by Judaism's imperative to pursue justice. AJWS is dedicated to alleviating poverty, hunger and disease among the people of the developing world regardless of race, religion or nationality. Through grants to grassroots organizations, volunteer service, advocacy and education, AJWS fosters civil society, sustainable development and human rights for all people, while promoting the values and responsibilities of global citizenship within the Jewish community."[14]

AJWS seeks to create partnerships for its projects with the communities it hopes to serve and remains humble about its performance and capabilities. Among its many projects are its efforts to bring an end to the genocide in Darfur. Jews have a proud tradition of defending the powerless. This is rooted in the story of our enslavement in Egypt. Having been slaves we are told that we understand the heart of the stranger and we are prohibited from harming and oppressing the stranger. Jewish tradition emphasizes that a society is judged by how it treats its weakest member. Our historical experience during the *Shoah*, or Holocaust, when most of the world was silent to our destruction, inspires Jews to speak out in the face of oppression of the other. Jews also take inspiration from those non-Jews who, at the risk of their own lives, saved Jews. They have been given the honorific title of Hasidey Umot ha-'olam (the Righteous of the Nations of the World), and there are memorials to them at Yad Vashem, the Israeli Holocaust Memorial, and other special memorials around the world. Jews' minority status, as well as a long history of facing anti-Semitism, has often helped to create a great sensitivity to oppression and injustice. Jewish history has taught the power of building coalitions and the need to engage other individuals and groups outside the Jewish community.

Isaiah's words, which are inscribed on the walls of the United Nations, have become the byword of the peace community:

> And they shall beat their swords into
> plowshares
> And their spears into pruning hooks:
> Nation shall not take up

> Sword against nation;
> They shall never again know war. (Isa. 2:4)

Israeli poet Yehuda Amichai added, in his *An Appendix to the Vision of Peace*,

> Don't stop after beating the swords
> Into ploughshares, don't stop! Go on beating
> And make musical instruments out of them.
> Whoever wants to make war again
> Will have to turn them into ploughshares first.

Jewish tradition sets peacemaking among its highest values, encouraging Jews to be, in the words of Hillel the Elder (c. 110 BCE–10 CE), disciples of Aaron, loving peace and pursuing it.

Christian Reflection

Duane K. Friesen

Just Peacemaking requires groups of citizens who take initiative themselves and encourage governments to do the same. Religious communities can be particularly important in forming persons with a deeper and more enduring commitment to peacemaking amidst apathy, indifference, and the tendency of xenophobic or ethnocentric fear to fuel violence. When grassroots peacemaking is not nurtured, religious traditions have a tendency to ignore injustice and succumb to the forces that encourage violence.

A brief sampling of a few case studies from the Christian tradition shows how important the practice of nurturing grassroots groups has been in contributing positively to peacemaking among Christians, and also how Christians are overtaken by the forces of violence when the practice of encouraging grassroots peacemaking groups is neglected.

The Biblical Foundations of a Christian Social and Peacemaking Vision

A Christian vision of peacemaking is grounded in three theological convictions.[15] The first is a call to discipleship, to live the ethical practices modeled by Jesus in his life and teachings. Jesus himself called disciples, asking them to follow him. His teaching known as the Great Commission (Matthew 28:19–20) commands his disciples to "make disciples of all nations . . . teaching them to obey everything that I have commanded you." As prophets before him had done, he organized a group of disciples—in effect his own grassroots group.

And he traveled from village to village, initiating grassroots groups of followers as he went. Jesus emphasizes community practices, not conversion to a set of orthodox beliefs. According to Matthew's interpretation, Jesus summons people to join a disciplined community who put his teachings into practice.[16]

He calls on us to forgive others as we have been forgiven by God (Matt. 6:12, 14; Eph. 4:32; Col. 3:13); to love indiscriminately as God does, which includes loving our enemies (Matt. 5:43–48, 1 John 4:7–12); to love as Christ loves, giving of himself (John 13:34, 1 John 3:11–16); to serve others as Jesus served (Rom. 15:1–7, 2 Cor. 8:7–9); and, as the Apostle Paul instructs, to look not to our own interests, but to the interests of others, humbling ourselves as Christ humbled himself (Phil. 2:3–14). Jesus's teachings became the community practices of the groups of followers that he began.

The second conviction is a call to justice—not to withdraw from society, but to seek the well-being of the city where its people dwell (Jer. 29:7). Jesus' statement that his followers are the salt of the earth may be a commendation of the Qumran community for its distinctiveness—definitely a community with a different flavor than most of society—and definitely located by the Dead Sea, where it was very salty. But he immediately followed that by saying that his followers are the light of the world, calling them not to withdraw, but to organize communities in the midst of the world where people will see their deeds of compassion and justice and give glory to God.[17] The story of Zacchaeus (Luke 19:1–10) shows the transformative impact of Jesus' vision of justice on a Roman tax collector: "Look, half of my possessions, Lord, I will give to the poor; and if I have defrauded anyone of anything, I will pay back four times as much."[18] Jesus' inaugural sermon in Luke 4:18–19 (quoting Isa. 61:1–2) expresses how justice is integral to his own calling.

> The Spirit of the Lord is upon me,
> because he has anointed me to bring good news to the
>   poor.
> He has sent me to proclaim release to the captives
> and recovery of sight to the blind,
> to let the oppressed go free,
> to proclaim the year of the Lord's favor.

The third conviction is love and community, the church as an eschatological sign of God's love and reign in the world. God's love (*agape*) does not distinguish between the worthy and unworthy. *Agape* love transcends the reciprocity of friendship (*philia*) and attraction for the other (*eros*). The church is called to follow Jesus's model of *agape* love, to build community with others, especially those who have been excluded or marginalized, and to relate respectfully and lovingly with other persons who need to be persuaded to follow Jesus in peace-making rather than to follow Mars, the god of war. Jesus's encounters with the Samaritan woman (John 4:1–30) and with the Syrophoenician woman (Mark 7:24–30) are stories about crossing boundaries to build a new inclusive community. Martin Luther King Jr. is an exemplar of this vision of love and community: "Agape is not a weak, passive love. It is love in action . . . It is insistence on community even when one seeks to break it . . . Agape is a willingness to go to any length to restore community . . . The cross is the eternal expression of the length to which God will go in order to restore broken community. The resurrection is a symbol of God's triumph over all the forces that seek to block community. The Holy Spirit is the continuing community-creating reality that moves through history."[19]

When we observe the rhetoric and practices of many Christians who focus on individual salvation for the life to come at the expense of a social vision for peacemaking and justice, it may be hard to understand how Christians got so "otherworldly," given the biblical vision. The bad news of church history is that we so often forget our own story. The good news is we have a story that can be a constant source of renewal. Grassroots groups cannot be sustained without intentional efforts in education, preaching, worship, and exemplary modeling to keep alive the memory of paradigmatic stories like the Exodus (God's compassion for the oppressed) and the Good Samaritan (the "outsider enemy" as a model of neighborly love: Luke 10:25–37).

From the beginning the followers of Jesus sought to create a new society, the church as a social body patterned after Jesus' life and teachings. The vision for the church is a reconciled body in which persons are set free from the natural cultural divisions of friend and enemy, rich and poor, male and female, Jew and Gentile,[20] slave and free. Though these divisions persisted in the church and throughout church history, one can nevertheless describe the early church as a grassroots peace movement, a vision that has served as a source of renewal throughout the centuries. The Apostle Paul probably best summarizes this vision in his letter to the Corinthians: "From now on, therefore, we regard no one from a human point of view . . . So if anyone is in Christ, there is a new creation: everything old has passed away; see, everything has become new! All this is from God, who reconciled us to himself through Christ, and has given us the ministry of reconciliation" (2 Cor. 5:16–19).

This social vision shaped a number of peacemaking practices: shared authority for decision making among members of the community; support for the variety of gifts among members that contribute to the common good; contribution of material resources to meet the needs of orphans, widows, and the poor; hospitality to strangers; restoration, healing, and forgiveness of those who have violated other persons; and peaceable relationships and nonviolence toward enemies.[21]

The Implication of the "Constantinian" Shift

After Emperor Constantine became a Christian, the church was transformed from its minority status within the empire to become the majority aligned with the dominant political and economic institutions. Christian ethics shifted its attention from unmasking the idolatry of empire as a "beast from the abyss" (Revelation 13) to how Christians like Constantine might manage the empire. This shift had disastrous consequences for the relationship of Christians to people of other faiths. The failure to emphasize the church as a grassroots movement of followers of the way of Jesus contributed to moral disasters like the Crusades, the Inquisition, and religious persecution.

According to ethicist Larry Rasmussen, "[d]evelopments after the ecumenical councils, including the Reformation, only solidified the massive shift from the God-centered Christology of an alternative servant community within the wider world to the Christ-centered theology of a universalizing empire . . . This absorption of virtually all of God into the Jesus of imperial Christianity is at the greatest possible remove from the theocentric Jesus and his yeasty, salty, seed-y community way. Deadly results for Jews, pagans, indigenous people and cultures would eventually follow."[22]

With St. Ambrose and Augustine, Just War theory was developed to guide Christian rulers in the conduct of war. Hospitality to the stranger in the Benedictine monastic tradition and concern for the poor among the Franciscans and Waldensians kept alive grassroots peacemaking as an alternative to empire.

Religious Dissent, the Birth of Democracy, and the Church's Struggle against Injustice

The Anabaptists (Mennonites) of sixteenth-century Europe and the separatists of the seventeenth-century Puritan revolution in England (Baptists, Quakers) challenged a monolithic Christian society. Voluntary faith based upon adult conviction broke apart the idea of a unified Christian society (*corpus Christianum*), sowed the seeds for the idea of the independence of the churches from the state (before the secular Enlightenment), and contributed to the development of pluralist societies with a variety of religious faith traditions, rather than one established, privileged religion.

These grassroots dissenting religious communities made several contributions to the emergence of democratic institutions and the practice of Just Peacemaking. The most important is their contribution to the development of "civil society"—mediating institutions that exist between "the state" and the masses of the people. Voluntary associations empower persons to take collective action for change and to resist injustice, oppression, and the ideology of nationalism.

We can see what happens when civil society is weak. German Christians succumbed to Nazi ideology because Germany lacked mediating structures and associations between the state and the individual. Hitler appealed to the unifying mythology of the German "Volk" without resistance from organized opposition. Though the Confessing Church, led by theologians like Dietrich Bonhoeffer (1906–45) and Karl Barth (1886–1968), valiantly opposed the "German Christians," their movement lacked an institutional base of resistance among the people of Germany. When push came to shove, even the Confessing Church pastors took an oath of loyalty to Hitler.

William Cavanaugh shows how a "Christendom theology" during the time of the Pinochet dictatorship in Chile undermined the church's capacity as a mediating structure to resist the state apparatus of torture and defend the plight of the tortured. He ponders the question of how both the torturers and persons tortured and disappeared could participate in the same Eucharist. The separation of the "spiritual" (the church's business) and the "temporal" (the state's business) undermined the church's ability to respond to the violation of real bodies. Cavanaugh argues that only in following Jesus and "bodying" Jesus' life politically and socially in the Eucharist, or communion meal, can the church "resist" the powers and stand with and advocate for the tortured. The church rediscovered its mediating voice in December 1980 when seven Chilean bishops excommunicated torturers in their respective dioceses as an action of resistance against the Pinochet regime.[23]

Dissenting religious communities can become a source of renewal and change in the larger society, sometimes even against their own religious traditions when the traditions become aligned with injustice. The abolition of slavery, the resistance to racism, and the struggle for human rights have deep roots in churches that join with persons of other faiths and secular traditions to work for change. Religious institutions (the small cell, congregation, base community, interfaith organization) can give leadership and provide "space" in a society for the development and practice of Just Peacemaking.

Michelle Tooley describes the prominent role of women in human rights organizations in Guatemala. The violence of the 1980s served as a catalyst for women to become involved in collective action for social change.[24] Martin Luther King Jr. cannot be understood without knowing his deep roots in the prophetic black church tradition, "the major institution created, sustained, and controlled by black people themselves . . . the most visible and salient cultural product of black people in the United States."[25] "Space" was created for change in the 1980s in supposed monolithic East Germany when weekly prayer services in St. Nicholai Church in Leipzig eventually grew to larger gatherings that challenged the all-pervasive power of the state, toppled the dictator, Erich Honecker (1912–94), and sowed the seeds for the eventual fall of the Berlin Wall.[26]

Transnational networks such as the World Council of Churches, the Roman Catholic Church, and international networks of the various denominations can sustain Just Peacemaking because they transcend the barriers and limits of cultural, national, racial, class, gender, and ethnic identities. In the 1980s, organizations operating in freer and less repressive societies stood in solidarity with the people of Central America. We see a remarkable number of connections as a variety of groups respond to injustice and violence: Witness for Peace, the Pledge of Resistance, the Roman Catholic Church and Catholic Action groups and base communities, the World Council of Churches, Moravian church leaders, the Mennonite Central Committee, the Nicaraguan Baptist Convention, and the American Baptist Churches.[27]

Grassroots Organizations and Public Policy

The bottom line is that we need the discipline to develop and maintain organizations to sustain commitment to peace and justice over the long haul, even when public interest wanes and when popular sentiment turns toward violent solutions. We see this discipline in Desmond Tutu and the South African Council of Churches in the long battle against apartheid. We see it in the Southern Christian Leadership Conference that stepped in to support the Montgomery Bus Boycott and help sustain the long struggle in the United States for civil rights. We see it in the contribution of the International Fellowship of Reconciliation and Roman Catholic nuns to bring down the oppressive Marcos dictatorship in the Philippines in 1986.[28]

Political scientist Robert Putnam shows the importance of linkages between the achievements in international negotiations and the pressures of domestic politics.[29] Public advocacy for peacemaking is important at this time in U.S. history when countervailing domestic pressures supporting militarism or the status quo ante could derail the peacemaking inclinations of President Obama to reduce and eliminate nuclear weapons, to reach out to enemies through diplomacy and negotiation, and to open up a positive conversation between the West and the Muslim world.

Grassroots peacemaking requires hard work and discipline. In these grassroots groups and voluntary associations people learn the disciplines required to function in a vibrant democracy: the patience of conversation that requires both listening to others and articulating one's own point of view, the capacity to work together and compromise to develop a shared course of action, the discipline of meeting together and sharing the burden of many mundane tasks that sustain action for causes over the long haul. It is easy to be enticed into grassroots involvement when it is glamorous, but most of the time we just have to slog it out. Faith-based peacemaker groups sometimes have more lasting power than do many other temporary cause groups that lack grounding in a theological calling. That is why religious communities are so important, because our special vocation is "nurturing a spirituality that sustains courage when Just Peacemaking is unpopular, hope when despair or cynicism is tempting, and a sense of grace and the possibility of forgiveness when Just Peacemaking fails."[30]

Conclusion

The Abrahamic faith traditions all teach that human beings have intrinsic and blessed worth. It is in human action, particularly uncoerced and unified human action, that agency and power are found. Grassroots organizations, which develop voluntarily out of shared affinity around a particular need or initiative, reassert this understanding of power, especially when such grassroots organizations stand in the face of unjust powers. Both historically and today these organizations are motivated by a dedication to justice, hope in the possibility of community transformation, and recognition of the importance of openness, interpersonal relationships, and community solidarity. Grassroots organizations also play particularly important roles in educating the public about justice issues and establishing the groundwork necessary for mediation and further peacemaking efforts.

Religious groups can be valuable leaders in the development of grassroots organizations and initiatives. As faith communities share stories of compassion and peacemaking, they help to cultivate in their followers a commitment to just action, cooperation, and solidarity with the oppressed. Just Peacemaking depends on groups like grassroots organizations that empower people to live out their commitments to peace and justice through sustainable cooperative action, particularly when the impulse to choose violence as a solution is so prevalent throughout the world.

Notes

1. "A Better Community for All Pakistan CC ABC4ALL," United Religions Initiative, http://www.uri.org/cooperation_circles/detail/abc4all.
2. (s) stands for "Salla Allahu 'alayhi wa sallim," the traditional blessing on the Prophet.
3. Jawat Said, "Law, Religion and the Prophetic Method of Social Change," http://jawdatsaid.net (accessed July 1, 2010). English slightly edited for clarity.
4. Ibid.
5. John Esposito and Dahlia Mogahed, *Who Speaks for Islam?* (New York: Gallup Press, 2007), 30–31.
6. Ibid., 40.
7. Ibid., 48.
8. Ibid.

9. Said,"Law, Religion."

10. "Project Profile for Aceh Peace Initiative-Phase II—Tsunami," Canadian International Development Agency, http://www.acdi-cida.gc.ca/CIDAWEB/cpo.nsf/vWebProjBySoFSCEn/CB7D37CB8237A2D1852571250036FD07.

11. "What Is Just Congregations?" Union for Reform Judaism, http://urj.org/socialaction/training/justcongregations/vision.

12. "About RHR," Rabbis for Human Rights, http://www.rhr.org.il/page.php?name=about&language=en.

13. "Our Mission Statement," Parents Circle-Families Forum, http://www.theparentscircle.com/pages.asp?page_id=4#1.

14. "Who We Are," American Jewish World Service, http:/ajws.org/who_we_are.

15. For a more complete elaboration of these three convictions, see the introduction to *Just Peacemaking: The New Paradigm for the Ethics of Peace and War*, ed. Glen Stassen (Cleveland: Pilgrim Press, 2008), 18–32.

16. Richard B. Hays, *The Moral Vision of the New Testament* (San Francisco: HarperCollins, 1996), 97.

17. W. D. Davies, *The Setting of the Sermon on the Mount* (Cambridge, UK: Cambridge University, 1964), 214ff, 249–56.

18. New Revised Standard Version.

19. Martin Luther King Jr. See the chapter, "Pilgrimage to Nonviolence," in *Stride Toward Freedom* (New York: Ballantine Books, 1958), 84–85.

20. The rhetorical style of the references to the Pharisees in the Gospel of Matthew and "the Jews" in the Gospel of John have unfortunately contributed to "anti-Judaism" among Christians, contrary to the irenic vision of the New Testament writings in general. The vast scholarly literature on this issue is beyond the scope of this essay. The problem is hermeneutics—how an "in-house" conflict among a variety of Jewish groups in the first century CE reflected in the New Testament writings gets "translated" in later centuries into a conflict between "us" (Christians) and "them" (Jews). The Jesus movement was from the beginning thoroughly Jewish.

21. John H. Yoder, *Body Politics: Five Practices of the Christian Community before the Watching World* (Nashville: Discipleship Resources, 1992).

22. Larry L. Rasmussen, *Moral Fragments and Moral Community* (Minneapolis: Fortress, 1993), 142.

23. William T. Cavanaugh, *Torture and Eucharist* (Hoboken, NJ: Blackwell, 1998).

24. Michelle Tooley, *Voices of the Voiceless: Women, Justice and Human Rights in Guatemala* (Scottdale, PA: Herald Press, 1997).

25. Cornel West, *Prophetic Fragments* (Grand Rapids, MI: Eerdmans, 1988), 4.

26. Duane K. Friesen, "Encourage Grassroots Peacemaking Groups and Voluntary Associations," in *Just Peacemaking: The New Paradigm for the Ethics of Peace and War*, ed. Glen Stassen (Cleveland: Pilgrim Press, 2008), 210, 233.

27. Ibid., 205–6.

28. Pacifist organizations play an important role, especially when public sentiment overwhelmingly supports war. It is much easier to start a war, and much harder to get out of one, as we can see in the U.S. war in Afghanistan. After nine years of war, countless lives lost, and about a trillion dollars spent, it is hard to imagine an exit strategy. Almost immediately after 9/11, the rhetoric of a "war against terror"

became the dominant paradigm. We might have engaged 9/11 not with a war, but as a "crime against humanity," with the strategy and tools we use in fighting crime. In the frenzy of national sentiment after 9/11, however, there was a rush to war with hardly any dissent: all U.S. senators voted for war, and only one member of the House of Representatives dissented. Was this a "war of necessity" as President Obama claims, or did we make a choice without seriously considering other options? It is especially in times like these that we need vigorous grassroots organizations (along with an independent press) to challenge policy makers.

29. Friesen, "Encourage Grassroots," 206–7.
30. Ibid., 212.

Conclusion

The twenty-first century is now described as "God's Century" because of the growing influence of religion on global politics.[1] New forces of modernization, including globalization, political liberalization, and Internet communication are helping to grow religious influence in the political sphere rather than abolish religion altogether, as secularization theorists had argued since the late twentieth century. This process is accelerating, whether for good or for ill, and religious influence in global politics contains elements of both.

Interfaith Just Peacemaking: Jewish, Christian, and Muslim Perspectives on the New Paradigm of Peace and War could therefore not be more timely as a resource for understanding how the Abrahamic traditions can be resources for building just and sustainable political, economic, and social systems through nonviolent means. This is, in fact, the only sensible way to engage the growing influence of religion in the public square today. The idea that what democratic progress and economic advancement require is to "keep religion out of it" has backfired in several ways. Trying to "keep religion out of it" by repressive tactics simply causes political theologies to radicalize and become more extreme, as happened in Egypt under former president Hosni Mubarak. "Trying to keep religion out of it" less by violence and more by legal restriction doesn't work either. Countries where religion is or has been sharply restricted, such as Christianity and Islam in contemporary China or the Catholic Church by the Communist regime in Poland, have seen religion grow, not decline. China, for example, is on track to become not only the largest Christian country in the world, but also the largest Muslim country.[2]

Religious actors can be a force for constructive political, economic, and social change, however, especially when they have practical tools at their disposal that have a proven track record of producing results and that have strong support within their sacred texts and traditions. That is exactly the toolkit that the ten practice norms of the Interfaith Just Peace paradigm provide. All ten practice norms have immediate relevance for the way religion is driving conflict today, and how religious institutions and individual religious actors can change that.

For example, the power of nonviolent direct action is just as well supported in Judaism, Christianity, and Islam as is war making; the authors in this volume argue that historical examples of individuals and their whole faith communities support this. Nonviolent direct action is a set of time-tested practices that produce societal transformation. These practices were employed, for example, in Tahir Square in Egypt during January 2011, as the whole world watched.

Just Peacemaking does involve pushing forward on new initiatives in interfaith perspective, while using sacred texts to inform the direction and provide guidance for new work. This is the case with a norm such as "taking independent initiatives," where contemporary psychology combines with religious tendencies but pushes them forward.

In the past and continuing into the present, religious division has been a significant source of conflict in the world. In employing the Just Peace method of cooperative conflict resolution, however, religious communities and individual religious actors have now developed a track record for changing this outcome, and challenging religious conflict at its source—that is, within religions themselves. This gives us a means to interrupt the "spiral of violence," in Dom Hélder Câmara's evocative phrase.[3] We cannot change the wrongs of the past, but we can change our relationship to the past and not let its horrors haunt our present and limit our future. The interconnected steps of certain practice norms help actually change the power dynamics that, left unaddressed, keep recycling conflict, especially in religious contexts.

The Abrahamic faiths clearly do not have economic theories, theories of democracy, or a set of human rights norms in their sacred texts and traditions. But it is also clear that broad support exists within these faiths for the kinds of practices that result when people have the means to live, can believe as they choose, can speak as they wish, and can participate freely in their political systems without fear of being violently suppressed.

State to state, as well as within states, there are new mechanisms for peacemaking in communications technology and the use of nonstate actors in using these new tools for social movements. Increased person-to-person communication through technology and globalization offers opportunities to advance international cooperation. The growth in the world's youth population necessitates the development of new platforms of interaction. Religious traditions are not only supportive of these kinds of new interactions, they are also one of the major reasons why religions around the world are growing at such exponential rates.

Despite their many differences of text, tradition, and worship practice, the Abrahamic faiths share a fundamental commitment to "preserve life"— especially the lives of innocents and the life of earth itself. Yet even this commonality can look different when it comes to looking at specific contexts and debates over "self-defense" as part of the Just Peace practices. A contextual approach to peacemaking is not a "one-size-fits-all" idealism.

The 30 Muslim, Jewish, and Christian religious leaders and scholars who have worked together for years to craft these spiritually based, constructive, and practical approaches to peacemaking called the Interfaith Just Peace paradigm are a microcosm of the painstaking, often frustrating work of peacemaking. Producing this book required each of us not only to challenge others, but also to confront our own faiths in historic and contemporary perspective. We do not all agree with each other on everything.

What we do agree upon, however, is that violence is not inevitable and that peace can be made, year by year, step by step, especially when we take concrete actions that have proven effective time after time. The actual work of Just Peace-making in interfaith perspective has never been more timely and more urgent.

Notes

1. Monica Duffy Toft, Daniel Philpott, and Timothy Samuel Shah, *God's Century: Resurgent Religion and Global Politics* (New York: W. W. Norton, 2011).
2. John Mickelthwait and Adrian Woolridge, *God Is Back: How the Global Revival of Faith Is Changing the World* (New York: Penguin Press, 2009), ch. 1.
3. Dom Hélder Câmara, *Spiral of Violence* (Lake Orion, MI: Dimension Books, 1971).

Definitions of Key Terms

Judaism

Covenant: The mutual agreement between God and the people Israel that begins with Abraham but evolves throughout the Hebrew Bible. Israel commits itself to be God's people and to the observance of his commandments, and God commits himself to rewarding Israel with prosperity and well-being.

Diaspora: Jewish communities outside the land of Israel.

Halacha: The corpus of Jewish law that is based on the Hebrew Bible and the literature of the rabbis, the Talmud being the most important.

Hasidism: A Jewish mystical revivalist movement that started in eighteenth-century Poland and spread throughout Eastern European Jewry. At present it is a way of life for a large portion of the ultra-Orthodox Jewish community.

Hebrew Bible: The Bible that is sacred to Jews. It consists of three parts: the Torah (the five books of Moses), the Prophets, and the Writings. In Hebrew, the first letters of these three words create the acronym *Tanakh*.

Holocaust: The German extermination of six million European Jews during World War II.

Jewish Denominations: The three most prominent Jewish movements are Orthodox, Conservative, and Reform. The Orthodox movement is focused primarily on the observance of Jewish law as the center of Jewish life. The Conservative movement has a similar emphasis but tends to be more open to shaping Jewish law in light of historical circumstances. The Reform movement de-emphasizes the observance of Jewish law and instead insists that the practice of proper ethics and social justice are the essence of Jewish life.

Kabbalah: Literally "tradition," it refers to mystical forms of Judaism that developed in Europe from the eleventh century onward and created a highly influential Jewish theology.

Messiah: Literally, "the anointed one," the term refers to the human agent of redemption at the end of history.

Midrash: A difficult word to define precisely, it most often refers to rabbinic interpretations of passages in the Hebrew Bible.

Mitzvah: Literally, "commandment," it traditionally refers to God's imperatives to the Jewish people that must be observed as part of his covenant with them. According to rabbinic tradition, there are 613 biblical commandments (365 negatives—thou shalt nots, and 248 positives—thou shalts) of which less than half are still operative. In its secondary meaning, the term can also refer to any good deed.

Rabbi: Clergy and teacher in Judaism.

Synagogue: The place of worship and gathering.

Talmud: A multivolume work redacted in the sixth century in Babylon that contains discussions of the rabbis regarding matters of Jewish law in prior centuries. It is the foundational text for all later discussions of Jewish law.

Torah: In its primary meaning, it refers to the first five books of the Hebrew Bible known as the Five Books of Moses. It is considered to be the most sacred book in Judaism. In its secondary meaning, it can refer to all of Jewish religious literature.

Islam

Allah: Arabic for the God, the single divine source for all of creation and things known and unknown.

Five Pillars of Islam: The five pillars of Islam (*arkan al-Islam*) comprise five official acts considered obligatory for all Muslims. The Qur'an presents them as a framework for worship and a sign of commitment to faith. The five pillars are *shahadah* (witnessing the oneness of God and the prophethood of Muhammad), *salat* (regular observance of the daily five prayers), *zakat* (paying almsgiving), *sawm* (fasting during the month of Ramadan), and *hajj* (performance of the pilgrimage to Mecca at least once in a lifetime).

Hadith: The collected sayings of the Prophet Muhammad; the Prophet's sayings, actions, and tacit approvals. The collection of hadith is the second most important source for Islamic teachings, after the Qur'an.

Ilm: A field of knowledge, research, developing and acquiring knowledge; usually associated with higher insight.

Imam: A person who has a command of the Islamic religious teachings and has the authority to lead congregational prayers.

Jihad: A term meaning exerting efforts according to the essential ethical principles of Islamic teachings. There are intellectual, physical, spiritual, and social categories within these ethical principles.

Mosque: English word for *masjid*, which means "place for ritual prostration," or the designated space for Muslims to pray the daily and congregational prayers.

Muhammad: Muhammad was born in 570 in Mecca, and died in 632 and was buried in Medina. He was the last Prophet of God to reveal a monotheistic message of the oneness of God and the hereafter. Muhammad is understood to be one of the thousands of prophets sent by God to instruct humankind of a divine message.

Qur'an or al-Qur'an: Literally, "Reading/Recitation"; scripture of Islam revealed to the Prophet Muhammad; the first source of jurisprudence and viewed as the God's revelation to humankind.

Ramadan: The ninth month of the Islamic calendar, during which Muslims fast from sunrise to sunset to bring about greater piety, self-awareness, and God consciousness.

Shari'ah: A body of literature elaborating on the rules guiding the life of a Muslim in law, ethics, and etiquette.

Shi'ite: A sect within Islam that acknowledges the Qur'an, the Prophet Muhammad's message, his family, and the successive 12 imams who guided the community of believers. One who is partisan of 'Ali and his offspring through Fatima, Muhammad's daughter.

Sufi: A group of Muslims who practice the esoteric mystical dimensions of Islam as well as adhering to the rules of the *shari'ah*.

Sulh: Peace, peacemaking, and reconciliation.

Sunni: Literally, those who follow and incorporate the customs of the Prophet; approximately 80 percent of the Islamic community are Sunni Muslims.

Taqwa: The consciousness of the divine in the moment.

Tawhid: Pure monotheism; the oneness of the Divine.

Ulama: Trained religious scholars in the field of Islamic theology, law, philosophy, history, ethics, and related fields.

Umma: Commonly refers to the transnational community of Muslims around the globe; in early usage *umma* referred to Christian and Jewish communities in addition to the Muslim.

Christianity

Baptism: Christian ritual of immersion (adults) or "sprinkling" (infants) as a sign of participation in Jesus's death, burial, and resurrection.

BCE: Before the Common Era.

Catholic: Catholic has several meanings, including "universal." It particularly applies to the Roman Catholic Church that considers it has continuity from the Apostle Peter, who led the churches in Rome, through the centuries, to present Christians who have loyalty to the pope and whose worship centers in the Eucharist and is called "The Mass."

CE: Common Era.

Christian Scriptures: Also New Testament or the Greek Scriptures, written in the second half of the first century of the Christian Era. Christians also consider the Hebrew Scriptures to be part of their sacred canon and include them in the Bible.

Eucharist, Communion, Mass, or Lord's Supper: An act of remembering the Last Supper that Jesus ate with his disciples on the evening before he was crucified. Some Christians hold that the body and blood of Christ is present in the ceremony or Christ is spiritually present; in others it is a ritual of remembrance and community.

Evangelicalism: Those Protestants who emphasize salvation and personal conversion through Jesus Christ and the Holy Spirit, with strong emphasis on Jesus's death on the cross; commitment to the Scripture as the completely true guide to salvation, ethics, and life; and commitment to spread the good news of the Gospel throughout the world. Some evangelicals are Calvinists or Anabaptists, fewer are Lutherans, and many are Pentecostals.

Gospel: Means "good news," *euangel* in Greek; used primarily to refer to the New Testament books of Matthew, Mark, Luke, and John.

Grace: God's loving action toward persons and all creation to give life and salvation, by mercy.

Holy Spirit: God as present in spirit.

Jesus Christ: Jesus of Nazareth was born in approximately 4 BCE, and tortured and executed by Roman authorities in or around 30 CE; according to Christians, Jesus rose from the dead and saved humanity from sin.

Kingdom of God or Reign of God: Jesus's central message identified with the prophet Isaiah's message that God was coming to bring God's reign—to deliver or save us and bring peace, justice, compassion, healing, joy, God's presence, and repentance or return to God—initially in "mustard seeds" of small breakthroughs here and there, and eventually in fullness.

"Peace" Churches: Often refers to those churches on the "left wing" of the Reformation, such as Quaker, Mennonite, and Church of the Brethren, which make pacifism a core principle of belief and practice. Other churches, such as the United Church of Christ, have declared themselves "Just Peace" churches out of the movement to establish the Just Peace paradigm in Christian thought and practice.

Protestant: In 1517, Martin Luther *protested* against what he understood as Catholic teaching that salvation depends on human righteousness and not solely on God's grace through faith; in 1525 Anabaptists sought independence of churches from the state and began baptizing only those who are taught, come to their own faith, and commit to discipleship (Matthew 28:19–20); and in 1535 John Calvin protested against French Catholicism, fled to Switzerland, and emphasized grace and God's sovereignty. In 1906, Pentecostalism protested against all of the above and emphasized present experience of the Holy Spirit and sanctification in holy living. Thus many varieties of Protestantism proliferate.

Repentance: Changing one's mind; a profound turning of our direction away from sin toward God. Many Christians consider the confession of wrongdoing and a change of direction in one's life to be integral to the practice of repentance.

Salvation: God's action for us and for all creation to bring deliverance from the power and effects of sin.

Sin: Literally, "missing the mark." Human rebellion against the will of God, both individually and corporately.

Theology: From *Theos* (God) and *logos* (word or logic). Faith seeks reasoned understanding of God's character and will. The study of theology has many subdisciplines—biblical, historical, philosophical, practical, and ethical.

Trinity: Refers to God as comprising God as Father, Jesus as Son, and the Holy Spirit. Also God's work as Creator, Redeemer, and Sustainer. Christians insist God is one, and the Trinity is not three Gods.

Contributors

Mohammed Abu-Nimer is a full professor at American University's School of International Service in International Peace and Conflict. He is the director of the Peacebuilding and Development Institute and the director of the Conflict Resolution Skills Institutes, both of which offer unique peacebuilding courses for professionals in the field. Dr. Abu-Nimer is also the founder and director of the Salam Institute for Peace and Justice, and the cofounder and coeditor of the *Journal of Peacebuilding and Development*. He has chaired and presented at a variety of conferences, including the Hague International Conference on the Role of Religion in Peace Processes, Nonviolence International, and United States Institute for Peace, and at numerous universities. Dr. Abu-Nimer has also led conflict resolution training workshops in many conflict areas around the world, including Palestine, Israel, Egypt, Northern Ireland, the Philippines (Mindanao), Sri Lanka, and the United States. He has written, edited, and coauthored ten books including *Peace-Building by, between, and beyond Muslims and Evangelical Christians: Reconciliation, Coexistence, and Justice: Theory and Practice*; and *Unity in Diversity: Interfaith Dialogue in the Middle East*. He has also published a plethora of articles about conflict resolution, interfaith dialogue, and peacebuilding in journals such as *Journal of Peace Research*, *Journal of Peace and Changes*, *American Journal of Economics and Sociology*, and *Journal of Law and Religion*, and in various edited books. Dr. Abu-Nimer serves on the boards of numerous organizations, including the editorial board of *International Journal of Transitional Justice*, the governing board of World Dialogue, and Abraham's Vision.

Zainab Alwani is an assistant professor of Islamic studies at the Howard University School of Divinity. She was the program director and an adjunct professor of Arabic and Islamic studies at Northern Virginia Community College, as well as adjunct professor of Arabic studies at the School of Advanced International Studies at Johns Hopkins University. She developed courses in Arabic studies that focus on the link between Islamic philosophy, language, and culture. She also taught Islamic history, law, and comparative religion at Wesley Theological Seminary and the Washington National Cathedral. She received her PhD in Islamic sciences from the International Islamic University in Malaysia. She is a researcher and social and community activist and the first female jurist to serve on the board of the Fiqh Council of North America. Dr. Alwani has authored and coauthored a number of scholarly articles and chapter books such as *Change from Within: Diverse Perspectives on Domestic Violence in Muslim Communities, What Islam Says about Domestic Violence,* and *Perspectives: Arabic Language and Culture in Films.* She has also published a variety of scholarly articles on the topics of Fiqh legislation, Maqasid Al shariah, peace jihad and conflict resolution in America, Al ghazali and his methodology, Aisha's "Istidrakat" Commentaries and the Methodological Premises: Reclaiming a Lost Legacy. She has several upcoming publications focused on Qur'an and gender relations, marriage and divorce in the American Muslim community, *shari'ah* and family law in America, scholarship among Muslim women, and *fiqh* for minorities. In addition to her academic and social activities, Dr. Alwani is an active member of the American Council on the Teaching of Foreign Languages, the Association for Supervision and Curriculum Development, the American Academy of Religion, the Abrahamic Roundtable at the Washington National Cathedral, the Woman's Faith and Development Alliance, and the African Studies Association. She was named to "Who's Who among America's Teachers" for three consecutive years from 2003 to 2006. She was also recognized by "Who's Who in America" for 2011.

Patricia Anton, originally from Medina, Ohio, accepted Islam in 1997 as a student at the Ohio State University, where she received her BA in international studies. She was awarded a graduate fellowship in nonprofit management and governance at Indiana University, earned an MA in Islamic studies from Cordoba University, and has continued her graduate studies at George Mason University's Institute for Conflict Analysis and Resolution. She has also studied Arabic at Yarmouk University in Jordan. Ms. Anton has worked for several Muslim organizations including the Islamic Society of North America, Islamic Relief, the International Institute of Islamic Thought, and Cordoba University. She has also worked on contract with the United States Institute of Peace, George Mason University, and the Institute for Defense Analysis. Ms. Anton has contributed to developing trainings and manuals for "Say Peace: An Islamic Model of Conflict Resolution," Project L.I.G.H.T. (Learning Islamic Guidance on Human Tolerance), and the Muslim-Christian Initiative on the Nuclear Weapons Danger. She is cofounder of Medina Center in Bethesda, Maryland, where she has served as board member. She has also served on the board of Asia Relief.

Alvin K. Berkun is a past international president of the Rabbinical Assembly, a worldwide organization of 1,600 Conservative/Masorti rabbis. A native of

Connecticut, Rabbi Berkun was ordained by the Jewish Theological Seminary, from which he holds a Master of Hebrew Literature degree and has received an honorary Doctor of Divinity. After serving in the Chaplain Corps in the U.S. Navy, Berkun served as the rabbi of Congregation Beth Shalom in Hamden, Connecticut, for 15 years. While there, he was a founder of the first Hospice and Hospice Home Care in the United States. He went on to serve the Tree of Life Congregation in Pittsburgh, Pennsylvania. He also helped found Pittsburgh's Community Day School, a Solomon Schechter School, and the Conservative Movement's Rabbinical Assembly Region of Southwestern Pennsylvania, Ohio, and Kentucky, which he eventually served as president. Rabbi Berkun was presented with the Rabbinic Leadership Award at the General Assembly of the Council of Jewish Welfare Federations, currently serves as chair of the National Council of Synagogues, and is a member of the International Jewish Committee on Interfaith Consultation.

Pamela K. Brubaker is a Christian social ethicist whose family roots are in the Church of the Brethren, a historic peace church. She is a professor emeritus at California Lutheran University and currently serves on the World Council of Churches (WCC) Advisory Group on Economic Matters. She has participated in several WCC consultations of the AGAPE (Alternative Globalization Addressing People and Earth) during the past decade and two recent Christian Peacemaker Team delegations to conflict zones. She recently authored *Globalization at What Price: Economic Change and Daily Life,* and coedited *Justice Not Greed: Ecumenical Perspectives on the Financial Crisis* with Rogate Mshana and *Justice in a Global Economy: Strategies for Home, Community and World* with Rebecca Todd Peters and Laura Stivers. She has contributed chapters to *Towards a Reconstruction of Mission Stories: Building Communities of Hope and Peace* and *Women and Religion in the World Series: Christianity,* and articles in the *Journal of Religion, Conflict, and Peace* and *Ecumenical Review,* among others. She received her PhD from Union Theological Seminary in New York.

James B. Burke is an assistant professor in the Department of Theology and director of the Lewis University Center for Ministry and Spirituality. In 2007, Loyola University of Chicago's graduate school honored his dissertation, *Crafting a Global Just Peacebuilding Ethic from Just War and Strategic Nonviolent Conflict,* as "outstanding dissertation of the year in the humanities." Prior to college teaching, he worked in justice-education programming and fundraising with the American Friends Service Committee, Chicago (1994–2002) and as director of Catholic Relief Services/International Affairs in the Archdiocese of Chicago's Office for the Ministry of Peace and Justice (1987–94).

Robert Eisen is professor of religion and Judaic studies at George Washington University in Washington, DC. He received his BA at Yale University in 1983, and his PhD in Jewish thought at Brandeis University in 1990. His areas of interest include medieval and modern Jewish philosophy, biblical interpretation, religious ethics, and comparative religion. He is author of three books: *Gersonides on Providence, Covenant, and the Chosen People* (State University of New York Press, 1995); *The Book of Job in Medieval Jewish Philosophy* (Oxford University Press, 2004); and *The Peace and Violence of Judaism: From the Bible to Modern Zionism* (Oxford University Press, 2011). He also coedited *Philosophers and the Jewish Bible* (University of Maryland Press, 2008) with Charles Manekin. He has received a number of grants and awards to support his research, including a Fulbright research grant at the Hebrew University in Jerusalem in 1999 and 2000. He is active as a consultant on issues of religion and international conflict with a particular interest in fostering better relations between the West and the Islamic world. He has participated in a number of high-level dialogs and consultations in Washington and abroad concerning this issue. He is a member of the C-1 Committee, an organization of Muslim and Christian leaders that grew out of the World Economic Forum and is devoted to improving relations between Muslims and Christians throughout the world. He is on the advisory board of the Center for World Religions, Diplomacy, and Conflict Resolution at George Mason University. He has also worked with the United States Institute of Peace in Washington.

Waleed El-Ansary is the Helal, Hisham, and Laila Edris El-Swedey University Chair in Islamic Studies at Xavier University, where he teaches comparative religion, Islamic studies, and Islamic economics. He studied economics at George Washington University (BA 1986) and the University of Maryland (MA 1998) and religious and Islamic studies at George Washington University (MPhil 2005, PhD 2006). He is a consultant to the grand mufti of Egypt and is involved in interfaith dialogue. He is coeditor of *Muslim and Christian Understanding: Theory and Application of "A Common Word"* (Palgrave Macmillan, 2010), and has authored numerous publications in the areas of religion, science, and economics, including "Economics and the Clash of Civilizations: Reexamining Religion and Violence," "The Economics of Terrorism: How bin Laden has Changed the Rules of the Game," and "Islamic Environmental Economics and the Three Dimensions of Islam: *A Common Word* on the Environment."

Reuven Firestone is professor of medieval Jewish studies at Hebrew Union College and founder and codirector of the Center for Muslim-Jewish Engagement (http://www.usc.edu/cmje). Dr. Firestone received his MA in Hebrew literature and history from Hebrew Union College—Jewish Institute of Religion and his PhD from New York University. He has lived in Israel and Egypt and has traveled and lectured extensively in Europe, Asia, and especially the Middle East. Firestone has authored more than 80 scholarly articles and essays and seven books including *Who Are the Real Chosen People? The Meaning of Chosenness in Judaism, Christianity and Islam*; *Jews, Christians, Muslims in Dialogue: A Practical Handbook*; *Children of Abraham: An Introduction to Judaism for Muslims*; and *Jihad: The Origin of Holy War in Islam.*

Duane K. Friesen is Edmund G. Kaufman Professor Emeritus of Bible and Religion at Bethel College (KS), and on the faculty of Associated Mennonite Biblical Seminary, Great Plains Extension. He has a doctorate in Christian social ethics from Harvard Divinity School. He has authored *Christian Peacemaking and International Conflict: A Realist Pacifist Perspective* and *Artists, Citizens, Philosophers: Seeking the Peace of the City*, and coedited with Gerald Schlabach *At Peace and Unafraid: Public Order, Security, and the Wisdom of the Cross.* Friesen has participated in interfaith conversation, organizing a symposium on the Middle East; as a fellow at the Ecumenical Institute for Advanced Theological Research, Jerusalem; in the Decade to Overcome Violence of the World Council of Churches; and on the Mennonite Central Committee Peace Committee. His recent work includes coauthoring with Bradley Guhr "Metanoia and Healing: Toward a Great Plains Land Ethic," *Journal of Religious Ethics* (2009), and organizing the Sand Creek Community Gardens.

Nancy Fuchs-Kreimer is the director of the Department of Multifaith Studies and Initiatives and an associate professor of religious studies at the Reconstructionist Rabbinical College. Dr. Fuchs-Kreimer holds an MA from Yale Divinity School and a PhD from the Temple University Department of Religion. She has pioneered the teaching of Islam to rabbinical students through service learning courses and through retreats she created for emerging Jewish and Muslim religious leaders. She serves on the boards of the Interfaith Center of Philadelphia and Clergy Beyond Borders. Dr. Fuchs-Kreimer blogs at Multifaithworld.org, and writes about current issues for The Huffington Post.

David Gordis is president emeritus of Hebrew College, having served from 1993–2008. Prior to assuming the presidency of Hebrew College, he was vice president of the University of Judaism in Los Angeles. Dr. Gordis is founding director of the National Center for Jewish Policy Studies. He is currently visiting senior scholar at the University at Albany of the State University of New York. He earned his BA and MA from Columbia University, as well as an MHL and a PhD from the Jewish Theological Seminary, where he was ordained in 1964. Among Dr. Gordis's publications are *American Jewry: Portrait and*

230 • Contributors

Prognosis, Jewish Identity in America, and *Crime Punishment and Deterrence: An American Jewish Exploration.*

Blu Greenberg is an active participant in the movement to bridge the gulf between Judaism and feminism. From 1969 to 1976, she taught religious studies at the College of Mount St. Vincent and lectured at the Pardes Institute in Jerusalem during her sabbatical year. In 1997 and 1998, she chaired the first and second International Conferences on Feminism. She also cofounded and was the first president of the Jewish Orthodox Feminist Alliance. Ms. Greenberg has also worked to build bridges between women of different faiths by helping to establish "Women of Faith," and through her involvement in the "Dialogue Project," which seeks to unite Jewish and Palestinian women. She lectures widely at universities and to Jewish communities in the United States and elsewhere. Ms. Greenberg received the Woman Who Made a Difference award on January 26, 2000, from the American Jewish Congress Commission for Women's Equality during a ceremony at the Israeli Knesset in Jerusalem. She received an MA in clinical psychology from the City University of New York and an MS in Jewish history from Yeshiva University. She has also been president of the Jewish Book Council of America and held the first chair of the Federation Task Force on Jewish Women. She serves on the editorial board of *Hadassah Magazine* and the advisory boards (among others) of Lilith and the International Research Institute on Jewish Women. Her publications include *On Women and Judaism: A View from Tradition* and *Black Bread: Poems, After the Holocaust.*

Matthew Hamsher is a doctoral candidate in Christian ethics at Fuller Theological Seminary and an ordained minister in the Mennonite Church. He is currently writing a dissertation on power and authority in the church while employed part time as a regional pastor for Ohio Conference of Mennonite Church USA and as an adjunct instructor in Christian ethics at Ashland Theological Seminary in Ashland, Ohio. He recently coedited a book of essays by John Howard Yoder, *The War of the Lamb: The Ethics of Nonviolence and Peacemaking,* and has contributed an essay, "Mu'tazilism and Arguments for Peace and Democracy in Contemporary Islam" for *Resources for Peacemaking in Muslim-Christian Relations: Contributions from the Conflict Transformation Project.*

Rabia Terri Harris serves as Muslim elder at the Community of Living Traditions, an intentional Abrahamic community dedicated to nonviolent social change located at Stony Point Conference Center in Stony Point, New York (http://www.stonypointcenter.org). In 1994 she founded the Muslim Peace Fellowship, the first organization specifically devoted to the theory and practice of

Islamic nonviolence (http://www.muslimpeacefellowship.org). Ms. Harris has been involved in interreligious solidarity work and Muslim community life as a writer, speaker, and organizer for more than 30 years. An adjunct professor of Islamic studies at Ursinus College and a practicing Muslim chaplain, Harris holds a graduate certificate in Islamic chaplaincy from Hartford Seminary, an MA in Middle Eastern languages and cultures from Columbia University, and a BA in religion from Princeton University. She is a senior member of the Jerrahi Order of America.

Susan Hayward is a senior program officer in the Religion and Peacemaking Center of Innovation at the U.S. Institute of Peace. She specializes in the role of religious leaders and communities in motivating violence and peace processes, and the development of conflict prevention, resolution, and reconciliation programs specifically targeting the religious sector. Prior to joining the Institute, Hayward worked as a short-term religious peacebuilding consultant for the Academy of Educational Development in Colombo, Sri Lanka, as a fellow of the Program on Negotiation at Harvard Law School. She has experience consulting on religious peacebuilding in the Conflict Resolution Program at the Carter Center in Atlanta, Georgia, and has done political asylum, refugee policy, and human rights work in Minneapolis and Washington, DC. Ms. Hayward holds a BA in comparative religions from Tufts University, a master's degree in law and diplomacy from the Fletcher School at Tufts, and a master of divinity from Harvard Divinity School. She studied Buddhism in Nepal and is ordained in the United Church of Christ.

Qamar-ul Huda is a senior program officer in the Religion and Peacemaking Program and a scholar of Islam at the U.S. Institute of Peace, specializing in Islamic theology, intellectual history, ethics, comparative ethics, the language of violence, conflict resolution, and nonviolence in contemporary Islam. Dr. Huda earned his doctorate from UCLA in Islamic intellectual history and his BA from Colgate University. Before joining the U.S. Institute of Peace, he taught Islamic studies and comparative religion at Boston College, College of the Holy Cross, and Brandeis University. In addition to numerous articles and reports, Dr. Huda has authored the books *Striving for Divine Union: Spiritual Exercises for the Suhrawardi Sufis* and *The Crescent and Dove: Critical Perspectives on Peace and Conflict Resolution in Islam.*

Matthew V. Johnson Sr. is national director of Every Church a Peace Church, an organization that equips people to transform their churches in response to Christ's call to implement justice through nonviolent means. In the ministry for more than 25 years, and serving as a pastor for over 15, he currently serves as pastor of Church of the Good Shepherd in Atlanta, Georgia. Dr. Johnson earned a BA degree from Morehouse College with a double major in philosophy and history, an MA degree in religious studies, and a PhD in philosophical theology from the Divinity School at the University of Chicago. He also completed two years of postdoctorate work in psychoanalytic training. Dr. Johnson is author of numerous articles, book reviews, and books including *The Tragic Vision of African American Religion* and a novel, *The Cicada's Song*.

Reuven Kimelman, an ordained rabbi, is professor of classical rabbinic literature at Brandeis University. Previously, he was Joseph Shier Distinguished Professor of Jewish Studies at the University of Toronto and Five College Professor of Judaism Studies at Amherst College. He has taught at Mt. Holyoke, Smith, Trinity, and Williams Colleges, as well as at the Jewish Theological Seminary of America, Yeshiva University, and the Hebrew University in Jerusalem. His PhD is from Yale University in religious studies. Professor Kimelman has published widely in journals of scholarly and popular interest on Bible, history, philosophy, ethics, liturgy, and current affairs. He is the author of the Hebrew work, *The Mystical Meaning of "Lekhah Dodi"* and "Kabbalat/Shabbat," and three audio books, two on *The Moral Meaning of the Bible—The What, How and Why of Biblical Ethics*, and one on *The Hidden Poetry of the Jewish Prayerbook: The What, How, and Why of Jewish Liturgy*. He is currently working on two books, one on the meaning and history of the Jewish prayer book, the other on terrorism, war, democracy, and the Jewish ethics of power. He has served as scholar-in-residence for many organizations including the former United Jewish Appeal Young Leadership cabinet, the Wexner Heritage Foundation, the Jewish Community Center Biennial Conference, the National Jewish Community Centers Association, and the General Assembly of the United Jewish Communities. He also was senior scholar of CLAL, the National Jewish Center for Learning and Leadership.

Peter S. Knobel has served as the spiritual leader of Beth Emet, The Free Synagogue since 1980. As of July 2010 Rabbi Knobel assumed the position of Rabbi Emeritus. A graduate of Hamilton College, he was ordained by Hebrew Union College–Jewish Institute of Religion (HUC–JIR) in 1969, and earned a master's in philosophy and a Ph.D. from Yale University. He came to Beth Emet from Temple Emanu-El in Groton, Connecticut. Dr. Knobel serves in many leadership roles within the Reform movement in Chicago and on a national level. He most recently served as president of the Central Conference of American Rabbis (CCAR) and on the Siddur Editorial Committee of CCAR. He is a past chair of the Liturgy and Reform Practice Committee and was a member of ad hoc committees on human sexuality, homosexuality and the rabbinate, and patrilineal descent. He is also a member of the Association of Reform Zionists of America National Board and chairs its Institute for Reform Zionism, and is a member of the board of trustees of both the Union for Reform Judaism and the HUC–JIR. Dr. Knobel is past president of the Chicago Board of Rabbis and the Chicago Association of Reform Rabbis and is active in the Evanston Downtown Clergy Association and a member of the board of the Council of the Parliament of World Religions. He is a member of the National Interreligious Leadership Initiative on Peace in the Middle East. Dr. Knobel has taught extensively at colleges including HUC-JIR, Yale University, Connecticut College, and Spertus Institute. He also has authored and edited numerous articles and publications in the areas of Jewish bioethics, liturgy, and Zionist thought and is the editor of *Gates of the Seasons: A Guide for the Jewish New Year.*

Andrew Sung Park is professor of theology and ethics at United Theological Seminary. He taught at the Claremont School of Theology after receiving his MA from the Claremont School of Theology and a PhD from Graduate Theological Union at Berkeley. He is an ordained minister of the United Methodist Church. While serving a church in San Francisco, he was actively involved in an interreligious movement for social justice. While teaching at Claremont School of Theology, he was engaged in racial and ethnic healing in the midst of the 1992 Los Angeles riots Eruptions. Out of that struggle, he published *Racial Conflict and Healing: An Asian-American Theological Perspective*, a Gustavus Myers Award winner for an outstanding book on the subject of human rights in North America in 1997. His other publications include *The Wounded Heart of God: Western Sin and Eastern Han, God Who Needs Our Salvation* (a videotape), *The Other Side of Sin* (coeditor), *From Hurt to Healing: A Theology of the Wounded,* and *Triune Atonement: Christ's Healing for Sinners, Victims, and the Whole Creation.* He has been involved in local and national interreligious and peace movements.

Zeenat Rahman is the deputy director of the Center for Faith Based and Neighborhood Initiatives at the United States Agency for International Development (USAID). She was previously the director of policy at the Interfaith Youth Core (IFYC), where she worked closely with the White House and various federal agencies including the U.S. State Department, USAID, and the Corporation on National and Community Service to advance programs related to youth, religious identity, interreligious engagement, and interfaith service. Ms. Rahman is a regular contributor to the *Chicago Tribune*, and has appeared in the *Washington Post*, on National Public Radio, and on CNN speaking on issues related to Muslim identity, civic engagement, and international affairs.

She previously built and managed international programs for IFYC in over a dozen countries and travels abroad frequently to speak about the importance of interfaith youth leadership in promoting civic engagement and healthy integration among youth. Ms. Rahman completed her master's degree at the University of Chicago's Center for Middle East Studies in June 2006. Her thesis work was focused on Muslim youth and the territorializing of Muslim religious institutions in America. She has spoken at the White House, the Nobel Peace Prize Forum, the Vatican, and many other venues. She is a term member of the Council on Foreign Relations and a fellow with the American Muslim Civic Leaders Institute at the University of Southern California. She is also a member of the Transatlantic Network 2020, a program sponsored by the British Council, which seeks to create sustainable, multilateral networks that engage future leaders from North America and Europe to collaboratively address global issues.

Louay M. Safi is an associate faculty at the Indiana University–Purdue University, Indianapolis (IUPUI) and a fellow of the Center for Christian-Muslim Understanding, Georgetown, and the Institute of Social Policy and Understanding. He is author of 11 books including *The Qur'anic Narrative, Tensions and Transitions in the Muslim World, Peace and the Limits of War, The Challenge of Modernity,* and *Truth and Reform.* A founding member and former board member of the Center for the Study of Islam and Democracy (1999–2007), he served as communications and leadership development director (2009) and executive director of the Leadership Development Center (2004–2008) of the Islamic Society of North America. He also served as the executive director (1995–97) and director of research (1999–2003) of the International Institute of Islamic Thought, editor of the *Journal of Islamic Social Sciences* (1999–2003), and president of the Association of Muslim Social Scientists (1999–2003). Dr. Safi has participated in numerous national and international forums and conferences, and appeared on many radio and TV programs, including CNN, BBC, Monte Carlo, Fox News, PBS, Middle East TV (MBC), Al-Jazeera TV, Voice of America, Malaysian Television, and Syrian TV.

Zeki Saritoprak has held the Nursi Chair in Islamic Studies at John Carroll University since 2003. He earned his BA in divinity, his master's degree in Islamic theology and philosophy, and his PhD in Islamic theology (the Science of Kalam) from the University of Marmara, Turkey. Dr. Saritoprak is the founder and former president of the Rumi Forum for Interfaith Dialogue in Washington, DC. He researched and taught courses at Harran University (Turkey), Georgetown University, the Catholic University of America in Washington, DC, and Berry College in Rome, Georgia. In addition to presenting at numerous conferences and universities over the years, Dr. Saritoprak is the author of several books and academic articles in Turkish, English, and Arabic and editor of *Fundamentals of Rumi's Thought: A Mevlevi Sufi Perspective* and "Turkey: Contributions of Fethullah Gülen" in *The Muslim World*.

Katherine Schofield is the editorial/conference assistant for the Interfaith Just Peacemaking project. She earned a BA in religious studies from Hamilton College and an MDiv from Chicago Theological Seminary in 2010. Her field education included internships with First Congregational Church of Chicago and Interfaith Youth Core, and a Beatitudes Society Summer Fellowship at Campaign for Better Health Care (Chicago). An ordained minister of the United Church of Christ, Rev. Schofield has served as Minister for Campus Outreach at United University Church in Los Angeles since April 2011.

Muhammad Shafiq is the executive director of the Center for Interfaith Studies and Dialogue (CISD), and is professor of Islamic and religious studies at Nazareth College. In addition, he is the Imam of the Islamic Center of Rochester, Inc. Dr. Shafiq holds a PhD from Temple University, and MA and BA degrees from the University of Peshawar. As executive director of the CISD, he participated in a conference on interfaith dialogue between Christian evangelicals and Muslims in Pasadena, California, in 2009, the theme of which was "A Common Word Between Us and You." Dr. Shafiq has written over 40 articles and several books, including *Interfaith Dialogue: A Guide for Muslims* and "Abrahamic Faiths: Models of Interfaith Dialogue in the United States (A Case Study of Rochester, New York)" in *Peace-Building by, between, and beyond Muslims and Evangelical Christians*.

Glen H. Stassen serves as Lewis B. Smedes Professor of Christian Ethics at Fuller Theological Seminary. Prior to his arrival at Fuller, he taught at Duke University, Kentucky Southern College, Berea College, and Southern Baptist Theological Seminary. Dr. Stassen graduated from the University of Virginia with a degree in nuclear physics, and he studied systematic and historical theology, Christian ethics, and political philosophy during his graduate work at Union Theological Seminary and Duke University. He has done postgraduate study at Harvard University, the University of Heidelberg, Union Theological Seminary, and the University of Notre Dame. Dr. Stassen's book *Kingdom Ethics: Following Jesus in Contemporary Context* received *Christianity Today*'s Award for Best Book of 2004 in Theology or Ethics. He has written several other books, including *Living the Sermon on the Mount* and *Just Peacemaking: Transforming Initiatives for Justice and Peace*, and coedited others including *Just Peacemaking: The New Paradigm for Ethics of Peace and War*, *Peace Action: Past, Present, and Future*, and *Authentic Faith: Bonhoeffer's Ethics in Context*. Dr. Stassen has served in leadership positions within the Council of the Societies for the Study of Religion, the National Association of Baptist Professors of Religion, the American Academy of Religion, and the Society of Christian Ethics.

Najeeba Syeed-Miller is assistant professor for interreligious education at the Claremont School of Theology, where she focuses on preparing students for interreligious leadership, designing interreligious dialog and educational opportunities. From 2004 to 2008, she was the executive director of the Western Justice Center Foundation, an alternative dispute resolution organization that works with communities, children, and courts toward peaceful conflict resolution. From 2001 to 2003, Ms. Syeed-Miller served as the executive director of the Asian Pacific American Dispute Resolution Center. She earned her JD from Indiana University School of Law–Bloomington where she specialized in conflict resolution and nonprofit management.

Susan Brooks Thistlethwaite is Professor of Theology and former President of Chicago Theological Seminary. Dr. Thistlethwaite received her MDiv from Duke Divinity School and her PhD from Duke University. An ordained minister of the United Church of Christ for over 30 years, she has authored and edited numerous works including *Dreaming of Eden: American Religion and Politics in a Wired World*, *Sex, Race and God: Christian Feminism in Black and White*, *Lift Every Voice: Constructing Christian Theologies from the Underside* (coeditor), and *Interfaith Just Peacemaking: Alternatives to War* (coeditor). Dr. Thistlethwaite also writes a weekly column for the *Washington Post* "On Faith" online section and is a frequent media commentator on religion and public events. She is serves as a Trustee of the Center for American Progress, Faith in Public Life and the Interfaith Youth Core.